EVERY FAMILY HAS A SECRET:

THE LIFE OF ROBERT EMMETT HICKS

MARGARET SAVAGE

Front cover and interior photos courtesy of Margaret Savage

Cover design and interior format by Debora Lewis
arenapublishing.org

ISBN-13: 978-1540461469
ISBN-10: 1540461467

Dedicated to the 56 living and deceased descendants of Robert E. Hicks

Contents

Prologue...1

1 Mea Culpa 5

2 Family Background 29

    Travel "Abroad"... 46

3 Coming Of Age... 53

4 The New York Years 95

    A New Beginning...110

5 The Chicago Years 119

    The Domestic Situation 144

6 The Association 163

    Back in South Whitley..................................173

    The Birth of Margaret 188

7 A Change of Direction 209

    Keynote Speaker for *Americana Encyclopedia,*
    1926 229

8 Travel...231

    The Governors' Convention 231

    Hawaiian Islands, 1927................................ 237

    A Foray into Politics 245

9 Retirement... 253

    Havana, Cuba 1929 258

    The Retreat from Havana 265

    Life at the Spanish Trail House 268

    The Last Years.. 272

    A Return to Havana 275

    St. Margaret Roman Catholic Church.............. 281

Appendices 297

PROLOGUE

It took far longer than I anticipated to write my father's biography. My interest piqued when I finally read, as an adult, his mea culpa, "A Conscience Unburdened". Who is this man who openly confesses his wrongdoings? Can he be the same loving old man who told me stories in the evening? He had little influence on my childhood; however, as I researched his life I became proud of his ability to turn a failed life into a successful one. He set high goals for himself and by his determination and hard work he achieved them. Today his descendants number fifty-six, and I am the only one still alive who knew him. We descend from hardy English – German stock, true pioneers who, at their peril, crossed the Atlantic Ocean in frail crafts. Peaceful farmers for the most part, they faced the formidable task of building shelters for their families and learning to live in an inhospitable land.

James Buchanan, the 15th president (1857-1861) of the United States, had been in office three months when my father was born in Knox County, Missouri. The Native American Indians had already been pushed farther to the West so my grandfather, Elisha

Hicks, bought land directly from the U. S. government. The family survived isolated and harsh conditions that decimated many another family. My father's lifespan extended through the election of Abraham Lincoln, the Civil War, the Spanish-American War, the annexation of the Philippines, World War I and the beginning of the Great Depression. He loved his country, but his patriotism did not include volunteering for any service in the armed forces. In his boyhood only horses, mules and oxen provided transportation until the coming of the steam engines and railroads. The first airplane he saw landed in his cow pasture in Indiana. The advent of the automobile delighted him but he never learned to drive. A restless man, it took him many years to find himself. Brash, boastful, arrogant and head-strong, he never became a 'gentleman'. Classical music and the arts interested him not at all. Four of his marriages are recorded but his love affairs remain unknown. His masculine energy and virility drew women to him and he, in turn, reciprocated by his admiration for them. He wrote passionate love letters to my mother, Mae, twenty-four years younger than he, and a reading of them makes it clear how easy it was for her to love a man who awakens the deep recesses of a woman's being. In his boyhood, he had many 'get rich' scams, and these continued into adulthood. Only when he hit the bottom as a dedicated alcoholic did he take stock of himself. He finally became a man with a purpose.

His Achilles heel, his lack of ability to judge the character of men, he never overcame. Time and time again he trusted so-called 'friends' who took advantage of his naive trust in human nature. I have tried here to put flesh on the bones of my father, dead these many years. Ecclesiastes reminds us in the passage "ashes to ashes, dust to dust" that we all will follow this well-worn path to our own rendezvous with Death.

1

MEA CULPA

Every family has a secret. I was a married woman with three children when I finally learned my family's secret. It crept out gradually through hints, allusions and then a question. Had I read "A Conscience Unburdened"? No, I hadn't.

"I'll send it to you," my nephew said and winked conspiratorially, but he never sent it.

A cousin said my half-sister had once threatened to tell me about this secret, but our mother suggested she leave well enough alone. I didn't know what my cousin was talking about. I only knew it concerned my father, Robert Emmett Hicks.

Now, looking back, I can't remember how I found out. When I did, I became overwhelmed with pride at the strength of my father, his determination, his obstinacy and his ability to turn a failed life into a successful one. My father wrote "A Conscience Unburdened" in 1915, but interestingly, it is included on the current reading list of several prestigious law schools, including Yale. It revealed that my father had been a flim-flam man, a drunk, swindler and cheat. To add to the disgrace, he had been convicted of a Federal crime, mail fraud, and sentenced to prison on Blackwell's Island, New York. Let my father tell his own story:

Canvassers Magazine

A NATIONAL MONTHLY FOR PEOPLE WHO SELL

Subscription price, $1.00 per year; single copies 10 cents. Postage on subscriptions to foreign countries, 48 cents a year additional; to Canada, 24 cents additional. Entered as second-class matter November 15, 1915, at the post office at South Whitley, Indiana, under the Act of March 3, 1879.

Published Monthly at South Whitley, Indiana

ROBERT E. HICKS CORPORATION, Publisher   ROBERT E. HICKS, Editor

The Official Organ of the Associated Specialty Manufacturers and Salesmen of America, Incorporated

VOL. I.   SOUTH WHITLEY, IND., OCTOBER, 1916   NO. 10

A Conscience Unburdened—Cowardly Attacks Refuted

To my loyal friends—canvassing salesmen everywhere—I owe it to you to tell the truth—to refute the terrible blows that are being hurled at Canvassers Magazine and at me personally in the hope of forcing the suspension of this publication. Underhand, cowardly, treacherous attempts are being secretly made night and day to poison your minds and if possible to destroy me. In this article I am telling you the whole truth—holding nothing back—revealing the darkest blots upon my life, that you may know and understand. It is for you to decide whether I am to be trusted or the mail-order pirates who are robbing you and your brothers of millions of dollars every year.

ROBERT E. HICKS
Editor Canvassers Magazine

Christ Jesus came into the world to save sinners; of whom I am chief—*Timothy 1:15*

THE past! When conscience has been brought to life, it is not always pleasant to think much of the past. I would if I could forget the shameful past for the reason that God forgets it. The Prophet Isaiah says, "God casts men's sins behind His back." In the words of the Psalmist, "God casts sins truly repented of into the depths of the sea."

* * *

It may interest you to know that Robert Hicks, the publisher of the magazine you mention has personal motives in slandering this Corporation, and it is unknown to the trade in general that said Hicks is an ex-convict, released last year from the federal prison, where he served a sentence for perpetrating a mail order fraud.

The above was the closing paragraph in a letter dated June 9th, 1916, written by the Mail Order News Corporation, Newburgh, N. Y., to the Vanilarine Company, Poughkeepsie, N. Y.

In the May issue of the Mail Order News there was nearly a page article, in which the same statements were made. I paid but little attention to this shameful outburst of hatred. I had expected that the more vicious of that class who are robbing the public would strike back —would try to cover their crimes by uncovering the darkest blot in my life.

In a recent letter from the Niagara Merchandising Company, Lockport, N. Y., which is in fact a business conducted by Wm. A. Heacock, signed by F. H.

457

Balliett, secretary, and addressed to Mr. R. Ghequiere, Calgary, Canada, I take the following paragraph:

Your favor under date of August 16th was duly received, making reference to Canvassers Magazine, and in reply would say that Robert E. Hicks, who is the publisher of that magazine, was a few years ago sentenced to ten months in jail and payment of $1,000 fine by Judge J. C. Pollock, United States Attorney, for violation of the postal laws, but he forfeited bail. He subsequently surrendered and served his term of imprisonment, although we understand that he was pardoned before the expiration of same through the intervention of some of his friends.

This perhaps is about as correct a statement as any of these firms engaged in robbing the public ever make. It is nearer the truth than any of the other letters that have been sent to me by canvassing salesmen who have received such letters.

The National Distributing Company, Chicago, by its manager, Mr. Walt. D. Munn, closes a letter under date of August 29th, 1916, to J. Fetter, Battle Creek, Mich. by saying:

This is a good deal more than your champion, Mr. Hicks, will do, who, I understand, is either an escaped convict or one who has served his term.

The National Clock & Manufacturing Company, Chicago, a powerful organization that boasts of its financial power, is not only writing letters in the hope of poisoning the minds of canvassing salesmen, but is quietly working among advertisers in Canvassers Magazine, endeavoring to induce advertisers to withdraw their patronage.

I would not pay any attention at this time to the letters that are being sent out by various fraudulent firms, or the article published in the Mail Order News in May, were it not for the fact that a number of firms engaged in conducting businesses of a fraudulent nature are quietly circulating reports concerning my past, in the hope of destroying Canvassers Magazine and forcing me out of the publishing business.

They have reasons for destroying Canvassers Magazine. At first they looked upon Canvassers Magazine as a joke, but now they know it is a reality, and they know that unless they can destroy Canvassers Magaizne the public will be protected against their fraudulent schemes, and they will be forced out of business and many of them sent to prison.

No doubt thousands of letters are writ-

ten every week by various fraudulent schemers to canvassing salesmen in every section of the country telling that which will injure me most—that which has a tendency to break me down and force Canvassers Magazine to suspend publication.

There is no way of knowing just how many letters are written by those whose fraudulent methods I have exposed, but this I do know, that a very large number of letters written have been sent to me.

All along I have refrained from telling the truth, hoping against hope that it would not be necessary to reveal the blackest blot upon my life. The time has come, however, when I must speak. I feel that it is a duty I owe to the thousands and thousands of canvassing salesmen throughout the country to tell them the truth—to conceal nothing. There is no other way by which I can refute these poisonous assertions that are hurled throughout the country every day for the sole purpose of forcing Canvassers Magazine to suspend publication.

*
* *

In my early days, away back in the seventies and the early eighties, when a boy in my teens, it was necessary for me to support myself. I worked on farms, as a canvassing salesman; served my time in the printing trade, and then returned to the business of selling things from house-to-house, and finally drifted into mail order schemes.

My first mail-order venture was to print fifty visiting cards for 10 cents. Then I sold school supplies by mail, such as reward of merit cards and other helps for school teachers. I was at that time publisher of the Lewis County Journal—a paper which I founded at Monticello, Mo. After a short time I sold the Journal and after spending the money received, I returned to the business of selling from house-to-house. I could always make a living in that way. I did not remain as a canvassing salesman for any great length of time—starting scheme after scheme of a questionable nature—selling mustache powders to make the mustache grow, and love powders to make any one love you. With the money made from these schemes I started such schemes as selling outfits for collecting names and addresses, start you in the mail order business, circular distributing schemes, medical schemes and schemes of all kinds by which money could be secured through the medium of the United States mails.

Let it be understood that in this article there is no attempt to justify myself—there is nothing to justify. When I was conducting questionable schemes, many of them actually fraudulent, I always justified myself. I sometimes tried to make myself believe that the schemes were legitimate. In the beginning I always justified myself with the thought that I was giving my victims more than they could secure elsewhere for the same money—that the stock catalogues and printed stationery which I was furnishing would cost many times the price that I charged if purchased independent of me by my victims from a printer.

It is not pleasant to look back, but often times when I do allow myself to think of the miserable past, I wonder if I really did not make myself believe that I was justified in what I was doing.

So far as making money was concerned, I was a success. It was in 1898 that I went to New York and started various mail order schemes, among which was the Geneva Chemical Company, a medical scheme which, like many other fraudulent schemes I had conducted, was a financial success until in 1902 when Anthony Comstock took a hand in my business and put me out of business. I was arrested, gave bond, and in May, 1903, was tried in the Federal Court in New York City before Judge Adams.

The trial lasted several days. I was convicted and sentenced to ten months in the Kings County penitentiary and to pay a fine of $1,000. An appeal was taken. I gave bond pending the appeal and immediately went to Europe. I remained there for some time, returning to this country in the fall of 1903.

There is nothing of particular interest in my life from the time that I returned to this country until I surrendered to the government on May 31, 1915, except that I engaged in various business enterprises with more or less success, and that I lived in continual fear of being taken into custody by the Federal authorities.

For thirteen years I went from city to city, from town to town, engaging in this and then in that, always living in the fear of being taken into custody and sent to the penitentiary where I rightfully belonged.

*
* *

Ever since I was twenty years old I had used intoxicants excessively—what is known as a "periodical."

My early life was spent in a Christian home. I lived in a home where the family altar was firmly established, but when it was necessary for me to go out into the world and earn my way as a canvassing salesman, or work on a farm, or work at the printing trade, I soon forgot the things that I had learned at my mother's knee and the prayers around the fireplace in the log cabin in Knox County, Missouri, where I was born. I longed for worldly pleasures and paid lavishly for them with the money which I had received as the profits from the businesses in which I had from time to time engaged. I did not then realize fully the wicked life that I was living.

"The wages of sin is death; but the gift of God is eternal life through Jesus Christ our Lord."

The wages of sin was death to me—death to my conscience, to truth, honesty and everything that was good. In that helpless, hopeless condition I followed where Satan led me and drifted back to New York City right under the shadow of the penetentiary to which I had been sentenced—a fugitive from justice. Sleepless nights, restless days, growing from bad to worse, trying to forget the shadow that hung over and around me—trying to escape from beneath the rock of despair that hung by a thread over my head—feeling that I was a hunted man, I went on and on to the edge of the precipice—a hopeless, friendless, penniless drunkard.

Every dollar, every cent that I had received by fraudulent methods—methods that were pleasing only to the devil himself, had been spent as the devil directed.

During all these years the devil had pointed out to me the pleasures of the world. I had followed the devil in securing the money to gratify these pleasures. I purchased these pleasures and paid the devil's price, until he finally led me where he will lead every one who follows him—to the end of the journey—to misery, shame and disgrace.

It was on the morning of December 1, 1912, that I wandered into the office of a business man that was once my friend when I had experienced more prosperous days. For weeks I had been helplessly intoxicated. In order to get rid of me this man had taken me first to one hotel on the East side and then to another, but on account of my filthy, drunken condition I was refused admittance, until at last, way down on Front Street, the proprietor of a low dive permitted me to enter and gave me a little room, without ventilation, on the third floor—no heat, just a cot in one corner of the room. I was helped to this room by two porters. I fell across the bed and went to sleep—a drunken, restless sleep.

It was late in the afternoon of that day that God sent to me the Rev. Dr. Robert G. Davey, who was then connected with the National Bible Institute in New York City. I am firmly of the opinion that if this good man had come a few hours later I never would have told you this story. In that room on that cold winter day, I was freezing. Hardly a breath of air could enter—I was sick from the effects of the poisonous, vile whiskey that I had been drinking for several weeks.

Dr. Davey aroused me from my stupor as best he could. He assisted me down two flights of rickety stairs and then to a street car and to Manhattan Gospel Hall, a light house of God, under the auspices of the National Bible Institute, at 101 Manhattan Street. It was late in the afternoon, I was given a clean, warm bed—something that I had not known for ten or fifteen days.

I can remember little of my first night in the Manhattan Gospel Hall. My poisoned stomach rebelled against food—10,000 pores in my body begged for whiskey.

It was some time during the early part of the night when I awoke; Dr. Davey was kneeling at my bedside praying.

I heard the music in the meeting room down stairs. They were singing, "Nearer my God to Thee." Dr. Davey finished his prayer and asked me to pray. I tried and could not. There seemed to be but one thought, just one desire, and that was to satisfy the 10,000 pores in my body that were begging for rum. Every nerve twitched—I longed to go to sleep and never

wake. I wanted to be alone. I wanted rest. I wanted above all things whiskey to satisfy that craving that I could not overcome.

Dr. Davey kneeled at my bedside again and prayed, and when he had finished a most earnest appeal, asking God to help me, he again asked me to pray. I mumbled something—it seemed like mockery. My mind was wandering, and in that condition I thought of the log cabin way back in Missouri and of years long ago, and I prayed a prayer that I learned at my mother's knee, "Now I lay me down to sleep, if I should die before I wake, I pray the Lord my soul to take."

Dr. Davey again asked God to help me, said "Good night" and was gone.

For perhaps an hour I lived again in the old log house in Missouri. I played again along the little stream that flowed back of the old barn. I enjoyed the sweet fragrance of the flowers that lined the approach to the old house in the front yard. I coud feel the warmth of the fire in the fire-place, and heard Mother read a chapter of one of the apostles, and heard my Christian father again ask God to guide, protect and keep us until the morrow. Basking in this beautiful reverie of the past I went to sleep.

The second day of December was a cold, beautiful day in New York, and when I awoke the sun was shining in at my window.

I was sick—unable to get out of the bed that had been so generously provided for me, but I felt much better. There had come into my life a hope.

On the third day of December I was able to be up although far from being well. There was that craving for rum—that something that for years I had used to quiet my nerves after a debauch such as I had just gone through, but I felt determined never to touch it again. I had felt that way before in my own strength, and it was my own strength that I was then depending upon. I knew of no other strength. I had not yet realized that there was other help.

I was able to attend the evening meeting in the chapel. Mr. Beggs was assistant superintendent of the mission and delivered the address of the evening. He spoke from Matthew 14:28: "Come unto me, all ye that labour and are heavy laden, and I will give you rest."

If there was ever a man who needed rest—if there was ever a man who was heavy laden, homeless and more friendless than I felt, I cannot imagine his position in life. Testimonies from converts were invited. These testimonies hardly seemed real—men told the wonderful story of how they had been saved. All of the stories were different and after all, they all told the same story. Lived lives of debauchery, wretchedness, drunkenness—had been picked from the gutter and brought to life through the blood of Jesus, who died for them and me upon the Cross of Calvary.

As I listened to these wonderful stories of redeemed lives, there would come to me the text that I had heard only an hour before, "Come unto me and I will give you rest." When the invitation was given I went forward and knelt at the altar and prayed the prayer of the publican. Mr. Beggs knelt and prayed with me, but I, unlike many who kneel at the altar in a mission, did not find Christ there. I was not in earnest—I had not surrendered myself unconditionally to Him. It seemed as though I could not make a complete surrender—perhaps I did not want to.

A short time after the meeting I went to my room. I was disturbed, troubled—conscience had begun to awake—I was now concerned with reference to my wife and little children. I did not know where they were and was not sure that they had proper food. I was nervous, wretched. There was something that troubled me as never before. I could almost, in my imagination hear little Helen and little Phoebe say to their mother, "Mamma, where is papa—mamma I am hungry—why don't papa bring us something to eat." When these thoughts would come over me I felt that I would go mad—conscience was alive again. I felt my responsibility and duty, something that sin and whiskey destroys. I cried out in anguish. I asked God to help me, but seemingly there was no help. I tried to sleep—sleep was impossible.

I got out of bed and walked the floor, I knelt at the bed and prayed. I would get back in bed and try to pray myself to sleep—no rest—no sleep. I was going through a hundred fiery furnaces.

The great East river was not far away. I felt if I could only let the waves as they rolled down to the ocean carry me with them, they would cool my burning head and perhaps bring the rest that I could not find elsewhere. How I longed for the waves to carry me down to sleep in the bosom of the restless ocean!

It was in the gray of the morning that I knelt again at the bed side and again prayed—the prayer that I learned at mother's knee: "Now I lay me down to sleep, if I should died before I wake, I pray the Lord my soul to take."

I could almost feel her dear presence with me again. I cried out to God to take me as I was and to use me as he pleased—no conditions, except God's own conditions—to serve Him and follow Him wherever He would lead me.

I was in earnest—no quibbling, "Just take me as I am, not one single plea, Oh! Lamb of God, I come to Thee." The surrender was complete and peace came over me—I was satisfied. I accepted God at His word. He searched my heart and He was satisfied.

I did not know where my wife and children were, but I was at peace with God and I knew that He knew, and I was satisfied. I was no longer restless, I did not now long for the waves to cool my burning head. The ten thousand pores in my body had ceased to cry out for rum.

It was late in the morning of December 4, 1912, that I awoke from several hours of the most peaceful sleep that I had enjoyed for weeks. I was far from being strong, but I was happy, except that I was greatly concerned as to my wife and children, and I realized now more than ever that I was a fugitive from justice.

Every hour I was getting stronger, and by noon I felt strong enough to help in the kitchen of the mission. I helped to cook and prepare the food for something like seventy or seventy-five homeless, wretched, hungry men.

I shall never forget watching the men eat the food that we had cooked and which the National Bible Institute had provided. I shall never forget the looks of despair on their faces, yet only a few hours before I had been one of them. There seemed to be just two things lacking in my life. I was satisfied, however, that God would arrange these two things for me—restore to me my wife and children and lift the awful load which I had carried then for about ten years—the load of being a fugitive from justice.

I left the mission on the morning of December 6th, two days after I was converted. I went immediately to the headquarters of the National Bible Institute. I was told by Dr. Davey that my wife and children had been located and I was given their address. Not necessary to tell of our meeting a few hours afterwards. We alone can live in the memory of that sweet hour—the memory of the tenderness of her caresses and the warmth of her kisses when she understood and believed that I was a redeemed man through the blood of Jesus Christ, will linger with me throughout this life. Let us live forever in the joy of seeing and feeling the happiness of our little children as they nestled in my arms and sat upon my knees on that never to be forgotten day!

They could not understand just why it was so, but they knew and felt that there was something that made them extremely happy. They were happy but they did not know why—they were too young to understand.

* *

During the months that followed God used me in many ways. He put it into the life of men to assist me in starting a small printing business in New York. It was not long until I had a comfortable little home. The days were busy days in a commercial way and the nights were busy nights—testifying first at one mission and then at another—telling what God had been to me in my life, but all the time I was realizing more forcibly that I was a fugitive from justice. In the old life there was nothing but fear of getting caught that made the load heavy. In the new life the load became heavier and heavier because my conscience was alive and I knew that I did not stand right before my fellow men. None of my new Christian friends knew that I was a fugitive from justice. It was then eleven years since I had been convicted—perhaps the Federal authorities had forgotten it, but I had not—the load was heavier day by day.

It was my privilege to testify to what God had done for me in many of the most prominent churches in New York and in various missions throuhgout New York City and Brooklyn. I was the speaker at many out door meetings in New York City. I filled the pulpits on Sundays in churches in New York. I was called to many nearby cities to help as best I could in the Master's work. The more that I would do, in my feeble way, for Him, the more I felt the load—the load of being a fugitive from justice.

Mr. Comstock's office was at 140 Nassau Street. Time and time again I would make up my mind to go to his office and surrender to the Federal authorities. On one occasion, without consulting my wife, I went to 140 Nassua Street, went up in the elevator and got off on the floor on which this good man's office was located. I did not have the strength or courage to open his door. I felt that I was not yet ready. I would put it off for a little while longer.

In the spring of 1915, I sent my wife and three children to spend the hot summer months in a nearby city out of sweltering New York. It was on Sunday evening, May 30th, that I spoke at the Bowery Mission, that famous old mission that has a reputation of making crooked men straight. More than 500 hopeless, helpless men listened attentively to my testimony as to what God had done for me. At the close of the meeting, a man past middle age, rose in the audience and said: "I want to live the life that I have heard about. Only a few days ago I was released from the penitentiary on Blackwell's Island. Everywhere that I go, I feel that every hand is turned against me. I am an ex-convict and I feel that everyone knows it."

I tell you what that man said struck home to me. He had served his time in the penitentiary. The man who had told him of the better life was a fugitive from justice. I resolved then and there that I would lift the load—that I would pay the price—I would stand in the presence of my fellow men, lifting up the cross of Jesus Christ, a free man.

After the meeting I went at once to my home. Alone in our apartment at 50 Horatio Street I talked the matter over with God—talked there with him just as I would have talked to an individual— told him all about how weak I was and how earnest I was in my plea for His strength to help me. Discussed it from every angle and asked God to guide me and He did. He guided me as He always guides us—to do that which is right.

I was up bright and early the next morning, Monday, May 31st. It was a holiday—New York was celebrating Decoration day which fell on Sunday but was celebrated on Monday. I waited impatiently until about nine o'clock, when I went to the telephone and called up Mr. Anthony Comstock at his home in Summit, New Jersey. It was a woman's voice that answered the telephone. I asked if Mr. Comstock was at home. She replied, "Who is it that wants to speak to Mr. Comstock."

For fear that I might lose my strength and again falter, I told her instantly, "Robert E. Hicks, 638 Hudson Street, New York City." So anxious was I to make the surrender and not again lose courage, I felt that by giving my name and address that I could not back down.

While I was waiting for Mr. Comstock to come to the telephone I commenced to sing, "Nearer my God to Thee," and never before in my life was I nearer to God than I was at that moment. I was singing when Mr. Comstock answered, "Mr. Hicks what can I do for you?"

"Mr. Comstock," I replied, "do you remember me?"

"Oh! yes, I remember you; where are you?"

"I am at 638 Hudson Street, New York, and after all these years I want to surrender to the Federal authorities. Shall I come over to Summit, or shall I call at your office in the morning?"

"Call at my office in the morning at ten o'clock," he replied, "and I will talk it over with you. Is there anything that I can do for you today?"

"Yes," I said, "Mr. Comstock you can pray for me."

"Oh! I will do that," he replied. "Mr. Hicks I have often prayed for you."

When I left the telephone I walked from room to room in my home singing, "Nearer my God to Thee." I was never happier in my life. I was happy all day.

I wrote a letter to my wife, telling her what I had done—telling her how happy I was, and while I had not been taken in custody yet, the surrender had been made

—I could not undo what I had done even though I should lose my courage and change my mind. I asked my wife to return to New York and take charge of my business.

I knew that she would receive my letter the next morning at about the time I would make the surrender to Mr. Comstock at his office at ten o'clock, Tuesday, June 1st. I had no other idea except that as soon as I made the surrender I would at once be taken to the penitentiary. Did not think I would have an opportunity to see my wife and children before going.

At ten o'clock Tuesday morning I called at Mr. Comstock's office. He was waiting for me. I was ushered into his private office and he greeted me cordially. "Mr. Hicks," he said, "I am glad to see you. I have just been looking over the records of your case and the trial. I have made some inquiry as to the work that you have been trying to do for the past two or three years. I recall thirteen years ago as if only last week. I remember how vindictive you were, how determined, and I remember how difficult it was to convict you. I had a hard time to get you in the penitentiary, and I fear now that I am going to have a harder time to keep you out."

"Why, Mr. Comstock, I did not come here to keep out, I came here to get in. This terrible load that I have carried for thirteen years must be lifted. God is with me in what I am doing today and I want to commence to serve my time and pay the price as soon as I possibly can."

"Mr. Hicks," replied Mr. Comstock, "I am not going to surrender you to the United States attorney today. I will go and see what I can do to keep you from going to the penitentiary. I will investigate further the work you have been doing in the slums of New York for the past three years and I am going to see if it is not possible to keep you out of the penitentiary. Go about your business and return here a week from today, and I will then let you know what I have accomplished in your behalf."

This was unexpected. I returned to my business. Wednesday morning my wife and three children arrived in New York. Mrs. Hicks was almost prostrated with grief. It is always the innocent that really suffer. The little children could not understand.

During the week I talked with a number of friends and most every one disapproved of the step I had taken. Just a few approved of the position in which I had placed myself. My Christian friends knew nothing about me being a fugitive from justice. They had supposed there was nothing in my life that I had been holding back and it was a great surprise to all of them. Many good Christian men contended that inasmuch as I had made it right with God, it did not matter as to man, but to me it did matter. As I stood in the Bowery Mission on the night of May 30th, talking to the 500 homeless, hopeless men I felt and knew that I did not stand in the right light. After the man in the audience had said that he wanted to live a Christian life and that every hand was turned against him because he had recently been released from the penitentiary, I felt more keenly than ever before that I was not doing that which God would have me do. As I stood among the Christian workers on the platform, as never before I felt a real shame—I felt that I had no right to stand among these men knowing that I was a fugitive from justice.

Except for the grief of my wife and the anxiety of my little children about something they could not understand, the week passed as pleasantly as, perhaps, any week during my entire life.

Tuesday morning with several friends I went to Mr. Comstock's office. The matter was discussed by all present. Mr. Comstock said there was nothing that he could do. He advised, as did the friends present, that I go home and settle up all my business affairs, arrange to continue my business during my absence and return to Mr. Comstock's office Thursday morning at ten o'clock, June 10th, when I would be surrendered to the United States District Attorney.

I shall never forget Thursday morning, June 10th, when I left home knowing that I would not return again for a long time. I would not even attempt to tell of my parting with Mrs. Hicks and the three little children. I was happy because I was going, and tried to look forward only to my return. Tried in vain to comfort Mrs. Hicks. Tried in vain to supress my sobs of grief at parting, yet all the time happy because I was going to go—to pay the price for crimes committed thirteen years before—the price for standing as a man, in the true light, before God and my fellow men.

When I arrived at Mr. Comstock's office on Thursday morning with a number of Christian friends, I found that a large number of friends had preceded me there and were awaiting my arrival. Mr. Comstock guided us to the United States district attorney's office in the Post-office building. The district attorney was waiting for us—shook hands with me cordially. Said he had gone over the matter carefully, had found the commitment papers issued thirteen years ago, and was sorry to say that there was nothing he could do.

I could hardly understand how the Federal authorities, who thirteen years before were so persistent in their efforts to convict me, were now just as persistent in their efforts to free me.

After talking the matter over for sometime it was decided that I should go before the judge of the United States district court which was in session. After waiting until some cases were disposed of the district attorney arose and addressed the judge, reviewing my case at length; telling the judge of the work I had been doing in the slums of New York. To my surprise he had a number of letters which he read, written to him by men of prominence in New York City.

The judge asked me if I was represented by counsel. I told him that I was not; that I did not feel the need of counsel, that I wanted to pay the price for crimes committed thirteen years ago.

"Mr. District Attorney," said the judge, "is it not possible that application can be made for a new trial?"

"No," replied the district attorney, "I have gone over the matter carefully and find that the time has long since past that a new trial can be applied for."

"I understand," said the judge, "that the Kings County penitentiary has been torn down and there is no penitentiary in Kings County. Will that have any bearing on this case?"

"No, your honor," replied the district attorney, "you have it within your power to resentence Mr. Hicks to some other penitentiary."

Turning to me the judge said, "There is nothing that I can do, Mr. Hicks, but resentence you. The sentence of the court is that you serve ten months in the New York County penitentiary on Blackwell's Island and pay a fine of $1,000."

Addressing the United States marshal, the judge said, "Mr. Marshall you understand the circumstances surrounding this case. I trust that you will extend to Mr. Hicks such courtesies as you feel are admissable in a case of this kind."

My friends present gathered around me speaking in low tones, all showing plainly their grief. I was the happiest man in the court room. After my friends said goodbye and slowly left the court room with bowed heads, the marshall asked when I wanted to go. I replied, "at once."

"Is there not something you want to see about—do you not want to go home and say good-bye to your family?"

"No," I replied, "but I would like to go and call my wife and have her meet me, as I have forgotten to arrange with the bank so that my wife and children can secure funds during my absence."

"All right," he said, "you go home, but if you want to go to Blackwell's Island today, the last boat leaves at three o'clock, and you must be here in time to catch that boat."

I went to a nearby telephone and called my wife and asked that she meet me at a nearby restaurant. I went to the restaurant and in a very short time she came. We had dinner together, then went to the bank and made necessary arrangements so that she would be supplied with means during my long absence from home. I then returned to the United States marshall's office in time for the three o'clock boat.

He informed me that it would be necessary for him to send a clerk with me in order that he might get a receipt for my body.

*
* *

June 10th was a beautiful day in New York. The prisoners that had been sentenced to the penitentiary on June 10th had been taken over on an earlier boat and I was the only prisoner that was a passenger on that boat. A large number of women were on the boat—in fact the boat was crowded, mostly with women going to see fathers, sons or brothers who were prisoners on Blackwell's Island—making monthly trips that my wife would soon make—to see her husband who was paying the price for crimes committed before she knew him.

As the boat pulled out and started up the river I could plainly see the penitentiary in the distance. I stood on the upper deck. I never went anywhere in my life with greater joy than I was making that trip to Blackwell's Island where I expected to remain for ten months. God was with me. God had given me the courage to do what I was doing. I did not have a single regret for the step I had taken—did not want to turn back—was anxious for the boat to land at the penitentiary.

It was just fifteen minutes before four o'clock when the great steel doors of the New York County penitentiary opened to receive me. It was four o'clock when I had finished answering questions, surrendered everything in my pockets, and sat down in the barber chair to have my head shaved.

After shaving my head and face I was taken to another room, stripped of the clothes I wore to the penitentiary, and for the first time in my life I was wearing stripes. I was put into a cell where I remained until time for supper.

In the mess room I tried to eat but could not—I had not become accustomed to the food. I might say right here that the food was far better than I had any right to expect. Every condition in the prison was better than I had a right to expect. I was their for committing crimes against the laws of God and man. I was not ignorant of the crime that I had committed. I deserved more punishment than I was receiving.

During the supper hour I sat between two negroes. I heard cursing and vile language in under tones all about me. Although I could not eat I bowed, after sitting down, and thanked God for His wonderful mercies, for His presence with me that hour and for the beautiful sunshine that was shedding its last rays for that day through the window of the prison near me.

The colored man on my right said in a low voice, "How long are you in for?"

I whispered my reply, "ten months and $1,000 fine."

"Two years and $500 fine for me; but I have been here a year."

"How do you find it here?"

With an oath he replied, "Tough—treated like dogs."

"I am sure," said I, "that if you will accept God into your life that things here will not seem so bad after all."

He laughed almost aloud and said, "I would like to see God or anyone else make things pleasant in this hell hole."

"They are pleasant to me," I replied. "Plenty of fresh air; this food is better than we have a right to expect; the East river flows around us, and certainly, under the circumstances, we have more than we have a right to expect."

He cursed me for expressing an opinion of this kind. The keeper heard him and rapped for silence with his club.

Thursday in the penitentiary on Blackwell's Island is concert night. I spent the first night in my cell near the chapel where the musicians assembled. It was possibly eight o'clock when the singing commenced. I knew that it had been dark only a short time. They do not have chairs in the cells on Blackwell's Island. You cannot sit on the cot as the upper cot is placed just over the lower cot, leaving only room enough to lie down. When in the cell one must lie down or stand up.

When I was first locked in the cell I asked the tierman to get me a Bible. With some little difficulty he secured one for me, which I was reading when the concert commenced. The first song that was sung was "Suwanee River." The singing made me melancholy—my mind involuntarily wandered to my home in the little apartment at 50 Horatio Street. I could see little Bob, Phoebe and Helen. I knew at that time they were waiting my home coming, and that they could not understand my absence or their mother's grief.

These were really the only unhappy moments that I spent while on Blackwell's Island. It was difficult for me to take my thoughts from 50 Horatio

Street. Tears for the first time filled my eyes. I opened my Bible and read, Malachi, fourth chapter. I was not at that moment interested in any particular chapter or verse—just wanted the comfort that reading any of God's promises would give me. My eyes fell on the tenth verse, and I read, "Prove me now herewith, saith the Lord of hosts, if I will not open you the windows of Heaven, and pour out a blessing, that *there shall not be room enough to receive it.*"

"Prove me now—*try me, test me*—if I will not open you the windows of Heaven and pour you out a blessing that there shall not be room enough to receive it."

Oh, it made my heart leap and my pulses beat fast when I read this word of our God. It was the full challenge of God to my faith.

He was telling me how willing He is, and bidding me test His willingness. Such impressive language—how could more expressive language be used?

"I will open the windows"—fling them wide! No stinting, no withholding, no grudging.

"I will pour you out a blessing." Not thimbles full, not buckets full, but poured out floods.

"Not room enough to receive it." Seemingly extravagant language, but I felt that that was how anxious God was to have me understand. He awakened my mind with this—"not room enough." I realized more fully the greatness of God's stored-up blessings, and that my shut-up life did not furnish room enough.

There in that prison cell, with the tierman looking on, I knelt at my cot and accepted God's challenge. "Oh! God, enlarge my heart! Make room for Thy blessing here. My heart is hungry within me—help me, dear Lord, to feel my need. Lead me, Heavenly Father, and I will follow."

The vision of home had passed from me—I was thinking of what I could do for His dear sake and my soul rejoiced. I said it over and over again: "Open windows! Open windows!"

A number of classic songs were sung by trained voices, male and female, such as, "My Old Kentucky Home," "Annie Laurie" "Suwanee River," and several other songs of this class. There was an intermission of possibly four or five minutes, and then the organist commenced to play, "Nearer My God to Thee." There were possibly ten or fifteen trained voices—they are now singing—the strains of music grow sweeter and sweeter. Now they commence to sing the chorus. Possibly five hundred prisoners in every part of the prison join in the singing—sweeter and sweeter—could I have ever been nearer to God than I was then?

Now a sweet, soprano voice sings the last verse alone. Seemingly seventeen hundred prisoners join in singing the chorus.

Everything is now quiet in the prison— for a few moments not a sound is heard except the rolling of the waves on the East river as they roll on to the great Atlantic ocean.

The windows of Heaven were opened. He had poured out a blessing that there was not room enough to receive it.

* * *

It is said that the first night in prison is the most miserable. In the earlier part of the day a number of convicts were brought in. The first-nighters all occupied cells near each other. Some were old-timers, having been there before. Others were not yet hardened, and their grief was pitiful to hear—sobbing bitterly throughout the night. All that I could hear after the lights were turned off at 10 o'clock was sobs from a few of the new arrivals and cursing and vile language from others. I spent the hours when not asleep in prayer. I was close to God that night, and I was happy.

You, who do not know God cannot understand.

In the mess hall the next morning at breakfast when I bowed my head to thank God for His wonderful mercies and for the food of which I was about to partake, those sitting near me cursed me in whispers, jeered and laughed. I was somewhat disturbed but I concealed my feeling as best I could. Breakfast consisted of bread and cereal with milk, and coffee. I could not enjoy the meal, although I ate rather freely of the bread which was much better than could have been expected. I spoke to the two men who sat on each side of me with reference to the better life and received curses in reply, but God was with me.

I was not discouraged. After breakfast

I was taken to the photograph gallery where my picture was taken, then into another part of the prison where I left an impression of my finger prints. After securing an impression of my fingers I was taken to the tailor and measured for a suit of regular prison clothes which consisted of coat and trousers. These two necessary articles of wearing apparel were given to me late in the afternoon.

I was assigned to the printing department, but did not go to work until Saturday morning.

I spent the day in reading God's word. I never knew before how interesting the book of Genesis was. During my stay in prison I read the book of Genesis several times and each time it became more interesting.

While in prison I read the old Testament through once and the New Testament through four times.

Saturday morning I was put in charge of four small printing presses. I worked faithfully and earnestly as I would have worked in my own office or for a firm outside of the prison. This was not pleasing to the other prisoners. At first they made it very disagreeable because I was striving with the best that was within me to do my full duty. I encouraged the men to do their full duty. There were five men working under me and while I had no particular authority over these men, yet they knew that if I reported them to the keeper that they would be punished. This I did not want to do and only once while in prison was it necessary for me to report any one of them to the keeper. I have always regretted doing it, for the reason that he was severely punished— sent to the cooler for five days.

The cooler is a cell in the back part of the prison, and it is seldom that a prisoner goes to the cooler the second time.

Prisoners in the printing department, shoe shop, spindle factory and tailor shop were given a bath on Saturday mornings. Many of the prisoners did not like the idea of taking a bath, but every one was forced to take a bath once each week.

After the bath I was dressing in a booth adjoining a safe burglar who had served time in several prisons. He was a man of more than ordinary intelligence. He had commenced a life of crime at a very early age. He told me that he was forty-two years old and had a year yet to serve on Blackwell's Island, and then had to go back to Sing Sing to finish a sentence of seventeen months, having been paroled from Sing Sing a few years before.

He cursed society, the police, judges of courts, the warden of the penitentiary, keepers, and in fact he cursed everything and every body.

"My friend," said I, "this is a beautiful morning, everything around us is ideal under the circumstances. The trouble is not with the police, the judges of courts, or of society, or the keepers of this prison or with the prison itself—the trouble is with us. If we had not been the enemies of society, we would not be here."

He flew into a violent temper and cursed me most outrageously—called me vile names, but God was with me. I did not lose my temper. Instead I felt more kind to him after he had cursed me in this most vile manner than I had before.

"My friend," said I, "this prison is not such a horrible place after all—it is just what we make it. Let God be with you in this prison and he will make it a place of happiness for you. Tonight when you go to your cell, go on your knees and ask God to forgive you—surrender everything and you will find that life in this prison is not to you what it is now."

Not necessary to repeat every thing that was said. Finally he cooled down and spoke more kindly. I told him that I was as happy in prison as I had ever been in my life.

He was working in the shoe shop. He was supposed to march back to the shoe shop, which adjoined the printing office, with the men that worked in the shoe shop, but he fell out of line unobserved by the keeper and marched back to his work with me. He was interested in what I had said as to what God could do for men in prison on Blackwell's Island.

The men in the shoe shop always stood at the head of the stairway, waiting for the men in the printing office to pass ahead of them. As we marched out of the printing office at the noon hour the safe burglar, who I will hereafter call Jones, was standing at the head of the stairway, and as I passed he said in a low voice, "I have been thinking seriously over what you told me in the bath room." He could not say more but I believe he wanted to.

Including myself there were eighteen men working in the printing office. There was one negro who was serving his first term in prison. This man had been on Blackwell's Island for more than two years. His sentence was for two years and a fine of $500.

A prisoner must serve one day for each dollar fine. This colored man had just begun to serve time on his fine. He spent most of his idle time reading the Bible while in prison, and he was the one man in the printing office that was glad to see me.

I am confident he was very much in earnest, but until I was placed in the printing office he did not have courage to talk to the men about the better life. We went to work at eight and worked until eleven, then had a half hour to wash up and get ready for the march to the mess hall. We returned to work at one and worked until four; had a half hour to wash before marching to the mess hall for supper. It usually required about five or ten minutes for the eighteen men to wash and get ready for the meal hour. I always had from twenty to twenty-five minutes to talk to the men, and I took advantage of every minute. My first day in the printing office I spoke to the colored man while waiting to go to the mess hall at noon. Some four or five other prisoners came up where we were talking, which gave me an opportunity to tell these men what God had done for me, and how happy He was making my life in prison.

Except for the colored man my talk was not received with much favor. Absurd foolish questions were asked me; vicious stories were told in my presence while I was talking, but God was with me, and I was determined to live in that prison in such a manner that He would open the windows of heaven and pour me out such a blessing that there should not be room enough to receive it.

Prisoners do not work on Saturday afternoons—they remain in their cells from Saturday noon after the dinner hour until Monday morning, except when they go to their meals and to church in the prison chapel.

I shall never forget my attendance at

church at two o'clock on Sunday afternoon, June 13, 1915. There are two services held in the chapel on each Sunday. The Roman Catholic services are held at nine in the monring, and the Protestant services are held at two in the afternoon. Each service lasts one hour and thirty minutes. There were something over seventeen hundred prisoners on Blackwell's Island at that time. At least 800 of these prisoners attended divine services in the afternoon of Sunday, June 13. The services were most impressive. Shut out from all the world, yet listening to the old old story, a story that is two thousand years old, but to those who know God it is always new.

The services were interesting and helpful, and every man, although ninety per cent were criminals, seemed to take a deep interest in every word that was said.

The closing song was one that will always remain very dear to me: "I need thee every hour, O! I need thee." Oh! that I could always feel the need of Him as I felt it during the singing of that song. With eyes toward heaven, with tears chasing each other down my cheeks, I sang that song as I had never sung it before. Nearly every one of the 800 joined in singing each verse. Many had good voices and some trained voices. Oh, that I could always feel the need of Him as I felt it then. I need Him now just as much as I needed Him then, but I felt His need then perhaps more than I ever have since.

Within a very few days it was generally known throughout the prison who I was, and that I had come to the prison voluntarily. I could see the men pointing me out as I marched in line to and from work, or at meal time in the mess hall.

I do not think that I was in prison more than three or four days before every one of the prisoners knew who I was and a great many never missed an opportunity to curse me or make vile statements when I passed them in going to and from the mess hall or to work. At times it began to have its effect, and if I had not kept in close communion with God I would have given up my determination to be of some service to my brothers while in prison.

God had challenged my faith when I read His challenge the first night that I was in prison, "Prove me, try me, test me,

and I will open the windows of Heaven and pour you out a blessing that there shall not be room enough to receive it." I was so determined to accept God at his word that I do not believe that any amount of jeers would have weakened my determination.

The spindle gang, as they were called, worked in a shop outside the prison. These men always lined up just outside their shop waiting for the shoe shop and the printing office men to pass by, when they would fall in line.

There was a young man not more than twenty-four or twenty-five years old in the spindle gang that hurled at me as I would pass at noon, and in the evening for supper, the most vile language that I had ever heard. I always spoke to him kindly, asked God to be merciful to him. This only seemed to enrage him, and one day at noon he cursed God in the most vile manner. He had been unsuccessful in making me angry. He had hoped by cursing God that I might take some exception to what he was saying.

Several days passed by and this man ceased to curse as I would pass. I shall never forget after having been in prison about ten days, possibly a little longer, as I was leaving the mess hall he managed to get past three or four men that were between us and came up behind me as we marched to our cells. In a very low voice he said, "Mr. Hicks will you loan me your Bible?" I turned my head and saw at a glance who it was and told him I would see to it at once. I had to pass his cell in going to my cell. We were on the first tier. I think his cell was number fourteen. I occupied cell number nineteen. We were locked in at the noon hour. When the tierman came to give us water I asked him if he would take my Bible and give it to one of the men in number fourteen, and if possible get me another one. He complied with my request. When I returned to my cell that evening I found two Bibles that the tierman had secured for me.

God had sent me two for the one I had given, and I have found through all my Christian life that this is just the way God does things. If we give Him a little He will give us a great deal.

It was the following Sunday when this man passed several men in line and came up behind me as we were passing from the mess hall after supper, and said, "Mr. Hicks I have about finished the book of Genesis."

"That's fine," I replied, "How do you like it?"

"Oh! it's wonderful, I can hardly wait until I get to my cell to finish this most wonderful story."

In another instant he dropped out of line and entered his cell. I passed on a few steps to number nineteen, and as the door was locked I felt that truly God was keeping His promise. The windows of Heaven were opened and the blessing which He was pouring out to me had filled me to overflowing. I just wanted to shout. I could hardly restrain myself from crying aloud the wonderful gifts of God.

I had not been in my cell long until the tierman slipped me an envelope containing a letter written on a sheet of brown paper. This envelope was one that had been sent to the man whom I have called Jones, the safe burglar, and he had enclosed in this envelope a letter to me. It was rather long, from which I take the following:

"Ever since having that talk with you in the bath room the other morning I have tried to do as you suggested. I want to thank you for your words of encouragement. From the test of the last two days I am at least convinced that there can be no peace without the grace of God. My life is much happier in this prison since meeting you the first time in the bath house."

After reading this long letter it just seemed that God was determined to pour out blessing after blessing. Shut out from the world I was not shut out from God. I had never been as near God in my short Christian life as I had been while on Blackwell's Island. I can now understand why it was that John Bunyan prayed that he might remain in prison so that he could be nearer to God.

The days were not long to me—they would come and go quickly. Every day I had a new experience. Every day I was permitted in some way or some how to speak to several prisoners with reference to their soul salvation and life eternal.

Twice a day for twenty to twenty-five minutes I had gathered around me all of the men in the printing office, except Saturdays when I was permitted to talk to them only at noon. There was only one man that continually interrupted the meetings in the printing office. Sixteen men listened attentively each day to what I had to say with reference to Him who died on the cross of Calvary that we might live. Often times the keeper would join us at these meetings. Every day God was opening the windows of heaven and pouring out His blessings.

* *

I could only write one letter each month to my wife, but she could write me every day, so could my friends. I could receive as many letters as were sent to me, but could only write one letter a month. These dear letters from my wife were always encouraging—full of hope. Always telling me about the children. Sometimes her letters would make me feel sad, when she would tell me how they missed me at home —tell me what the children had said —that "Papa has gone away off" or "that papa would not be home for a long time." "Mama, why don't papa come home?"

In one letter Mrs. Hicks wrote: "They miss you so much. Dear little Helen prayed for you tonight, "Dear Jesus won't you send papa home, we miss him all the time."

Helen was then four years old.

Every day except Monday I received these loving hopeful messages from Mrs. Hicks, but during my stay there it was only possible for me to write two letters to her. Mrs. Hicks visited me three times while I was in prison. I did not feel that I wanted her to see me there. It always made her grief greater. I could only see her for a few minutes, and then stood in line with other prisoners, with a wire screen separating prisoners from visitors.

I do not remember how long I was in prison, possibly about two weeks, when I was called into the warden's office to meet a lawyer from New York who had come to see me. He said that a large number of my friends had interested themselves in my behalf and that a petition had been sent to the President asking for my pardon. He had with him a large number of legal papers and I could see among these papers letter after letter from Christian friends to the President of the United States, asking for my release. I do not know how many. I was not permitted to see all of the letters. I just had an opportunity to glance at them. These letters were from religious friends, and pastors of various churches and mission workers of prominence in New York City.

I was informed by this attorney that these friends had sent this petition to the President, but that it could not be acted upon until I myself asked for a pardon. He handed me a sheet of paper upon which was written an application for my pardon which I signed. I was told by this attorney that just as soon as he returned to New York that Dr. Hallimond, superintendent of the Bowery Mission, would leave for Washington and present the petition in person to President Wilson.

I did not seem to realize what was being done. I could hardly understand.

Ever since I had been in prison—day by day and night by night, God had opened the windows of heaven and poured me out a blessing. I had never asked any one to intercede in my behalf. I did not feel then and I do not feel now that I deserved a pardon. I was guilty and I felt that my sentence of ten months and fine of $1,000 was really less than I deserved.

If I had gone to prison when I should have, thirteen years before, I do not believe that there was a man in the United States who would have interceded in my behalf. After all it was not me—it was God who had put it into lives of these men to intercede in my behalf, because of the life that I had lived and the work that I had tried to do for three years and five months.

As I dictate this and think back over the years, I wonder what would my fate have been if I had gone to prison when I should have gone, thirteen years before.

Thirteen years before I was a coward—thirteen years before I went to Europe to escape prison. I did not know God then.

A man once said to me, "Hicks it required a great deal of courage to do what you have done."

"Perhaps so," I replied, "but do you know that it was not Hicks' courage, because when Hicks did not know God, Hicks did not have the courage—he was a coward and like a thief in the night he went to Europe."

I had a horror of the penitentiary. I felt that ten months in the penitentiary would kill me. Whether or not it would have killed me, I do not know, but I would rather have been dead than to have gone to the penitentiary thirteen years before. Here is the difference: I had accepted God in my life. On the night of May 31 I prayed most of the night asking God for courage, help and strength. God answered my prayer. God gave me the courage. With God's strength I was a coward no longer, and was anxious to pay the price that would lift the load that I had carried for thirteen years—to pay the price for freedom—to pay the price that would enable me to stand clean before God and clean before my fellow men.

* *

The morning and evening meetings of from twenty to twenty-five minutes were growing in interest daily. I think it was just before July 4th that a new arrival in the prison was assigned to the printing office, making a total of nineteen in that department.

He was a young man, not more than thirty years old—I doubt if he was that old. He had commenced a life of crime very early in life. When twelve years old, he told me, he was sent to the Catholic Protectory in Winchester County, near New York City. After being discharged from the Catholic Protectory he served a term in a reform school. Released from the reform school it was only a short time until he was of lawful age, when he was arrested and sent to Sing Sing. Was paroled at Sing Sing some four or five months when he committed a burglary and was sent to Blackwell's Island.

Although a young man he was a hardened criminal. He had known nothing else, he said. Had never had a chance to know anything else—was brought up in the slums of New York. All of his associates were criminals.

When I talked to him and told him what God had done for me, he would often reply that he didn't want God to do anything for him. No one had ever done anything for him. About all that he had known was knocks, kicks and clubbing from the police. He had never attended school except in penal institutions.

This young man, at first, would always sit in a distant part of the room during the meetings, but it was only a few days until he would come closer and closer, and finally joined in the meetings, asking questions and drinking in every word that was said.

A few days before I left the prison this young man told me, and he could hardly supress th/ tears, that in his cell the night before, "I found your Saviour and He is my Saviour, too."

I had a long talk with him and am confident that he was in earnest.

I sometimes wish that I could have remained in the prison, that I might continue to help him and help others who I feared might go back to the old life when left alone and the meetings no longer continued.

When I left the prison and after devoting two or three days almost exclusively to my family—romping and playing with our three little children, I wrote a number of letters—letters of encouragement—to those I had left behind on Blackwell's Island. Among others, I wrote to this young man. I doubt if there was anyone else in the world that would care to write to him.

Under date of August 7, 1915, he answered my letter. I have his letter before me, and I am going to print here the closing paragraph just as he has written it:

"Very thankful I am as you haven't forgotten me and for the hearty remark in your letter—that a complete surrender to God will make life pleasing even in prison. After studying so many opinions of great men which brought me only in a state of confusion I came to the conclusion, "Our Lord" can only be the real saviour of my soul. I have been doing wrong but the "Almighty" gave me will power enough to become a better man, and so Mr. Hicks, I must let you know that the spiritual influence you had upon me was great and I never will forget the plain and simple way by which you brought me to satisfaction."

I have more than a hundred letters received from prisoners on B'ackwell's Island. I do not believe that any amount of money would induce me to part with these letters. I sometimes thank God

that I did not go to the penitentiary thirteen years before. If I had gone then I would not have been of any help to my brothers. I sometimes feel that if I could continue to do as much for the Master, for Him who has done so much for me, that I would willingly return to Blackwell's Island.

The sweetest recollections of my life are the days spent in the penitentiary.

Oh! that I could feel the need of Him always—feel the need as I felt it while there. I realize the need as much now as I realized it then, but I do not feel the need as I felt it then.

I need Thee, O, I need Thee;
Every hour I need Thee,
O, bless me now, my Saviour,
I come to Thee.

Daily, almost hourly, God was opening the windows of heaven and pouring me out a blessing. The last few days that I was in the New York County penitentiary were filled with such a joy that at times I almost regretted that my friends had interceded in my behalf. Occasionally a keeper would tell me that he had read in the newspaper something with reference to what was being done at Washington. Newspapers were not permitted in the penitentiary. My wife would write and tell me of what was being done—friends would write and tell me that my release was expected every day.

At times this was good news, but there were times when I did not fully appreciate my expected freedom. The work that I was doing in the penitentiary for the Master seemed to be of greater interest to me than was my freedom. Had it not been for the little children at home and for the constant grief of Mrs. Hicks, I firmly believe that I would have refused to sign the petition for a pardon, so great was the opportunity to do something for the Master.

* *

July 4th fell on Sunday, but was celebrated on Monday. There was no celebration in the penitentiary on Blackwell's Island. We were put into our cells on Saturday after dinner, about 12:30. We remained in our cells until Tuesday morning, except one hour and thirty minutes for regular services on Sunday, and some twenty-five or thirty minutes at meal time three times a day. This is a long time for a well man to lie in a little cell, no exercise except by walking in the little room. Prisoners dread, more than anything else, a holiday that falls on Sunday. It means that they must go into their cell on Saturday at noon and remain Saturday afternoon, Sunday and Monday—until 8 oclock Tuesday morning. Seventeen hundred prisoners were more restless then—more dissatisfied than at any other time. They would curse and swear and use the most vile language that can be imagined. It was different with me—it gave me an opportunity to read my Bible—to read it slowly, thoughtfully and earnestly. The time with me flew swiftly. I would lie on my cot for hours and read and pray; occasionally getting up to stretch myself and exercise by jumping up and down.

* *

It was on the morning of July 18th—I do not know just what hour, but it was sometime before the break of day and the tierman had just come on duty. He came to my cell and woke me up.

"Mr. Hicks, the head keeper told me to tell you that President Wilson at his summer home signed your pardon yesterday. He read it in the New York World as he came to the prison this morning, and wants you to know the good news."

The thought of home, my wife and children, made the news most acceptable. I was overjoyed for a minute—for a minute only I had forgotten about the work that I had done in the prison. I had forgotten about the men in the printing office who were helping me in the daily meetings—the men who testified in these daily meetings and who would join me in prayer. I was thinking of my wife and children—of home, and was overjoyed.

What could I do to atone for the wrongs that I had done? The thousands whom I had defrauded in various mail order schemes, I could never repay in dollars and cents. I asked God to help me to come to a decision.

It was just before we were called to get up and prepare for breakfast that I decided that when I was released from that prison, I would start a magazine in which I would expose every firm that was engaged in the business of defrauding and robbing. While I could not make restitution to those whom I had defrauded, I felt that it was God's will that I should protect the innocent from men engaged in the same business that I was engaged in thirteen years before. My cell was number nineteen, section two, tier number one, in the New York County penitentiary. It was while on my cot in this prison cell, on the morning of July 18, 1915, shut out from the world, that I decided to start Canvassers Magazine and expose fraudulent firms engaged in the mail order business.

I had been a canvassing salesman in the early years of my life. I knew their needs—their struggles, how they were being deceived and robbed.

I knew what it was to sell things from house-to-house, and realized that it was canvassing salesmen that were being robbed the most, and that seventy-five per cent of all these fraudulent firms advertised under the classification of "agents wanted." It was for that reason that I decided to publish a magazine devoted absolutely to the interest of canvassing salesmen and protect them against fraud and deception.

I have been accused of having an axe to grind. I have been accused of having personal motives. I have been accused of many other reasons for making a fight for clean advertising and for honest methods and a square deal every time for canvassing salesmen.

I have no ill-will against any of the men engaged in robbing canvassing salesmen, but I have a burning desire to protect the public, and especially canvassing salesmen, against the fraudulent methods of mail order pirates doing business in nearly every city throughout the country.

I promised God while lying on that cot before the rising of His sun over the East river, on the morning of July 18, 1915, that when I was released from the prison on Blackwell's Island I would do just what I am doing, and I feel and know that what I am doing is with His approval.

I know and feel that I could not have accomplished what I have accomplished if God was not with me. I know and feel that I would not have had the courage to go ahead against the powerful opposition,

474   *CANVASSERS MAGAZINE*

unless that courage was supplied and strength given me by God.

Just so long as my strength and courage come direct from God, all the influence, all the wealth and all the power of the mail order pirates can not break me down.

* *

On the morning of July 20th, as I was going from the mess hall to my cell, the young man in the spindle gang, who, when I first entered the prison, cursed God in my presence in the hope that he could irritate me, stood in the door of his cell, having preceded me from the mess hall, handed me a note. As I have before stated, my cell was only a few doors beyond his. When the cell doors were closed and locked I unfolded the piece of paper and read: "I prayed last night." For an instant I could read no further—my eyes were filled with tears—this man who, some four or five weeks before had cursed God in my presence, "prayed last night." Surely God had opened the windows of Heaven and was pouring out such a blessing that there was not room enough to receive it. I read on:

"I prayed last night that the sun would never set today until you were released from prison. To be frank with you, Mr. Hicks, when I cursed God in your presence I did not believe there was a God; I did not feel that I was cursing anything, but since reading your Bible I am a changed man; there is a God and I am striving to lead the life that He would have me lead. When I am released from this prison on April 16th, 1916, I am coming first to see you."

I did not know that I was to be released that day, but in a very short time I was notified to get ready, to fold my blanket, to get my water cup and towel.

As I stepped from my cell I said "good bye" to the man in the next cell—the man who had persistently interrupted the meetings that were held twice a day by me in the printing office. "Good-bye, Mr. Hicks, and God bless you."

He shouted this out rather loudly—those near him repeated in a loud voice "Good-bye Hicks," and almost instantly seventeen hundred prisoners shouted time and time again, "Good bye, Hicks," and many added, "God bless you, I am glad."

I was not long in preparing to leave the prison. When word was received by the warden that President Wilson had signed my pardon he immediately had my clothes pressed and made every preparation for my departure. In less than an hour the great steel doors were opened and I left the New York County penitentiary on Blackwell's Island—a free man, having paid the price for a crime committed thirteen years before.

I looked back at the grey prison walls and truly regretted that I was leaving so soon. I felt that just another day in that prison might have been the means of helping some man to a better understanding of his need of Him who had been so much to me. As I looked at the grey walls I again promised God that so long as I lived, if it was His will, I would right the wrongs that I had done by protecting canvassing salesmen against the fraudulent schemes of firms who were engaged in the same kind of business that I had been engaged in thirteen years before. I could not make restitution, that was impossible, but I could, through the medium of a magazine, published solely in the interest of canvassing salesmen, expose the firms who had been and were robbing them.

I did not know how this was to be accomplished; I did not have sufficient means to launch a magazine but I was determined and God provided a way. Mr. F. E. Miner, president of the Atoz Printing Company, at South Whitley, Ind., had read in a western paper of my surrender to the Federal authorities. He wrote me a letter, addressed in care of the Bowery Mission. After I was released from prison I answered Mr. Miner's letter with the result that after the exchange of some four or five letters, Mr. Miner came on to New York and I explained to him my plans and what I wanted to do. It is not necessary to go into all the details but it was finally agreed that I was to go to South Whitley and that the Atoz Printing Co. would assist me in starting Canvassers Magazine. Mr. Miner had known me for a number of years and has extended me credit that possibly no other large printing house would have extended at that time under the circumstances. Mr. Miner believed in Canvassers Magazine and when he was convinced that I had given up drinking and that I was leading a Christian life, he believed in me. With the credit which the Atoz Printing Co. extended to me and with the small capital which I had, I undertook the publication of Canvassers Magazine and have succeeded so far, far beyond anything that I could have hoped.

During Mr. Miner's stay in New York he accompanied me to various missions for the purpose of seeing for himself the wonderful work that is being done for the underworld in a great city. We visited the Bowery Mission, the Water Street Mission, and at midnight the All Night Mission in the heart of Chinatown. When we entered this mission we were invited to sit on the platform. At the close of the meeting I was asked to address the homeless, helpless, hopeless men that were present. I told these men, as I always did, what God had done for me, and told them of my plans to leave the city in a few days. At the close of my remarks the superintendent of the All Night Mission asked Mr. Miner if he would not say a few words of encouragement to the men present.

Mr. Miner talked at some length, closing his remarks, in substance, as follows:

About eight years ago the Robert Hicks who has just addressed you was in my employ in a little Indiana town. Mr. Hicks had come to work for us with the hope of getting away from the temptations of the city. After being with us for nearly six months, and having worked himself into a very responsible position, as well as into the confidence and respect of the people of our little village, he was sent away on a short business trip. While on this trip, he met an old friend who, for old time's sake, urged him to take just one drink. That one drink was the undoing of all his resolutions, hopes, and ambitions, and he was brought back to our town a few days later a drunken wreck. After much annoyance, persuasion, reasoning, we had to give up trying to get him back on his feet. I finally gave him a hundred dollars and told him to leave town and never return.

Strange as it may seem, I have come all the way from that little Indiana town to New York for the sole purpose of inducing Mr. Hicks to return with me.

Eight years ago I told him to go and never return, but today I am willing to make almost any concession if he will come back and become a part of our organization again. But this is not the same Hicks that I sent away, but a new man. I am thoroughly convinced that that Power which is greater than any mortal man can give, has entered into his life and has made him what every one of you men can be if you are willing to accept

that same Power and place your faith in Him who alone can give it.

From the very start obstacles were placed in my way—stumbling blocks at times lined the road to such an extent that it seemed impossible for me to go ahead. When days seemed to be the darkest, when forging ahead seemed to be impossible, I would ask God to guide me and He did. Loyal canvassing salesmen everywhere would not only send me words of encouragement but extended to me, so far as possible, their financial support. A very few advertisers who commenced with me with the first issue remained loyal, and relying always upon God to guide me I have met with success that possibly no other magazine has ever met with in the first nine months of its existence.

Firms engaged in the business of robbing the public, and especially of robbing canvassing salesmen, many of them very wealthy, have combined to destroy Canvassers Magazine. They dare not come out in the open—they dare not have me arrested—they dare not bring me before a court of justice, but in a quiet, underhanded way, they are writing letters telling that which is not true—telling that I am an escaped convict, that I have served a sentence in the penitentiary and that I am an all around crook. They hope in this way to poison the minds of those loyal to me and thus destroy Canvassers Magazine.

I have a letter before me in which it is stated:

We merely give you this information to show you what kind of a man he is whose testimony you are taking and we are sure that as soon as we bring this to the attention of the U. S. Department of Justice that they will stop this man Hicks from sending out his publication.

This is their hope, and they know that if they continue in business Canvassers Magazine must be destroyed.

I want to say to the loyal friends of Canvassers Magazine that the firms whom I have exposed in this publication can never destroy me or the influence of Canvassers Magazine. They may cripple it—I confess that they have crippled it, but it is only for a time.

On the pages that follow I am reprinting newspaper comments from such papers as the New York World, the New York Herald, Times, Press and other publica-

476 *CANVASSERS MAGAZINE*

tions that will bear out the statements which I have made in this extended article. Canvassing salesmen—the loyal friends who have stood by me from the very start, to you I owe much—without you I could not have accomplished what I have accomplished, and altogether we could not have accomplished anything unless God had guided us.

Holding nothing back, I have stated the facts, and it is for you to decide whether or not that because of the dark spots upon my past life, with all of its disgrace and hideousness, you can take me for what I am now and for what I have been since the early morning of December 4th, 1912.

It is for you to decide whether or not I am your friend, your true champion, and whether or not I am worthy of your confidence, moral and financial support.

I need your moral support—I need your financial support, but I need more than anything else, the prayers of Christian men and women.

* *

There are those of my loyal friends who fear that eventually the mail-order pirates will succeed in their efforts to break me down. I realize the power that their ill-gotten wealth has given them, but why should I fear the power and influence of wealth wrung from hungry children and hard working, ambitious men and women, so long as I am guided by God? So long as my determination and strength come from God, and so long as I am doing the things He would have me do, all the wealth, all the influence of these men that are robbing and deceiving cannot force the suspension of the publication of Canvassers Magazine.

They may succeed in poisoning the minds of thousands of canvassing salesmen—of influencing advertisers to withhold their patronage—they may make the forging ahead more difficult than it now is—they may do all this, but so long as I live, so long as it is God's will, Canvassers Magazine will be published—will expose frauds and protect canvassing salesmen against injustices of every kind.

Break me down! Never! If every advertiser withdraws his support Canvassers Magazine will continue to be published. If the time ever comes when I must reduce the number of pages for the lack of patronage, I will make the reduction, work during the day for some firm that I know can make use of my services, and at night set the type, make up the forms and continue to print Canvassers Magazine, even though its size be reduced to sixteen, twelve or eight pages.

Break me down! Not while there is life in my body and God guides me.

Comments of New York City Newspapers

GOES TO PRISON VOLUNTARILY ON AN OLD SENTENCE

It Was Imposed on Hicks 13 Years Ago, Since Then He Has Been a Fugitive Drunkard and Mission Worker

(From the New York World, June 11, 1915)

"Blessed are the pure in heart, for they shall see God," said James T. Hunt, manager of the Bowery Mission, in opening the meeting last night. He then asked prayers for the wife and three children of Robert E. Hicks, who a few hours before had gone to Blackwell's Island voluntarily to serve a sentence imposed thirteen years ago.

"Hicks has become one of the pure in heart," Mr. Hunt continued. "Though he walk in the valley of the shadow of death, he need fear no evil."

For two days before he voluntarily appeared in the Federal Court and offered to serve a term of ten months in prison. Hicks was an associate leader of the mission. Before that for ten years he was a fugitive from justice, and earlier still a printer prosecuted by Anthony Comstock. In the interval between his prison sentence and yesterday he had married and established a small job printing shop at No. 638 Hudson Street. He lived across the street with his wife and three children.

None Knew of His Sentence

Neither the wife nor his associates in the mission knew of the prison sentence. The Federal authorities had dismissed him from their mind. Hicks, a forceful speaker, had become one of the mainstays of the mission and had been welcomed as a speaker by several churches. But the weight of his crime weighed on his mind and swayed it to confession when on May 30, Mr. Hunt spoke on the theme, "Be on the level with yourself." The next night Hicks, who was scheduled to lead the meeting, got up and said:

In 1918 Robert Emmet Hicks, Bob, was 58 years old. He had married for the third time and his trade magazine, *Canvassers*, enjoyed a national distribution. He could look back over more than half a century to his birth in a family-built log cabin in Knox County, Missouri. He could reflect on his turbulent youth, his career as mail-order swindler and his sojourn as a hopeless alcoholic in the gutters of the Bowery of New York City. By 1916 his self-confidence, paired with hard-earned success, made it possible for him to write his 'mea culpa'. What brought about this change of fortune?

2
FAMILY BACKGROUND

Bob's parents, Elisha and Sarah Seltzer/Selser Hicks, met about 1844 on the Seltzer farm in Scott County, Virginia. Matthias Seltzer, Sarah's great- grandfather, had immigrated to America in 1723 from the Kraichgau region of Germany. He had a reputation as a church-going, hard working, prosperous, respected member of his community. When Matthias died in 1766 on his own land holdings in the Shenandoah Valley, Virginia, he left substantial property to his sons and a slave to each of his daughters.

Sarah's grandfather, also named Matthias, in 1782 married Eve Heintz/Haines, a fine looking, capable German girl. The land the young Matthias inherited, he sold and moved to North Carolina. Old Matthias could not bequeath his sterling character to his son, Matthias, Jr. His namesake failed to inherit those industrious, admirable qualities. Young Matthias came to a violent end when shot and killed by a planter, Alexander McMillins, in Knox County, Tennessee. *"Matthias Sulfer (sic) was an infamous character known in North Carolina for his horse* *stealing and abuse of peaceful citizens." *Tennessee Ancestors, vol. 3.*

A local jury quickly exonerated McMillins of any wrong-doings because Selser/Sulfer had a bad reputation and probably meant physical harm to McMillins, a solid citizen in Knoxville.

Matthias's attractive widow, Eve Haines Selser, with her brood of young children, immediately moved to Russell County, Virginia, married a substantial farmer, George Kuntz/Counts, and produced six more children. One of Matthias and Eve's sons, Larkin Selser, Sarah's father, moved to Scott County, Virginia, prior to Sarah's birth in 1824.

Elisha Hicks (b. 1824/25 d.1875)) came to work for the land-owning Selsers. From the description on his Civil War pension papers, he was six feet tall with dark hair and blue eyes. He was a fine looking man according to the one extant photo of him taken around 1865, possibly when he enlisted in the Union Army at Hannibal, Missouri.

The Selsers were not amused when their daughter, Sarah, became adequately enamored with Elisha to become pregnant. Family legend has it that two of her brothers chased the couple to the Tennessee border where they were married in Bristol, in 1846. Their first child, James Claiborne, was born in Russell County, Virginia, a few months after their marriage. By the time the second and third babies arrived, they had moved to Hawkins County, Tennessee. Evidently Elisha earned his bread by the sweat of his brow, having to move from one farm to another to get work. Why not go to the West where land could be homesteaded or bought for a dollar? In 1853 the couple packed their meager belongings and with their young children crossed the great Mississippi to seek their fortune in Knox County, Missouri. The North American Indians had been driven farther to the West, so Elisha homesteaded a piece of land four miles south of Novelty in an area called Cherry Box. It was raw, untamed country, sparsely populated. The first priority was to cut down trees to build a one room cabin of rough-hewn logs. James, the oldest child, would only have been eight or nine years old – not much help in putting a house together and Sarah was heavy with their fifth child. That 24th of January, 1855, Sarah gave birth to Henry Franklin, their first baby born in Missouri. Three years later, Robert Emmett Hicks, the 'Bob' of this biography, came into the world on February 25, 1858.

Four months prior to Bob's birth, Elisha purchased 80 acres of land for $60.00 from the U.S. government. (Book R, page 8, Knox County Clerk's Office.). Knox County's seat is Edina, a village with a population of 1,207 according to the census of 2003. In 2010 census takers counted 132 citizens in Novelty, Bob's birth place. The Chariton River, or a branch of it, ran near their log cabin providing water for the family needs. For a boy, that wilderness with the forest animals and streams must have personified freedom itself. Long summer days spent exploring the woods, hunting rabbits, squirrels and wild turkeys, fishing in the creeks with a home-made line and hook – what more could a boy want. In autumn the leaves on the trees turned scarlet and yellow. The boys chopped wood for the winter fire. A hog was slaughtered, smoked and hung to cure in the woodshed for the cold months ahead. Winters could be bitter with the wind howling about the eaves of the cabin, snow banking against the walls making the trip to the outhouse miserable at best. Fires burned all day in the cabin stove and banked at night as matches were rare and precious. Spring arrived with the red breasted robins, crocuses and budding oaks. Bears with cubs awoke from hibernation and "the voice of the turtle was heard in the land." Then the oxen were hitched to the plow to turn the virgin soil in order to sow corn, beans, potatoes and flax. All the family worked together to provide their living.

At the age of 66, Bob wrote a tribute to his mother for Mother's Day, April 18, 1924:

Today, I am thinking of my mother. There are millions of wonderful mothers, but, somehow it seems to me, as I look back over the years of long ago, my mother was so wonderful, so wonderfully patient, so good, that other mothers could hardly equal her. This may be just a fancy of mine, but I love to think of her as the most wonderful mother in all the world.

The mother of nine children, eight of whom lived to adulthood, her life was not easy; it was drudgery, but she was always happy. My father was a poor man, but from the day she married him my mother stood by his side, fighting as a woman had to fight in the long ago. She worked, not the eight or ten hour day of the union, but the twenty-four hour day of the poor. She scrubbed and patched and nursed and worked in the fields side by side with my father from early dawn until bed time; even in the hours of the night she was up and down, getting drinks for thirsty lips, covering restless little sleepers, listening for croupy coughs. She had time, however, to listen to my stories of boyish fun and frolic and triumph. She had time to say the things that spurred my ambition. She encouraged me as no other human being could have done.

I recall an incident the memory of which shall ever remain with me. I was just a little boy. It was in the Chariton Hills of Missouri. For two days and nights I had visited a cousin who lived two or three miles from our home on the other side of the Chariton Hills. When I returned, Mother said, "Bobby, I am mighty glad you are home again. I could hardly cook with the wood the men chopped for me. The wood you chop burns so much better." It was just like Mother and I remember that I felt of great importance as I piled the wood high back of the stove. It was a pleasure for me to do the things that pleased her. It is such encouraging words that increases our determination, makes our burdens light and our work a pleasure.

My mother went without that her children might have. She gave her all for us that we might have some of the pleasures of life. The dresses that she needed were made by her own hands for her daughters that they might not be ashamed when in company with their girl companions.

It is thirty-six years since Mother left us, since she went to the home of which the Christ said, "I go to prepare a place."

I would not take her back, if I could, but oh, so often I long for her kindly advice, her wonderful presence and cheering words to guide me in the right and through the struggles that come to me in the work I am striving to do."

Bob continued with advice to his readers:

Men, not only on May 11th, as never before, think of your mother; don't wait until May 11th, but think of her always and remember now while there is yet time, while she is yet living, to pay back to her in love and tenderness some of the many thousand debts you *owe her and remember also that you can never pay in full the debt to your mother."*

In May, 1926, Bob wrote another editorial tribute to his mother in his publication, The *Specialty Salesman Magazine:*

My memory takes me back to the days when, a bare-foot, tousle-headed boy, I wandered among the Chariton hills of Missouri. I remember the creek that ran near our little log house in the new country. I see myself playing among the pebbles on the bank of that little stream while my mother, as was the custom of pioneer women, built a fire under the big iron kettle on the bank and prepared to wash the clothes where water was most available. And sometimes I would stub my toe and howl in anguish. Busy as she was Mother would take time to minister to my hurt, her treatment being mental much more frequently than it was physical.

By 1864, when Bob was six, a one room schoolhouse had opened in the neighborhood. The teacher, a Mr. Watson, received his small stipend from the students' parents. Bob never forgot Mr. Watson and many years later said that the school day began 'with a reading from the Scriptures and whipping Bob Hicks." He added, *"of course, doubtless there were times when I deserved exactly what I got. I hold no brief for myself. I was not an angelic boy, misunderstood and abused. I was merely a healthy young animal who wanted to be treated as a human being rather than as an idiot who had to be told to wipe his own nose."*

Mary Ann, Bob's oldest sister, told a story of her brother in those early school days. She and eight year old Bob arrived late one winter's day. Bob always lagged in the rear, hating another day with Mr. Watson. When they arrived they found the teacher and students held at bay by a snarling dog in front of the school door. Mary said that Bob snatched a large club protruding from the snow. Without a word, he charged the vicious creature, with club swinging, and won. Mary didn't remember whether or not Mr. Watson praised the boy, but when their mother, Sarah, learned of the incident she added the story to her list of family tales to be repeated with pride to all who would listen.

The life of the family changed dramatically the last of April, 1865, when Elisha and the oldest son, James Claiborne, left for Hannibal to enlist in the 14th Missouri Calvary of the Union Army. They left Sarah with seven young children to run the farm. Bob had celebrated his seventh birthday two months earlier. How could one know that three months later Elisha would return home a sick man, debilitated by chronic bronchitis?

Bob's father, Elisha, did not endear himself to his children. He was a stern patriarchal 19th century father. "Spare the rod and spoil the child" seemed engraved on his heart. Bob gave him credit for being an honest, just man, but there appears to have been little affection lost between them.

Many years later Bob told a story about his father, Elisha, to his executive secretary, George Peabody. Bob's maternal grandmother (Sarah Finney Selser) came to visit the family in Kirkville, Missouri. She and Bob had a special bond between them. In a few days Grandma Sarah would leave and Bob wanted to give her a present. It seems the old lady habitually smoked a pipe and Bob wanted to buy her a new one. Where could he find the money?

"I tried every way I knew to earn the five cents the pipe cost, but it just couldn't be done. Then it happened that Mother needed some vinegar and sent me to the store to get it. John Hope ran the little store and it seems I can still see him dozing in the sun as I approached with the vinegar jug. I followed him into the store. It was a fatal decision for there, on the counter, was a tray of brand new, shiny clay pipes. The price was five cents. Instantly my wish for a pipe to give my grandmother rose up with uncontrollable force. I knew it was wrong. I knew I should not do it, but the store was empty, the tray full of pipes and I wanted one tremendously. At the time I was wearing leather boots and it was a simple act to transfer one of the pipes to the leg of my boot. It slipped down comfortably, out of sight. No sooner did I have it than

more heartily than I had desired it, I wished I did not possess it. But there was no chance to put it back. Johnny returned with the jug and there was nothing I could do but go.

Down the street I went as miserable as I have ever been in my life, wondering how I could get rid of it for now I knew I could never give it to Grandmother. I'd not gone far when Johnny grabbed me by the shoulder.

"Better give me that pipe."

"I haven't got a pipe," I lied.

"Oh, yes, you have," he replied as he pulled up my trouser leg and extracted the pipe from my boot.

Johnny made no comment but returned to his store.

Later that afternoon I saw my father walking down to the store as was his custom. He walked slowly with his hands clasped behind his back. He and Johnny were friends and those afternoon meetings and discussions were a great pleasure to Father. I knew Johnny would tell him about my stealing the pipe and I knew Father well enough to know what would happen after that.

Within twenty minutes I knew my fears were well founded. I saw Father coming back. He was striding rapidly, his arms swinging vigorously to and fro. On his face as he neared, I could see a look of deep hurt mixed with stern lines of determination. My father *was a strict man. I have no wish to show him as being brutal or extraordinarily severe. He never punished without cause but when his established rules were violated or his code of honor flaunted, he dealt with the offender as he thought the occasion demanded. Honesty was almost a fetish with him and the letter of the law was sacred. I am sure he would rather have heard of my death than to have learned I had stolen a five cent pipe. In our house Father was the head. Mother never interfered with his direction or chastisement of the children. What he did was supposed to be his right and priviledge. That beating was administered with the hitching strap and was calculated to be one I would never forget. I never did. But I recall how after the whipping was over, Mother laid me across her lap in the kitchen and as she gently rubbed goose grease into the open wounds and red welts across my back, her tears fell to mingle with the blood drawn by the stinging lash."*

Sarah's children loved and respected their mother. Time and time again Bob wrote of her courage, her loving kindness, her unremitting work for the good of the family.

Years after she died, he remembered her with these words: *"I think most of us try hard to be men because our mothers want us to be. Not always are we successful in justifying her pride in us, yet Mother does not need much justification for pride in her boy. She, more than any other mortal, can see beneath the sins and the shortcomings of her sons and daughters the spirit of right and truth and honorable conduct striving to push up into the daily life of even the most thoughtless of her children. There were times when I was glad my mother could not see me. There have been other times when I have wished I might go to her and see the dim eyes light up and the worn face become beautiful with the gratification of motherly hope and love as I told her that I was playing a man's part in the world. This I can no longer do. But I do believe that my mother is watching from the windows of Heaven and waiting for me to come some day and tell her all about it. That is one of the joys of holding to the faith of a Christian mother. She watches over us from the cradle to the grave."* Bob published few words about his father.

In the summer of 1869, Bob went to work for a neighboring farmer named Mote. The eleven year old Bob had the job of breaking new sod with a team of oxen, whose names, Bright and Bill, he never forgot. The work day began at six. Following the plow, barefoot, the stiff, wiry grass with razor edges cut into his legs and feet. On the frontier, a boy was expected to do a man's work. About noon the farmer's wife called them in for the mid-day meal. "Then," as Bob finished the story, *"they hustled me through my* dinner and while the farmer and the oxen rested in the shade, I took mine by chopping wood. By one thirty we were back in the field and worked until Mrs. Mote rang a bell to tell us supper was ready. After supper I fed the pigs, watered Bright and Bill, cleaned the stalls, chopped more wood, and so on, until bed time."

"But one night I recall I was more than ordinarily tired and my feet hurt so badly that I could not bear to put them in the cold water drawn from the well. I fell asleep with my legs hanging over the side of the straw tick cot. For some reason Mote came down to the barn, woke me up and told me to go to the well to wash my feet. Now, in those days soft soap was made at home and was just a little milder than concentrated lye. In fact hickory ash lye formed a large part of it and small imagination is required to understand what that soap did to my cut, scratched and chapped legs and feet. I can clearly recall how I sat on a stone by the side of the well, crying in agony as I applied the caustic stuff to my skin. And right there I swore when I was big enough I would thrash Clark Mote for every stinging pain he had caused me. However that was the resolution I never carried out, since by the time I was big enough to make good on it, Clark Mote was an old man." Bob added with a chuckle, "and my feet had stopped hurting." The job lasted seventeen days. Mote paid him in script "which *was the only kind of money we saw in Missouri in those days."*

"Indeed it seemed to me there was nothing in the world I could not buy if I wanted to. At present I own property in many different states, I have stocks that represent interests in many different industries, I have funds in a number of banks, but even now I know I will never be so rich as I was on the day Mote paid me off. I had in my own hands $4.25 earned at the rate of twenty-five cents per day .I remember that so long as any portion of that money was in my possession I counted it upon every possible occasion, but I am under the impression I had small conception of just how much wealth four dollars and twenty five cents was and therefore, I was soon broke again."

Bob seldom lost an occasion to tell of his accomplishments and, less frequently, his failures.

About 1871 Elisha decided to sell the farm and move to Kirksville, a town with better schools. As far as Bob was concerned, the school in Kirkville appealed no more to his liking than Mr. Watson's school in Novelty. His parents tried all the tricks of the parental trade to no avail. Then someone suggested to Elisha that Bob be apprenticed to the local printer and Bob stepped into his destiny. The boy became intoxicated with the fumes of the ink, the setting of type and the noise of the press. He had found his niche. Within a short time Bob graduated from apprenticeship as a printer's devil to take his place beside the men. Twelve hours a day he worked at whatever job came to hand in the shop, then went to the house of the owner to chop wood. After that he was free to go home and he thrived on the diet. That year he earned $96.00. Elisha, however, fared little better in Kirksville than on the farm. He tried running a boarding house with the ever-faithful Sarah as cook and housekeeper. It became a losing proposition. Next he ran a small grocery store. Failure again. Finally he bought a farm near Williamstown only to discover after the transaction had been completed, that the farm was heavily indebted and he had unknowingly taken over the debt. Still suffering from the bronchitis contracted in his few months as a soldier in the Union Army, Elisha took to his bed. Sarah, in desperation, asked a Dr. Neeper to treat her husband but to no avail. Elisha died 21 April 1875. Sarah and the children buried him in the Liberty Cemetery across from the Baptist Church. His age, 53, is engraved on the tombstone.

Of their nine children, they had reared eight to adulthood. They had been married for 29 years. Were they happy? Were there times when they sat together in front of the dying fire, and Elisha ran his fingers through Sarah's graying hair and whispered that she was still his sweet, pretty girl? If so, memories were all he left her. When the family moved to the Williamstown farm, Bob and Henry stayed in

Kirksville and continued to work at the printing office. At 15 Bob thought himself a man. He was living away from his parents, possibly with his oldest sister, Mary Ann, who had attended the Normal School in Kirksville and become a teacher. Bob innocently answered an ad guaranteeing the recipient that for one quarter, only 25 cents, the preparation advertised would grow hair on the upper lip or head of any man. Bob told the story: *I mixed the powder as the directions indicated, then I scrubbed my lip with a coarse towel and soap until the skin was almost raw. Following that I vigorously rubbed in the magic preparation that within a fortnight was to give me the beginning of the finest mustache to be found in all Missouri; however, within a few days my upper lip became exceedingly sore and then, raw. I happened to meet old Doc Neeper on the street, a gruff old chap, a typical country doctor.*

"Bob, what's the matter with your lip?" he asked.

After some hedging and dodging I told him what I was doing.

"Humph," grunted Doc,"let me see some of that stuff."

I went home and got some of the powders and took them up to Doc's office. After a short examination he looked up at me and grunted in characteristic fashion:

"Hell, boy, 'nuthin but sugar of milk. Git all you

want of it at the drug store for ten cents a pound. It wouldn't grow hair on a monkey."

Thus I met my first mail-order thief and from him I not only got a sore lip but the idea that money could be made by printer's ink in other ways besides printing hand-bills and newspapers.

By that time he had left the print shop and with his older brother, Henry, worked for the Kirksville Journal, a weekly newspaper. He also procured a small U. S. Army printing press and could print cards and small circulars. He decided to go into business on the side for himself, selling the same fake 'mustache powder' that he had bought. He printed circulars describing what his 'magic powder' would do, most of it copied from the original ad, and sent them out. *The response was entirely satisfying. I found that old Doc was away high in his estimate of the price of sugar of milk. By purchasing it in quantities I could get it for four cents a pound and a pound made a great many of the small packages I rolled up as doctors used to roll up their doses of medicine and sent out to unsuspecting and credulous boys.*

For a considerable time I did very well considering the limited circularizing I could do. I think, as I remember it, that I took in an average of two to three dollars a week and that amount represented quite a spare time income for a boy in that day. Along with what I earned it made me independent. But it did more than that for me, and something infinitely worse: it introduced me to the possibilities of making easy money. It gave me entrée into the evil fraternity who got without giving. It convinced me that I was keen enough to live by my wits and that I did not need to depend upon the sweat of honest labor to take care of myself. At a most impressionable age that puny but significant success gave me a philosophy that finally brought me to the very brink of ruin and took me through as bitter a Gethsemane as any man ever endured before I learned that happiness, success, peace and comfort could never be found over that road.

TRAVEL "ABROAD"

With Bob's new sense of independence following the death of his father and money in his pocket, he set out to see something of the world. From Kirksville he went to Canton on the Mississippi, then West Quincy and Palmyra, stopping in Hannibal to work for the *Hannibal Courier*, a newspaper made famous by Mark Twain. That first six months of travel had only taken him within a hundred mile radius of his home.

The centennial of 1776 would be held in Philadelphia that year and Bob wanted to be there. He crossed the great Mississippi for the first time and hopped an east-bound freight traveling through Illinois, Indiana and into Ohio. At Sandusky he saw the Lake Erie lighthouse and had to ask what it was. By the time he got to Cleveland his money had evaporated.

I had five cents left. With that I bought a glass of beer in a free lunch place somewhere near the railroad yards and then proceeded to sip the beer while I made vast inroads on the plates of the free lunch. I was doing first rate until the German proprietor noticed me and served notice that my operations on the free lunch must cease until such time as I saw fit to buy more beer."

Cleveland may have overwhelmed Bob, an 18 year old farm boy, as he spent no time there; however, undaunted, he traveled along the lake shore northeast and when he came to Painesville he got a job at the *Northern Ohio Journal* run by W. Chambers and Son. James Clayton, a fellow printer, and Bob roomed together to save money. Perhaps because Clayton played a violin in the evenings, Bob hit upon a novel idea that appears so bizarre as to be fanciful. Why not use steel strings? So Bob bought a few yards of steel wire, cut it up into the size needed, printed circulars, and orders and money rolled in. The bubble burst when Bob got the first letters demanding money back because the steel wire had ruined the violin bows. Incredible as it seems, Bob had amassed a fortune of several thousands of dollars (or so he wrote) and he left town.

Bob returned to Kirksville in the autumn of 1877. Sarah, his mother, had been dispossessed of the farm near Williamstown and lived with one of her children, perhaps Mary Ann, who had married Simon Doran. Elisha had left his wife virtually nothing other than a brood of children and debt. Crippled by arthritis and hard work, Sarah tried to get a pension as a widow of a Union Army veteran. The application had been returned to her as she had no proof of her marriage to Elisha in 1846 at Bristol, Tennessee. During the Civil War, the courthouse there had burned, destroying all records. The witnesses at the marriage had been a couple named Milton and Sarah Jaynes, but Sarah had no idea where they could be found thirty years after the fact. Bob took up the quest, writing letters to postmasters in Bristol, Tennessee and Virginia, as well as the surrounding villages. Finally he found them in Sneedville, Tennessee. Mrs. Jaynes testified in an official document dated 27 February 1879 that she had been present at the ceremony. Sarah got the pension and gave Bob the credit.

At some time during the 1870's Bob became a house-to-house 'peddler'. He wrote: *Farm houses were few and far apart and at almost every house there was one or more vicious dogs – generally more. I sold a cement to mend broken dishes, wood-work, etc., and as a side line I carried a few "chromos"*[the definition for which this author has been unable to find]. *The houses were built of logs and quite often were located a long distance from the main road in the center of the farm. Farmers had but little money. I visited house after house where I could have easily made sales if money had not been lacking. Cement and "chromos" were fairly good sellers. There was not many patented specialties. But my greatest success was as a subscription book agent. I sold Bibles, what was then known as the Family Bible, a very large edition with pages for the complete family record. Country people were inclined to be religious – a home without a large Family Bible and a card hanging over the door "God Bless Our Home" was hard to find after I made deliveries. I was very particular to make deliveries late in the fall after farmers had sold what they could spare of their scant farm products. After my success selling Family Bibles and motto cards, "What is Home Without a Mother", I secured a prospectus of "Livingston in Africa". I now had confidence in my ability. I no longer hesitated to go right up to a prospective subscriber: I would go to the home, to the store, to the office, everywhere and anywhere – I did not 'skip'- into every house I went into every store and place of business and if I failed, I went again. I believed in my book. I felt that it was the greatest book ever published- I was in earnest and I loved the work. I talked "Livingston in Africa" from early morning until late at night and when I was sleeping I was dreaming of" Livingston in Africa". I knew my story well and I told it well and I sold so many books that the publishers found it necessary to send a man to help me make deliveries. Their generous offer of help, however, was no doubt for their own protection as I did not have the money to pay for the books until they had been delivered and as my sales amounted to something near eleven hundred dollars, they could well afford to be generous in protecting themselves.*

I do not at this late date remember just how much I made, but I can safely say that my weekly profits were as much as fifty or sixty dollars. As much as I loved the work, after all deliveries had been made and I had a few hundred dollars capital, I decided that I would employ others to sell for me – I would be the general agent and employ sub-agents. Easy as it was on paper, the plan did not work out. I was 'busted'.

Bob failed to explain his rise and fall in the business of 'peddling' but it seemed to be a pattern in his life. Drinking may well have been the problem. He never refused a good whiskey, or a cheap one either, but learned moderation in later life. Selecting 'sub-agents' who pocketed the money and disappeared also could have been the cause. As good a salesman and as clever as Bob was, he never developed an intuition about men. More than once a man he considered 'fair and square' turned into a 'con man', who dipped into the money drawer, leaving Bob to pay the bill.

3

COMING OF AGE

By December, 1877, Bob had moved on to La Belle in Lewis County, Missouri, taking his mother, Sarah, and his youngest brother, Thomas Elbert, with him. He was nineteen years old. The youngest girl in the family, Virginia, went with her older brother, Henry and his bride, westward to Grouse Creek, Kansas. At La Belle, he initially worked for the *Lewis County Journal.* Then, in September, 1879, Bob founded *The LaBelle Journal,* which ran for 21 weeks. When it proved financially disappointing, with his printing press and family in tow, he moved on to Monticello, the county seat of Lewis County, Missouri.

The short biography of Bob published in the 1926/27 *Who's Who in America* cites 1877 as the year he founded the *Lewis County Journal*; however, the four-county history of northeast Missouri states that John Moore established the *Journal* in 1872. Although the founder's identity is difficult to prove, the newspaper survived another half century. During the time Bob worked with The *Journal,* perhaps as advertising and subscription agent as well as a journalist, a grisly murder occurred in Clark County. The Spencer family had a farm in the area. A bachelor, Bill Young, owned the farm adjacent to the Spencers'. Young was a man who kept to himself, but the community respected him as a hard worker. One morning Mr. Spencer's 'hired hand' discovered that Spencer, a recent widower, and his four children, had been murdered. Spencer lay hacked to death with a hatchet and the children killed with a pitchfork. From somewhere a private detective, Frank Lane, appeared, offering his services to the local constabulary. Lane found out that Bill Young had quarreled with Mr. Spencer and set out to pin the killings on Young. He successfully aroused the citizenry. Young was arrested and a trial date set. Because of the heated tempers of the people around Monticello, the trial was moved to Kahoka, the county seat of Clark County.

Bob visited Young in the county jail, decided he was innocent and stoutly defended him in the *Lewis County Journal*. He defended him as well in town meetings, church groups and bars. Whether or not Bob influenced the court decision is another question, but the jury did indeed render a verdict of not guilty. Young, strongly advised to leave the district, refused. He had been acquitted. He promptly returned to his farm. It was a fatal decision. Fifty years later, Bob summed it up: *Bill was acquitted on Friday, went away and was married on Saturday, returned to his home and hanged on Sunday.*

The mob, supposedly led by Lane, captured Young, placed him with a rope around his neck in a wagon, threw the rope over the crossbars of the gate to his farm house and within a few minutes it was over. For 125 years, an annual picnic continues to be held by the townsfolk on the grounds of the church where the Spencer family is buried. The murder remains unsolved.

Monticello in the 1870's and 1880's had a substantially larger population than today. The 2003 census report gave the population of Monticello as 122. Only the fine old courthouse remains to attest to its vanished prominence. As a young editor Bob took advantage of his opportunity to join the Missouri Press Association. That year the Association held its meeting in Columbia and Bob duly received his invitation and railway pass. Years later Bob enjoyed telling the story of his bravado and brashness on the way to attend the meeting.

When the conductor entered the car I was in, I recall holding that pass high over my head, not so he could see it but rather that the other people in the car might behold it. I wanted them all to know I was a personage, that I was important – I rode on the railroad without having to pay.

A number of important Missouri editors and

publishers attended that meeting, among them Bob Wallace of the *LaGrange Democrat*, Eugene Field, poet and secretary of the Missouri Press Association and Jim McCullough, influential editor of the *St. Louis Globe Democrat*. Bob tells his own story:

In my own mind I was the most important man there and I saw to it that I got the attention such importance was entitled to have. Nor, seemingly, was anybody loath to give it to me. I must have made a complete ass of myself.

Indeed Bob made a correct assessment of himself according to Mr. Wallace, who included Bob in his article of the meeting in the *LaGrange Democrat: For copper-plated, double riveted, old dog-iron brass, that young idiot who calls himself the editor and publisher of The Lewis County Journal, Robert E. Hicks, takes the band wagon. The unmitigated fool made of himself a nuisance and a bore to everybody at the convention. To see him parading around, blowing off, and butting in on the conversations of men who really knew something one speedily gained the impression that Hicks thought himself the most important editor there. The poor simpleton didn't realize every man there was making sport of him and using him as the butt of their jokes.*

It is to Bob's credit that he not only accepted the scathing remarks but kept a copy. Did it alter his behavior to any great extent? Evidently not, as Bob recounts another tale:

I visited St. Louis a few months later and went to call on Mr. McCullough at the offices of the Globe Democrat. I barged into the editorial sanctum. I recall how McCullough turned to meet me in some surprise, though this seemed to fade when he saw who I was. Another man, large, well dressed and important appearing, was leaning over the editor's desk talking to him. Their conversation stopped at once. McCullough did not introduce me but I learned afterward that his caller was a United States Senator, come to see him on important matters. I at once informed McCullough that I had met him at the Press Association meeting, that he and I exchanged papers and therefore, being in the city, I felt I ought to call on him. I'll never forget McCullough's smile. I can understand it now, five decades later, but then I felt sure he read my paper as carefully as I did his. For a few minutes we gravely discussed the politics and crop conditions of northern Missouri and then I was politely bowed out. Never the less, the meeting was grist for my mill and on my return home I made much of my visit with the editor of one of Missouri's greatest papers. It had its effect too. After that people began to wonder if maybe I didn't amount to something after all."

Neither Bob's ego nor his ambition faltered.

Bob never wrote about his early marriage in 1879 to a French girl named Rosa E. The 1880 census in Lewis County, Missouri, lists Bob (age 22) as the head of household with Rosa E. (21), a baby boy born in August, Sarah (Bob's mother) and Thomas E., (Bob's youngest brother). The census taker carelessly wrote 'farmer' for Bob's occupation. No doubt Bob had been absent when the census taker stopped by because Bob had inordinate pride in being an editor of a newspaper, no matter how small or insignificant. By 1877, Henry Franklin Hicks, Bob's older brother by three years, had moved with his wife, Mollie Ann Gollihar, to Grouse Creek, Cowley County, Kansas. In February of 1880 the Kansas City, Lawrence and Southern Kansas Railway crossed Cowley County a few miles south of the area where Henry lived. Henry and seven other men saw the golden opportunity of plotting a town site along the rail line because the railroad was the life blood of any community at the time. Henry and his friends made a smart decision. On the third of May, 1880, a few families gathered to welcome the incorporation of the town of Cambridge, named by the wife of one of the founding fathers. Other hamlets a few miles away from the tracks withered and died. The entire population of Kansas numbered less than a million souls. The new railroad companies set about contradicting the image of

Kansas as an area infested with plagues of grasshoppers, known for interminable drought and the wholesale starvation of animals and men. Public Relation agents hired by the railways were sent to towns all over the eastern part of the United States to promote immigration westward. Urged by Henry to join him, by November of 1880 Bob, Rosa, their baby son, James Robert, Sarah, Bob's mother, and Thomas E., the youngest son of the family, took the train from Missouri for Cowley County. Their arrival coincided with the death of little Clarence, Henry and Mollie's only son. Bob wrote the obituary published in the *Winfield Courier*:

Clarence H. Hicks, infant son of Henry F. and Mollie Hicks, died on Thursday morning, Nov. 11th, 1880, aged two months and eleven days. Thus passed away one of earth's brightest flowers, one who was the light of a happy home, his father's idol and his mother's joy. But little Clarence, like the flower that blooms in the morning and withers under the sun's blighting rays, was given to his parents but for a season and was not allowed to live to experience the hardships of a prolonged existence. He who rules over all things called him home while yet in his purity and while yet too young to revel in the sinful pleasures of earth and he now rests in peace in the bosom of his Heavenly Father, never more to be afflicted with disease or pain. He will there await the coming of those who now so deeply mourn his loss and may then not grieve but rather console themselves with the thought that Clarence has only flown to that better world and that they have the blessed privilege of joining him one day on that beautiful shore, never more to part.

REH Torrance, Nov. 13, 1880

The maudlin sentimentality of the obituary was accepted as the norm for that era.

By February of the following year the two brothers were comfortable enough with their situation to found the first newspaper in Cambridge which they named the *Cambridge Commercial*, a newspaper that lasted from February 18 to November 19, 1881.

Posthaste Bob and Henry sent a copy of the new paper to the editor of the Kirksville's *North Missouri Register* who promptly replied:

We have received number one and two, Vol.I of the Commercial, published at Cambridge, Cowley Co., Kansas by Henry and Robert Hicks. We spell Kansas with a C, in order to keep that letter uniform throughout. The Hicks brothers learned the printing business with us at Kirksville, Missouri, and Henry was the best "devil" we ever had. He never learned the wayward ways of the majority of 'devils' but was always on hand and attentive to his duties. We cannot say so much for Bob, but he has married and settled down and we learn is very attentive to his business. We wish them success in their Kansas venture. The Commercial is a neatly printed, well edited 8 page, 28 column paper. (North Missouri Register.)

Bob, the editor of the *Cambridge Commercial,* replied, "We always thought that we were as good as any little "devil" that ever lived, but the above from our old 'boss' and a good 'boss' too, does not prove the fact, but Major does not say we were not good, but that we were not as good as our senior. At any rate, we will be content if the *Register* will say that we were the next best 'devil' he ever had and then the *Commercial* will be run by two of the best "devils" that ever worked in the *North Missouri Register* office."

But not all editors welcomed the new Cambridge paper. McCray, the editor of the *Enterprise* in the neighboring town of Burden, evidently wrote some slanderous words concerning the Hicks boys' new paper. In the April 16 edition, Bob printed the following:

STOP MY PAPER

We were somewhat surprised Thursday morning when we received the following card which will explain itself and we will leave it to our readers to pass upon:

Torrance, Kan., April 13, 1881.

R. E. Hicks

Sir:- You will please stop sending me your paper, as I will not patronize no man hoo will not defend his own reptation when assalted by a nother. D. Elliott. We mailed the following reply to Mr. Elliott Thursday evening: Commercial Office, April 14, 1881, D. Elliott, Torrance, Kas.-

Sir- Your card requesting a discontinuance of the Commercial to your address received. I can, I think, survive the shock of your withdrawal from my subscription list; but, sir, you order your paper discontinued with somewhat of a flourish, simply because I do not desire to participate in a disgraceful newspaper fight with the Enterprise. No, sir, I looked upon you as a man that would not approve of the language McCray has been making use of in his paper and if you have ordered a discontinuance of your paper because I will not reply to such language as "damn villains, liars, puppy, etc., etc.," I will say that I can afford to part with every man of this kind on my list and really desire to be rid of them. R. E. Hicks, Editor of the Commercial. It was perhaps not kind of Bob to ridicule Mr. Elliott by printing his misspelled words.

The Cambridge Commercial received news of the bigger world by telegram:

DOOMED TO DEATH

The Murderers of the Czar Sentenced to be Hanged

St. Petersburg, April 14 – Prisone Jeliahoff, in a

speech at the conclusion of the trial of the Nihilists, asked as a favor that his last speech in his defense might be printed and published, word for word. Sophia Pieoffsokv asked that she be dealt with regardless of her sex. The prisoners received their sentence of death by hanging with the calmest indifference.

A brief profile of the new Czar, Alexander lll, followed: *The new Czar leads a very simple life. He rises early and takes a long walk, then breakfasts with his family. After dinner he spends a long time amusing himself with his children. Still, he don't know what moment he'll be sent to kingdom come by a bomb-throwing Nihilist.*

One can see that the war with revolutionaries has a long history.

Immigration also posed a problem in the 1880's

The increasing tide of immigration to the United States is attracting the attention of European governments. Seeing that Germany and other Continental States are pouring Westward a larger contingent than Great Britain, English economists no longer account for the partiality shown to America by the subjects of Queen Victory, by putting it upon the ground of community of language, laws and blood. These things exercise an influence but they should determine the course of immigration quite as strongly toward English colonies as toward the

United States. The fact is 73% of last year's emigration from Great Britain was to America. A nasty incident occurred on 27 July 1881 in Silvercrest Township, Cowley County, when Bob found himself hauled into court on criminal charges that he did *"unlawfully feloniously beat and bruise one Wm. Elliams, a minor of the age of eleven years, with the intent of bodley harm* [sic]." A Catherine French signed the complaint. The court convened on 4 August and the jury found Bob guilty as charged. He paid a fine of $5.00 plus court costs of $50.00, a considerable sum of money at the time. What had prompted Bob to beat a young boy? The life of small town newspapers hinged on local gossip that traveled quickly from one community to the next. Bob's trial and subsequent conviction stirred several editors of neighboring settlements to repeat the story and give their opinions, in this instance fairly unanimous.

On 6 August the following appeared in the *Winfield Courier*:

Another outrage has been perpetrated on the privileges of the press. Neighbor Hicks of the Cambridge Commercial has been arrested for 'licking' a boy'. It has come to a pretty pass if an editor can't "lick a boy" without having a row made about it. We had begun to feel it our duty to 'lick' the boys who have been breaking the windows of the school and other buildings, ransacking unoccupied houses, stealing fruit from gardens and committing other diabolisms in the city, but now we won't do it, but demand that Shenneman shall board them in his hotel.

The *Enterprise* followed suit the same day: *R. E. Hicks , editor of the Cambridge Commercial, was arrested last Thursday and brought before his honor Judge Smith, charged with striking a small boy in Torrance with a buggy whip. Bob gave bond and the trial was adjourned until August 4th. The trial will afford abundant opportunity for the exhibition of the jealousy existing between Torrance and Cambridge.*

The following appeared in the *Enterprise* on August 11:

Esq. Smith of Burden had an interesting trial before his magistrate one day last week in the trial of Hicks, the editor and French, the sawyer, in which the editor got badly beaten. The defendant was charged with striking a small boy with his buggy whip, as he drove through Torrance. It cost Hicks about $60.00. It is rather hard on the editor, but it is the making of the boy."

Bob told his side of the story in the *Cambridge Commercial* August 6, 1881, using the 'royal we', as follows:

Since our arrest has been made public throughout Southern Kansas, we shall give to our readers and friends the cause of this difficulty: On the 26th of July in company with S. B. Sherman, we passed through Torrance enroute for Burden. Just as we got opposite Mr. Lyons' barn a boy by the name of Wm. Matthews ran after our team, evidently trying to scare it and in order to protect ourselves and to keep the youth from running too near the wheels of the buggy and getting hurt, we struck towards him with the whip, not intending to hit him but accidently did so. We should not of even struck towards the boy, not withstanding he needed a good flogging, but only a few weeks ago when we were driving through that town in company with Dr. Pleasants, a boy ran up to our team and struck one of the horses with his hat and we found it very difficult to manage the frightened animal. The team ran away only a few days ago and has run away several times. We were arrested as above stated and by false swearing of the witnesses for the State fined five dollars and costs. Not feeling that we have done anything but what we were justified in doing, we have appealed it to a higher court and will fight that envious and lying crowd across the creek as long as we have got a dollar. Mrs. French swore that the boy was coming to his dinner in a little trot. Mrs. French saw the boy and knows very well that he was running after the team as fast as he could. We have nothing to say about what was sworn to by the ladies but there was one C.C. Collins who has endeavored to do everything in his power to injure us. He swore that he saw the boy trotting slowly beside the road when we came by and struck him. This one Collins knows very well that the boy was running after the team as fast as he could. But this is as much as we could have expected from this scoundrel Collins; a man that is known throughout this neighborhood as one whose word is very unreliable and one of the biggest liars in Kansas and honest and decent people should refuse to associate with him. ...Collins has expressed a desire to give us a good thumping. We are not anxious for a thumping but we are not that sort of a journalist who stands bulldozing in this way but if he really desires to thrash us and will furnish us with reliable proof of his respectability, we will give him an opportunity of carrying out his threats at such time and place as he may designate. Collins evidently swallowed his pride and did not 'thump' Bob, as no more is recorded of the matter. A month or so later the *Cherryville Globe* characterized Bob as follows:

The quiet and bashful editor of that excellent local paper, the Cambridge Commercial and postmaster at that thriving town, favored the Globe with a pleasant visit Wednesday afternoon. The editor of *The Globe* used gentle irony describing Bob as 'quiet and bashful,' personality traits he totally lacked. Other editors called him boastful, arrogant and bull-headed, crass, plus adjectives not normally applied in print without a libel suit being threatened. Bob usually gave as good as he received, taking it all as grist for his mill. Not a tall man, he carried himself well and gave the impression of being taller than his five feet-six inches. He had thick, dark hair and blue, wistful eyes. Bob emanated a masculine energy, a great appetite for life that men respected and women liked. All in all, he was a fine looking fellow and knew it. On 5 August, 1881, Bob became postmaster. As no post office building had been built in Cambridge, Bob had the facility moved into the front room of the printing office. His wife, Rosa, established a millinery and dress-making shop there as well, so the premises were crowded. Then perhaps that little red spot of larceny in Bob's heart began to palpitate and postal funds went missing, or did they?

At some time prior to the first of November, 1881, a shocking event occurred when Bob was arrested by Sheriff Shenneman for embezzlement of post office funds. Whether or not he was jailed when taken into custody is not known; however, on the Bar Docket, District Court of Cowley County for November, his name appeared in the criminal docket. No documents have been found as to the outcome of that serious charge, however.

Embezzling post office funds is a Federal crime—a felony. Why were there no headlines in the local papers about the trial? With Bob's arrest, the

Cambridge Commercial sadly sold its subscription list to its competitor, the *Burden Enterprise,* as reported in the Winfield *Courier* on Thursday, December 1:

The Cambridge Commercial dies with last week's issue. The Burden Enterprise takes its subscription books. This leaves the Enterprise the only paper in the third representative district, with an excellent subscription list and on a first rate paying basis. Enos, there are many anxious hearts who would like to know something about this business. Henry Franklin revived the paper but with a new name, *The Cambridge News* and Bob went on with his life, but not especially well.

From the time of his arrest in November, 1881, until December, 1882 there's a hiatus in Bob's story. Did the shame of being arrested for embezzlement, even if found innocent, make him leave Cowley County? It would be unlikely. If found innocent, he would have proclaimed his virtue far and wide. Where did his wife and baby go? What happened?

The first snippet of news of his whereabouts after the arrest came on December 9.1882, published in the Mason City, Missouri, *Register* and re-printed in the *Cambridge News.*

Henry and Robert Hicks, two boys who learned the 'art preservative' in the Register office at Kirksville, have started more papers in the last four or five years than any two boys (now men) in the country.

They have made their debut at various places in Missouri, Kansas and Texas. The last we heard of Bob, he was running a paper in Texas and Henry has been for some time in the same business in Kansas and comes to us from Kansas the Danville Argus, volume one, number two, Horn & Hicks, proprietors, an eight page, forty column paper. We presume the 'Hicks' is Bob, as an X is asked-(incomplete—the extant copy is torn).

Macon City, Missouri, Register

If Bob was 'running a paper in Texas', where in Texas? He definitely returned to Kansas by the beginning of the winter of 1882.

Danville lies 75 miles due west of Cambridge. Both towns had been founded in 1880. Both were rough and raw. Danville, laid out along the tracks of the K.C. I. & S. K. Railway, had a blacksmith shop, a general store, and a home moved in from the country by a family named Mott. Had it grown much by 1882 when Bob, presumably with his family, was joined by his older sister, Martha Jane, and her husband, J. R. Horn from Missouri? According to the *Kansas: a Cyclopedia of State History* "In 1882 a newspaper, the Danville Argus, was established by R. E. Hicks, and in that year the Presbyterians built the first church." More information comes from a history written in 1912:

The press history of the town is summed up in that

of the *Danville Argus*. *This paper was started on November 10, 1882, by R. E. Hicks. After two months, it was sold to J. R. Horn and in February, 1883, it passed into the hands of a stock company. It was started as a Republican sheet but changed to Democratic views upon coming into the possession of J. R. Horn. Its form is that of a "patent" five column quarto.*

On 23 December 1882 a reprint in the *Cambridge News* from the *Danville Argus* reports that *Mrs. Sarah Hicks, mother-in-fact and in-law, of ye editors, arrived at this place from Torrance, Cowley County, Monday night and will spend a week with us. Like all others who come, she is profoundly impressed with our beautiful town and country and is equally so over The Danville Argus.*

As soon as his brother-in-law bought Bob's interest, he was gone, leaving the 'beautiful town and country' to move once again. By 5 July 1883 he had established himself and Rosa and three year old James Robert in Grenola, Elk County. Had Bob been convicted of a federal embezzlement charge in Cambridge, it is highly unlikely he would have had the opportunity to go to Texas, then Danville and on to Grenola to publish newspapers. It is far more likely he would have been escorted to Leavenworth Prison for considerable 'time out'. Editors had long memories, never hesitating to dig up old scandals when it suited their purposes. In October, 1883, when Bob's political views didn't coincide with the editor of the *Courier*, that editor's rebuttal reminded his readers that Bob "had been under arrest for embezzling post office funds..." Being convicted and sentenced to a Federal prison was far more serious than being under suspicion for embezzlement.

Brother Henry, of honest character, remained a solid citizen in Cambridge. In September, 1882, he established another newspaper, *The Cambridge News,* this time in partnership with Sam B. Sherman, the attorney who had acted as Bob's counsel in the assault case. The two men also established a profitable land and loan business known as Sherman & Hicks. Henry, hard working and honorable, was appointed postmaster by Republican President Chester A. Arthur and re-appointed by two more presidents until 1895. Henry continued to live in Cambridge, his home for 60 years, until his death on 2 June 1938 at the age of 83 years, four months and eight days. His wife, Mollie, had died in 1925. They reared four children of whom only one daughter, Anna Belle (Mrs. H. R. Gailey), lived to bury her father.

Part of Henry's obituary in the *Winfield Courier* reads as follows:

H. F. Hicks, 83, pioneer resident of Cowley County and founder of the city of Cambridge, died at his home in Cambridge at 1:45 Thursday afternoon. He had been in failing health for several months and became critically ill a few days ago.

Mr. Hicks had lived in Cambridge nearly 60 years. He laid out the original town site. For 20 years he was postmaster of Cambridge and also owned and operated a newspaper there for several years. Surviving Mr. Hicks are his second wife, Anna D., one daughter, Mrs. Belle Gailey, six grandchildren and four great grandchildren. In childhood and as young men, Henry and Bob had been close; however, there is no record of their seeing each other after Bob left for New York City and then Chicago. They each became absorbed in their individual lifestyles. The two brothers shared the trait of being hard workers but were of different character. Henry settled into life in Cambridge with his work, his wife, children and friends. As one of the city founders, postmaster and business man, he died respected and mourned by all. On the other hand, Bob yearned for a larger world. He took chances with life, losing at some games, winning others. He battled inner demons—a restless spirit that gave him no peace, a fight with his craving for whiskey and the temptation of women. Turning again to the early years, Bob left Danville in the spring of 1883 for Grenola to establish yet another paper:

R. E. Hicks, late of Cambridge, has started a new paper in Grenola named the 'Grenola Chief'. Robert is an accomplished newspaper man, and give him a good town where there is plenty of business and he will make a success every time. The first number is before us and comes out in good shape.

The Grenola Chief, a paper just started at our neighboring town of Grenola, made its appearance Monday last. It is a newsy and wide awake paper and starts out with a very good patronage in the way of advertisements. We wish Bro. Hicks, the editor and proprietor, success. (Moline Mercury).

We have received the first number of The Chief, Grenola's new paper. R. E. Hicks editor and proprietor. The paper is neat and tasty. Mr. Hicks has had lots of experience in the newspaper business and will doubtless succeed at Grenola. We extend our best wishes. (Howard Journal).

So by 1883 Bob, his reputation restored one may presume, had moved on to Grenola, Elk County, Kansas, a few miles to the east of Cambridge. Between 1881 and 1884 Grenola was the largest single cattle shipping point in America. The Longhorn cattle were driven along the Chisholm Trail that stretched from south of San Antonio through Oklahoma to Kansas. Bob established the *Grenola Chief* on 6 July 1883, publishing and editing the paper until 24 October 1884. Grenola prospered in the late 19th century and into the early 20th. By 1900 the population had grown to 11,443 but times change, and by 2000 the population shrank to a mere 2000. In the first issue (6 July 1883) of the *Grenola Chief* the *Winfield Telegram* published a salutary welcome to the new little paper that was re-printed in the *Chief*:

From the ashes of the Grenola Chief, lately destroyed by fire, has arisen another paper, The Chief, by R. E. Hicks. It is neat, well made up, and newsy. We hope Mr. Hicks may be more fortunate than Mr. Crotsley." Bob added a laconic "Well, yes, we hope so, too."

The Cambridge News announced the arrival of the *Chief* with the following: R. E. Hicks, editor and proprietor of the Grenola Chief. It is a five column quarto, is well filled with home news, and judging from its first appearance, will be worthy of a liberal support from the citizens of Grenola and vicinity. It is independent in politics and will advocate the up-building of Grenola and is to be run for the money there is in it for its proprietor.

But not all editors wished Bob and his new paper success. On 13 July 1883 Bob printed the following:

The Burden Enterprise, with its usual kindness, last week published the following highly complimentary notice about the editor of The Chief. We always feel thankful for any words spoken in our behalf:

Bob Hicks is saying some naughty things in The Grenola Chief about the editor of this paper and says privately that he can afford to say meaner things than we can. This is true. Bob is known by our citizens to be a 'notorious liar and incurable deadbeat.' Having no reputation to sustain, and being nothing but a newspaper tramp, anything he says will be passed by those who know him as the vaporings of a fool who aspires to a position many degrees above his caliber. However, Bob has one friend down here who wants to see him 'BAD'.

The readers of *The Chief* no doubt waited with baited breath for Bob's rebuttal which came out in the 27 July issue as follows:

That alleged newspaper man over at Burden is saying some naughty things about The Chief. Now if he had sense enough to herd sheep we might get mad or say something, but as it is we feel like the boy when the long eared animal kicked him – we just consider the source- the idiot doesn't know any better.

Thomas Elbert Hicks, Bob's youngest brother, joined the newspaper as a partner in August, 1883. As of 1880 Tom had been living with Bob, his wife and son and their mother, Sarah, in Lewis County, Missouri. They had all come to Kansas together. He remained with the newspaper until April, 1884 when he returned to Cambridge to buy half interest in the Weaverling & Co. mercantile business owned by his sister's in-laws. The former editor of the *Grenola*

Chief, A. M. Crotsley, was arrested in Kingman, Kansas, according to the following article in the CHIEF Sept. 7, 1883:

The news has reached us from Kingman that A. M. Crotsley has been arrested for stealing $35.00 from the money drawer of the hotel where he has "cheeked" his board for the past several months. If the report is true, and it is on the best authority, the scoundrel will get his just dues without further expense to Elk County. From what we can learn of him, he should be sent to the penitentiary on general principles. He is a dead beat of the first water and the sooner he is taken care of and given a boarding house where he will not be obliged to 'stand off' the landlord, the better. There is room for such men at Leavenworth and by all means let the citizens of Kingman provide him with a free pass and as a matter of business, send the sheriff along to keep him company.

Well, so much for Mr. Crotsley.

A poignant article followed:

Sheriff Gary of Cowley county was a passenger on the east bound train Monday morning, having in charge General A. H. Green, who was pronounced insane some time ago. Mrs. Green was accompanying her husband to the insane asylum at Ossawatomie. We got a glimpse of this unfortunate man as he lay upon a couch in the baggage car; and he looked like anything but the live, energetic business man whom we were intimately acquainted with only a few months ago. It is thought that his case is a hopeless one and in this misfortune Winfield has lost one of her most active business men.

The insane asylum in Ossawatomie had been built in 1866 at the end of the Civil War. A two storied structure with a porch on the front, by 1883 it became totally inadequate for the number of patients incarcerated there. Overcrowded and understaffed by brawny illiterates who shackled and beat recalcitrant inmates, it was typical of the mental hospitals of the nineteenth century. If General Green (titles were often honorary) had fought in the Civil War, his illness today might be diagnosed as post traumatic stress disorder and treatment could alleviate symptoms. In the 1800's mental patients were treated worse than criminals, excepting horse thieves. who were promptly hanged. On Friday the 12th October, 1883, Bob wrote an editorial, in response to the *Burden Enterprise*'s article, regarding the Republican candidate for commissioner of Cowley County, Mr. James A. Irwin:

The Burden Enterprise this week makes the statement that the editor of this paper circulated false reports regarding the character of Jas. A. Irwin, Republican candidate for commissioner of Cowley County. We do not believe that Mr. Irwin ever told the Enterprise's hired man anything of the kind, but if he did, he lied, and is not worthy the respect of any community. We have always held Mr. Irwin in the highest esteem, having known him several years ago in Lewis County, Missouri. We have never made any statement to any one regarding the character of Mr. Irwin, for we believed him to be a man worthy of the confidence of the people. In our last issue we said that the Republicans had made a mistake in nominating Mr. Irwin as their candidate for commissioner, and we are yet of that opinion. If elected he will prove a burden to the party, from the fact that he has never been successful in conducting his own business, let alone the affairs of Cowley County. He is not competent, lacks all the qualifications to make a good officer and his election would certainly be a detriment to the party to which he belongs. The Republican party had better be defeated than to elect a man that would disgrace it by his official acts. We have known Mr. Irwin for a number of years; we know that he has not the education, that he has not the business qualifications to conduct his own affairs and we know that the Republicans of Cowley County will regret the day that they nominated him as their candidate for commissioner. As to the Enterprise editor, we have but a few words. He is ignorant and does not know the first principles of the profession to which he aspires, and when he made the charges in this week's Enterprise, he lied and in his craven, black heart, he knew he lied. He is not worthy of the respect of a dog, is a disgrace to the profession and a burden to the community in which he resides. He is not worth a dollar, has nothing but his little salary of four dollars per week and he dares to make assertions about the editor of this paper, who could buy him a hundred times. Henthorn, we say you have lied and if you are a man you will resent it.

The above blast was followed on Friday, 3 August 1883 by the following:

The Enterprise, an alleged newspaper at Burden, is again trying to slur and say something naughty about the editor of this paper. He calls us a dead beat and c., which we pass by with the best of feelings, considering the source it originates from. We have in these columns noticed the editor of that sheet simply because he was ignored by all other papers. We done so more because we pitied the varmint more than on account of malice, for we hope never to be guilty of letting our angry passions rise at the remarks of any nincompoop. If Henthorn was even a third class newspaper man or actually knew the first principles of journalism, we would consider him worthy of a name in the journalistic field, and as to the Enterprise and its editor they are unworthy of notice. Yellow dogs cease baying at the moon and fly to the woods, tail between their legs, howling at every jump, when he appears. A wanderer on the face of the earth, an outcast from the pale of refined society, a cumberer of the ground, he yet dares to assume he is a journalist, when he has not the faintest idea of the rudiments of the profession. A 'thing' unworthy the name of man, who should, in reality, belong to the paternal ancestors of the long-eared illegitimate children of the female members of the horse family, he dares to make assertions in regard to ourself which are false and which in his cowardly craven heart he knows to be false. He lives merely because the earth refuses to receive him to her bosom. With less brains than a mullet-head, he is yet conceited enough to think he is a man. Unworthy of consort with the jackal, scorned by the hyena and shunned by the buzzards, he is really deserving of pity. Trusting that our words of friendship may fall upon his alleged mind like dew upon the parched earth, we bid him adieu and hope he may sufficiently reform during this life to be deemed worthy of a snug corner in purgatory.

The *Winfield Courier* on 25 October 1883 whose editor formerly had been supportive of Bob, then published the following article supporting Irwin and heartily condemning Bob.

SLANDER AS A POLITICAL WEAPON

Knowing that James A. Irwin, the Republican candidate for Commissioner of the Third District is too popular and highly respected to be defeated by honorable means, his political opponents have resorted to innuendo and slander. Two weeks ago the *Grenola Chief*, edited by Bob Hicks, uttered the following:

The Republicans of eastern Cowley County made a grand mistake when they put in nomination James A. Irwin as their candidate for commissioner. We fear that the Republicans will regret this step after the election, if not before.

The Telegram seized upon this as a sweet morsel and added several innuendoes that there must be something bad in his old home record in Lewis County, Missouri.

The hostility of The Telegram to Mr. Irwin is easily explained by the fact that he is a Republican nominee and by its own admission in last week's issue that it is fighting Irwin for official patronage. Then came the *Burden Enterprise* to characterize the hostility of Bob Hicks in the following language:

When Hicks was under arrest for embezzling post office funds, he went to Mr. Irwin and asked him to go on his bond. Mr. Irwin refused, giving as a reason that he had no confidence in Hicks and did not care to risk what little property he had in such a manner. Again, at the reunion at Topeka, Hicks went to Irwin and wanted to borrow money from him, which was refused. This made the galled jade wince and if any person will take stock in a dirty personal fight upon a man of Mr. Irwin's standing, then we are very much mistaken in the intelligence of the citizens of Cowley County.

The Enterprise also squelched the insinuation that there is something bad in Mr. Irwin's Lewis County record by publishing the following testimonial from the leading men of that county.

We, the undersigned citizens of Lewis County, Missouri, take pleasure in stating that James A. Irwin was a resident of this county for a number of years and while he lived here was honored and respected as an honest upright citizen and fair in his transactions with his fellow man and acted in such a manner as to command the respect and confidence of the people generally.

This complete and thorough vindication was not needed among the people who have known Mr. Irwin well for years in Windsor Township as an honorable, upright man, of rare intelligence and worth. With these, no slander or innuendoes against him would be believed, but it is well to publish the vindication for the benefit of such voters in that district who have not had the fortune to become personally acquainted with him.

Newspapers played an inordinate role in the promotion and politics of Kansas. Bob was typical of the editors of papers who took a biased role not only in promoting or slandering a candidate but in encouraging the growth of a cluster of houses to become a township. Newspapers sprang up in the 1880's like prairie grass and withered just as quickly. It has been estimated that in 1888 Kansas had over 300 papers, more than any other state in the Union. Editors sparred endlessly with each other, competing for advertisers and readers. Far more papers died than survived.

The 21 June 1884 issue of the *Arkansas City Republican* noted that *The Grenola Chief has completed, this week, the first year of its existence. Brother Hicks understands well the management of a paper and has achieved success. To newspapers of this standing, Kansas owes much of her unexampled prosperity.*

Bob, once again, seems to have regained his respectability.

On the 24th of October, 1884, Bob wrote his final editorial in *The Chief:*

One by one roses fade away. With this issue my connection with The Chief ceases. Having sold the paper together with all the patronage and good will to Abe Steinberger, it is only left for me to return to the good people of Grenola and vicinity my sincere thanks for the liberal patronage I have received from them and to extend to them my sympathies in the afflictions which are bound to follow the change in the office. R. E. Hicks.

Directly below these cryptic remarks, the new owner wrote as follows:

I have bought The Chief because I wanted it and trust the change will be satisfactory to the patrons. The Chief will be its own boss, independent in everything, neutral in nothing. Abe Steinberger

In the same issue we learn what Bob was up to:

R. E. Hicks, manager of Gunn's Opera house, has secured Neff's Chicago Opera company for the last three nights in November. This is a splendid company and they will have the honor of opening this new place of amusement.

So Bob had gone into the entertainment business.

The following month, 14 Nov.1884, we learn that the Opera house continued being under construction.

Work on Gunn's new Opera house is progressing but not as rapidly as the amusement loving public would like to see it as the season is shortening rapidly. Would it be ready for opening night the last of November?

In the same issue is a notice about Bob's wife, Rosa:

Mrs. R. E. Hicks was taken seriously ill Wednesday evening. Mr. Hicks who was absent from the city on business was notified by telegraph.

Rosa recovered because on 19 December 1884 she went to Cambridge to 'spend the first part of the week with friends and relatives, returning in time to attend the opera. A number of articles in the re-named *Grenola Hornet* indicated that the Opera House had not been completed; however, it must have served its purpose, although unfinished. Bob made arrangements for veterans to have special excursion rates on the Southern Kansas railroad in order for them to attend "The Spy of Atlanta" on the 18th, 19th, or 20th of December. Eli Perkins had been booked for a lecture on January 15, 1885, and Bob informed the newspaper that "he is receiving a great many letters from first-class companies who are desirous of procuring dates."

Around this same time, on Friday, 30 January 1885 Rosa gave birth to their second child, another son, named Elisha Elmer. Bob's youngest sister, Virginia E., called "Jennie," had moved to Kansas at an earlier date than Bob. More than likely she came with Henry Hicks, her brother and his wife, Mollie, in 1877. In 1881 the Cambridge Committee invited her to be the school teacher for the first six grades. Classes took place in a private home until the one room schoolhouse opened in October, 1882. Later in that year, her name became linked with Bill Weaverling, son of a prosperous local merchant, when they worked together as type setters for the *Tattler*, possibly the school paper. Their friendship grew and the following year she and William A. Weaverling married on March 6, 1883, in the Torrance home of her mother, Sarah.

John Q. Knight, preacher of the Gospel, officiated. Jennie's life can be followed by the snippets of newspaper articles such as the poignant little notice that appeared in the *Cambridge News* on July 7 asking if anyone had found Jennie's "gold pencil and a green cross on a broken chain between Torrance and Mr. Williams' house." Had it been a treasured gift from her husband? Did someone find and return it to Jennie? After the birth of her nephew, Elmer, she traveled to Grenola to visit Rosa and Bob and to attend the opera. A year later her brother, Thomas Elbert Hicks, bought half interest in Weaverling's Emporium, her father-in-law's business. Early in 1884 Jennie and Bill had a baby boy whom they named James A. Weaverling. The infant lived but a short time and was buried in the Cambridge cemetery. The parents placed A Card of Thanks in the *Cambridge News* on March 22, 1884: *The friends who so kindly with devoted attention assisted us during the short illness of our little darling, have our heart-felt thanks and are especially remembered by us when at the throne of Grace. Our prayer is that God will reward them. Mr. and Mrs. Wm. Weaverling."* Jennie became a leading light among the young matrons. She took part in amateur theatricals, headed various women's organizations, and continued her interest in the school, although she could no longer teach now that she was a married woman. The last of February, 1885,

Jennie gave birth to a second child, a daughter. Ill health plagued Jennie. In 1886 she had a severe attack of malaria that lasted for weeks. Malaria does not fade away but continues to recur time after time, leaving the victim weak and exhausted. Then the doctor diagnosed Jennie with consumption and she died on March 12, 1888, aged 27 years, 8 months, 27 days. *The Cambridge News* ran the obituary on Friday, March 16.

It becomes our painful duty this week to chronicle the death of Mrs. W. A. Weaverling which occurred at her home two and one half miles east of this city last Monday morning about seven o'clock. Her death had been expected for several days as her life's blood was being slowly but surely preyed upon by the dread disease consumption. She was conscious almost to the last and gave directions concerning her funeral. Mrs. Weaverling was well known in this part of the county and especially in Cambridge and her death cast a gloom over all. She was nearly twenty-eight years old, a devoted wife, strong in her likes and dislikes, a zealous worker in all good works and had been an active member of the Methodist Episcopalian church for about thirteen years. Hers was a restless spirit, not contented without being engaged in some good work calculated to elevate mankind. The deceased leaves a husband, an aged mother and a number of sisters and brothers to mourn her demise. She was buried in the Windsor cemetery west of town on Tuesday afternoon. In compliance with a request made on her death-bed the remains of her first born were taken up and buried with the mother. On the 19th of March of that year, a short obituary followed in the Winfield Courier:

Mrs. W. A. Weaverling, of Cambridge, aged 28, and well known as formerly a teacher in Cowley's schools, died last week. In compliance with a request made on her death-bed, the remains of her first born were taken up and buried with the mother.

Neither obituary mentions the little daughter born in 1885. Had that child also died? It remains a mystery. Two months after Jennie's untimely death, her mother, Sarah Selsor Hicks, passed away. Perhaps Sarah's will to live died with her youngest daughter. Sarah had left her prosperous home in Virginia to marry a man who never prospered. She bore him baby after baby in straightened circumstances and followed him until his death, then took what charity her children offered. Jennie's passing may well have sounded her death knell. Grief can kill. Her obituary, published in the *Cambridge News* on 25 May 1888, follows:

Died at her home east of town on May 21, 1888, of heart disease, Mrs. Sarah Hicks, aged 62 years. Funeral services were conducted by Rev. D. E. Hoover. Grandma Hicks, as she was familiarly called, suffered a great deal during her sojourn in this unfriendly world, being an invalid for a number of years, and doubtless the Angel of Death was gladly welcomed by her waiting soul. She had been the mother of nine children, three of whom passed on before. She had been the member of the Methodist Episcopal Church for many years, was a kind and affectionate mother. Her husband died in Lewis County, Missouri, April 2, 1875, leaving her to care for quite a family of children, whom she labored earnestly to bring up in the path of obedience and rectitude. She has gone to meet her reward. Peace be to her ashes.

In the Cambridge Cemetery just west of town, the grave of little James is flanked by that of his mother, Jennie, and his maternal grandmother, Sarah Selser Hicks. They sleep quietly together under the broad Kansas sky. In April, 1885, the *Grenola Hornet* noted "R. E. Hicks has sold his residence in Smith's addition to Ike Campbell, who will occupy it in a very few days. Mr. Hicks has commenced the erection of another dwelling in the same locality."

The vagaries of Kansas weather were notorious—droughts, locust plagues, torrential rains and blizzards were commonplace. The great blizzard of the winter of 1885/86 lives on in histories of the Great Plains. It is estimated the chill factor of that January dropped to 100 degrees below zero. In southwestern Kansas fully

80 percent of all range cattle died from cold and starvation. Cattle 'barons' were ruined. Six to seven feet snow drifts blocked trains, literally cutting off transportation. The summer of that year had gentle rains with an abundant crop, but was followed in 1887 by a devastating drought as hot, dry winds swept the prairies. A number of pioneer farmers turned their covered wagons eastward with awkwardly painted words on the wagon canvas- "In God we trusted, in Kansas we busted". Bob just kept founding newspapers. By 1887 Bob had moved farther to the west, establishing the *Seward County Courant* in Springfield, Seward County, Kansas. He published and edited that newspaper from May 30, 1887 to May 4, 1889. Seward County is in southwestern Kansas almost on a straight line across the state from Cambridge. Wife Rosa and the two boys? Did they tag along or did they stay in Grenola? Considerable light is shed on Bob's whereabouts by a newspaper article published in Topeka when a journalist interviewed Bob in the summer of 1926:

Before leaving, the casual visitor met Robert E. Hicks and he turned out to be "Bob' Hicks, who edited and owned half a dozen or so Kansas newspapers back in the 'eighties when county seat fights were the popular diversion. He got out papers in Cambridge, Grenola, Springfield, Syracuse and participated in county seat fights from Morton County, up thru what was then Hamilton County, bigger than Rhode Island, to Clark County.

The Topeka article quoted Bob extensively:

"Tells of Exciting Kansas Days."

"Why, we voted 900 ballots after the polls closed when Syracuse and Kendallville were fighting for the county seat," said Mr. Hicks. "I was with a party of 100 rifles strong that started for Kendallville one night to get some records we needed. It rained. We argued. Finally better judgment won and we counter-marched. The next morning we learned that 200 yards further down that road where the grass on both sides was better than waist high in a draw, the Kendallville crowd was waiting in ambush, nearly 100 rifles in the hands of men that could shoot."

"Hicks saw Col. Sam Wood shot at Woodsdale."

Hicks continued. "That wasn't a county seat fight, but grew out of a railroad that we started, the Wichita and Trinidad and something else, on $200.00 cash and a lot of bond issues. And then in Grant county, over at Ulysses—" and Bob Hicks talked until near midnight of his early days in Kansas when they fought county seat wars with ballots in the second line and bullets in the front line trenches."

If Bob witnessed the murder of Colonel Samuel Wood, he was in Hugoton, Stevens County, Kansas, on 23 June 1891. Wood was a man of substance and prominence in Kansas. In 1854 he left his birthplace in Ohio to establish a home near Lawrence. He became the leader of the free-state party, opposed to slavery. Wood established three newspapers and was an original stockholder of the Atchison, Topeka & Santa Fe railroad. Just where and when Bob came to know Wood is unknown, but they had common interests. The *Kansas Cyclopedia of State History* laconically writes that Jim Brennen killed Wood as a result of a county seat fight in Stevens County. Although the murder was witnessed by a number of people, including Bob, Brennen, because of the tricky laws at the time, was never convicted and ended his days as a prominent and prosperous rancher in the Oklahoma Territory.

4

THE NEW YORK YEARS

By the time Bob reached 40, Kansas had become too small to hold him. In 1896 he turned up in New York City. Trow's Directories listed him as a publisher working at 113 W. 31st Street and living at 510 W. 29th Street. By 1900 Bob had been in New York for three years. No longer a newspaper man, he ran a publishing business, moving his printing presses to new locations on a yearly basis. New York City had the largest population, 3.5 million, of any city in the United States. One could get lost in New York City and that seems what Bob tried, unsuccessfully, to do. The centennial of 1900 witnessed the beginning of the technological age. Queen Victoria continued to reign supreme over the British Empire, but her days were drawing to a close. She died January 22, 1901. In both London and New York City an occasional automobile could be seen driven by a uniformed chauffeur or a proud young dandy wearing a bowler. In Madison Square Garden the first national automobile show took place with record attendance. Bob fell in love with the first car he saw, and for the rest of his life cars fascinated him. It's a sure bet he attended the exhibition. On Fifth Avenue the first electric omnibus served women wearing ankle length dresses with tight-laced waists, extravagant hats and high-heeled boots. The first excavation for the New York City subway system was being dug with pick and shovel by Irish 'navies' and other newly arrived immigrants. In Philadelphia the Republican National Convention took place that June. President Wm. McKinley was renominated with Theodore Roosevelt as his running mate. McKinley would be assassinated the following year with Roosevelt succeeding him. The French Count de la Vaux landed at Kiev after flying in a hot-air balloon 1,304 miles in 36 hours from Vincennes, France. Kodak Camera Company made photography available to the average citizen by selling the first Brownie Box camera for $1.00. A tidal wave swept the Galveston coast of Texas killing hundreds, and St. Louis witnessed riots when tram system workers struck for better working conditions and higher wages. The turn of the century brought with it new concepts, new inventions and new expensive toys for the few who could afford them.

The 1900 Federal census taker recorded Bob in New York, then 42 years old and listing himself as a widower. Rosa, then, had supposedly died. His two sons, James Robert (20) a printer pressman, Elisha Elmer (15) a student and the surprise, Elizabell Smith

(32) an Irish widow and a 'vocal singer', lived with him. Mrs. Smith's position in the family was given as a 'partner'. How could this be? Bob was a married man.

Sometime prior to 1900, Bob had married a certain Jeannette Wren, possibly in Kansas City or St. Louis. In March of 1900, she filed for legal separation in the Superior Court, New York City, but it dropped off the Court calendar, as she did not pursue it; however, in 1901 she filed for a divorce. A titillating account of Bob's domestic problems, as reported by a New York journalist, follows in part:

Hicks obtained a dismissal of his wife's first action and 13 days after was served with the complaint for the divorce suit. He alleged in his answer that his wife at Kansas City had admitted that she had been guilty of misconduct with Dr. Wainwright who had attended her professionally. He denies that he has been guilty of improper conduct with Mrs. Smith, the co-respondent, a widow with whom he and his two sons by a former marriage have been boarding for the last three years.

Mrs. Hicks denies her husband's allegations as to infidelity on her part.

In spite of the bickering and evidence of infidelity, later events indicate the divorce did not occur.

Bob moved again in 1901 to 45 E. 99th Street, with his publishing business at 49 W. 28th. Why so many moves? He lived well, had his suits tailored, frequented the higher class bars and enjoyed being a 'man about town.' How did it come about? He again had decided to try his hand at making money the easy way. He remembered the scam of the mustache powder from those early years in Missouri. Certainly there were more gullible 'suckers' available in New York City than Kirksville, so he established the Geneva Chemical Company, printed pamphlets on his own printing press and sent them through the postal system. Two of his most popular remedies, both targeting women, were pills for 'bust developing' and a specialty advertised as 'if you want to have a baby, don't take this pill." The pill, a concoction of sugar and a harmless binding substance, did no harm but was worthless as a contraceptive. The money rolled in and the living was easy.

The halcyon days of 1901 ended abruptly on May 31, 1902. Bob, riding the subway to his office, opened his issue of The New York Times to read the following account:

AN AERONAUT'S FATAL FALL

Harry Hicks killed at Kingston Point, N. Y. while Descending in a Parachute. Kingston, N. Y., May 30.

Harry Hicks, an aeronaut, was killed at Kingston Point, a summer resort, today. He had been engaged to make daily balloon ascensions, and this afternoon was booked for his first exhibition.

When the balloon had reached an altitude of about

2,000 feet, Hicks commenced the descent by means of a parachute, coming down slowly to about 800 feet above the Hudson River.

For some reason the aeronaut lost his hold and fell, striking head first on a sand bar in the river.

The dead man was a nephew of Charles Kabrick, well known as a balloonist.

It was Memorial Day. Bob's oldest son had tired of working as a printer pressman. He joined a so-called 'famed balloonist' Charles H. Kabruch/Kabrich who made his living by parachuting out of a balloon at State Fairs, national holiday gatherings and organizational picnics. James Robert, taking the euphonious name of Harry Hicks, became Kabruch's apprentice. On that particular Memorial Day they were performing at Kingston Point, Ulster County, N.Y. Other newspaper accounts claimed that Harry's body was swept away by the current before men in a rowboat could rescue him. Rescuers pulled his corpse from the river at Rondout, downstream from Kingston Point. Eventually the body was taken to Rhinebeck, directly opposite Kingston. No explanation was given. Could it be there was no coroner to issue a death warrant in Ulster County in 1902? James Robert "Harry" was barely 22.

The *Kingston Daily Freeman* remembered the young man in the newspaper column entitled "Ten Years Ago Today": *The body of James R. Hicks, aeronaut, found in a net by Isaac Schultz.*

Years later Bob confided in his wife, Mae, that on reading the news of his son's death, his hair turned white overnight.

Bob continued to print his pamphlets advertising fallacious medical remedies. His new stenographer, Viola Wilmot, a former actress from San Fransisco, stuffed circulars into envelopes, typed letters with two fingers and made coffee on a small Bunsen burner.

'A sprightly young woman brightens an office,' Bob thought.

Perhaps Viola introduced Janette Colepaugh to Bob. Bob became infatuated with her, though she was slightly younger than the son he had lost; however, his blandishments left her unmoved. "If you love me so much, marry me," she told him.

Try as he did, he failed to change her mind, but not his determination.

A journalist reported the ensuing scenario as follows:

The *Jersey Evening Journal*, Jersey City, N. J., Thursday, April 14th, 1903.

Couple in Hansom Cab to be Wed

Some little excitement was created about the Gregory Street Police Station last night when a stylish hansom drew up to the door. In it were two women and a man, all of them stylishly dressed. The excitement was slightly increased when the man said he wished to marry one of the women.... Police Inspector Archibald sent them to the house of Justice of the Peace Martinez at 41 Gregory Street. The man said he was Robert E. Hicks, 45 years old and engaged in the 'mail order' business at 1193 Broadway, his house being in Passaic, N.J. He said it was his second marriage but did not say whether his first marriage ended with the death of his wife or through divorce. The bride, who was a very pretty woman, described herself as a stenographer and said she was 21 years old and lived in Passaic. All legal questions being answered, the ceremony was quickly performed and the judge rewarded with a substantial fee. Mr. Hicks seemed to be plentifully supplied with yellow backed oblong paper said to be able to hold its own in an ordinary conversation. A peculiar feature of the wedding was the fact that while both bride and groom lived in Passaic, the driver of the hansom said that Mr. Hicks had hired him at Broadway and Twenty-seventh Street in Manhattan and after the ceremony, he drove the party back to that city. Miss Julia Bloch, the witness they brought with them, said she lived in New York City but did not give her address. The other witness was Mrs. Martinez.

Two days later, the same journalist wrote a follow-up story:

Hicks' Bride Finds Him A Prisoner

Miss. Viola Hicks, a bride of two days, went into the office of her husband, Robert E. Hicks, on the second floor of 1103 Broadway, New York, yesterday afternoon, only to find Anthony Comstock in charge and learn that her husband was under arrest on a charge of violating the postal laws by sending medical advertising circulars through the mails....

Another newspaper, The *New York World*, picked up the story, giving more details:

Estelle Wilmot, a California Actress, in Trouble in New York—

Sentence Suspended

Today's session of the criminal branch of the United States Circuit Court closed with two women in hysterics. In the trail of Robert E. Hicks and Estelle Wilmot, a stenographer employed by Hicks, who were charged by Anthony Comstock with conspiracy to use the mails for carrying on an illegal medical business, the jury had returned a verdict of guilty. Hicks' wife rushed from the courtroom wailing and moaning, and fell into a fit of hysterics in the corridor. Miss Wilmot, who came to N. Y. from CA a year ago, said while on the witness stand that she was an actress, but had given up the stage for steadier employment in the Hicks establishment. She denied knowing that she was assisting in an illegal business. She is now engaged as a chorus girl in a Brooklyn theatre. The court suspended sentence in *her case after she was revived. Hicks got ten months in jail and $1000 fine.* As he wrote in "A Conscience Unburdened", his success, built on sand, sifted away when arrested for mail fraud in 1902 by Anthony Comstock. Who was this Anthony Comstock who had the authority to have Bob arrested and brought to Federal Court? *The Dictionary of American Biography* calls Comstock a 'reformer', but rank and file reformers have no legal jurisdiction. Comstock, in one sense, predated Senator Joseph McCarthy of the 1950's, and on the other hand, was a protector of the innocents who could ill afford to lose money through mail fraud. Comstock came of New England stock and early developed an acute conscience aided by his adherence to strict Christian Congregational discipline. He took the place of his older brother, a Union Army soldier, who had been killed at Gettysburg, but the younger Comstock saw no action. By 1868 he had become active in the YMCA movement against obscene literature, securing the arrest of two publishers, one of whom attacked him with a knife. Through the auspices of the YMCA he formed a committee for the Suppression of Vice that supported his going to Washington where he became a special agent of the Post Office Department. Comstock in 1873 persuaded Congress to pass a law prohibiting any obscene matter, especially contraception or birth control information, to be carried through the mail. He gained notoriety by banning the sale of George Bernard Shaw's play, *Mrs. Warren's Profession*. In retaliation, Shaw coined the word 'Comstockery' meaning "censorious opposition to alleged immorality (as in literature)." The word soon took its place in dictionaries.

Comstock hunted Bob down, arrested him and appeared at his court hearing. After posting a thousand dollar bond, a large sum of money in 1903, the Judge released Bob until the court set the date for his trial. He was a bigamist. He was charged with a felony. Bob secretly decided to skip bail and leave the country. From New York he made his way to Canada, taking ship in Montreal for England, where he proceeded to go on a drunken binge until he had only sufficient money left for passage back to America. A memento of that troubled time is a postcard of London's Charing Cross station that he later gave to his daughter, Sarah Phoebe. In the October, 1924, issue of *The Specialty Salesman,* Bob wrote an article briefly referring to his London sojourn:

A long time ago I went to England. I landed in London with a little money but not enough to enable me to buy the Tower of London. I walked the streets of that old, old city and poked my nose into a number of places where it had no business. One time I spent a day trying to cash a draft for a hundred pounds. It was what I had left and it was a lot of money but I couldn't buy a penny's worth of anything with it. It took me a day before I learned that the American consul could cash it for me. In my hurry to get there I took a tram, forgetting that I had not a penny in my pocket. When it came time to take my fare, the conductor called a "bobby" and I was nearly arrested, but, the policeman, being a decent chap, took my pocket knife as pledge and paid my fare. I got the knife at the station the next day.

London has probably changed some since then. But, if it had not changed, I could be dropped in the city today without warning and find my way about.

By Christmas Bob had returned to America, possibly through the port at Philadelphia. He was on the run from the Federal authorities, and his funds were running out. He took the name of 'Gammon'. Why Gammon? Was Bob being a little too clever? 'Gammon' is defined in a variety of ways e.g. a smoked or cured ham, to stand close to a person while a confederate picks his pocket, and one that may have especially appealed to Bob's ironic sense of humor— 'to stuff with nonsense, to humbug, to hoax.'

No arrest followed. He disappeared from 1904 until 1905. No trace of him during those two years has been found. What little is known, he told to his great-nephew (the grandson of his sister, Mary Doran) who worked for him at the *Specialty Salesman Magazine*. In 1980 Cleon Fleck of the Whitley County Historical

Society, interviewed Harold Doran about his uncle, and published the article entitled "The Amazing Robert E. Hicks" in the Society's quarterly:

Uncle Bob's arrival in South Whitley in 1905 was recalled by James Remington, a bank cashier at the time. Mr. Hicks impressed Mr. Remington as a portly gentleman, bold and loud in speaking, and very convincing in his speech. At South Whitley he worked at the Atoz printing plant at his commissioned work for a salary of $15.00 a week, later raised to $50.00. But his associates sensed the 'shady side' nature of his enterprise and disapproved of his propensity to drink. They gave him $100.00 and ordered him out of town. The story is told that Mr. Hicks, on leaving South Whitley, chartered a railroad dining car on a siding and invited associates and business men of South Whitley to dinner on the day of his leaving. Then after the farewell visit, he announced before his guests finished their brandy and fruit, "Gentlemen, you will have to leave now, as this car is leaving with the train for New York." And he disappeared for some years.

Now past 45, Hicks drifted for the next 12 years, to Kansas City, to Denver, back to Chicago, to St. Louis, and to New York City. He continued primarily to print and mail catalogs in exchange for dollars from the unsuspecting public.

In Chicago he headed an apparently flourishing

business that occupied an entire floor of one of the Dearborn Street skyscrapers. He soon had two Harris two-color presses and a corps of stenographers and girls busy in his offices. As explained by Mr. Remington, Hicks refrained from drink when starting an enterprise but when business was once established, the old appetite would return with overwhelming force. So he left Chicago in 1908 or 1909, financially poor again. He jumped then to St. Louis where he failed, surprisingly, as promoter of the R. E. Hicks Mercantile Company. Then he drifted well out of sight until the year 1915.

Well, not quite. By 1907 he had become a distinguished member of the Chicago Publishers Club. In November of that year he gave the annual presentation speech, introduced by the program chairman as 'the silver-tongued orator'. His photo, along with other members of the Club, appeared in the annual bulletin. One must remember the U. S. Federal agents were looking for him, a felon.

Bob's niece, Kate Larue Hicks Ohi, remembered visiting her Uncle Bob at his Chicago office in 1908. She was 10 years old at the time. In October, 1962, she wrote a letter to her cousin, Roger Putnam, recalling that summer:

One summer in Chicago in 1908 there I met Uncle Bob and his third wife, Margaret – he married her in Seattle, Washington. She was a large beautiful woman and was a well trained singer, concert, opera and church. She could not be the mother of the two girls and one boy as she was about 40 years old. Uncle Bob had a large mail order business at that time. Later he had a mail order house in St. Louis. When in Chicago he seemed so fond of me I went to see him at his office. I had my sister's child with me. He told me where Aunt Margaret lived and she would love to see me but I could not take the child with me, so I never saw her again.

The memory of a 72 year old woman can play tricks. 'Margaret' is the last wife whom Larue never met. The 'well-trained singer' was the Elizabell Smith listed as Bob's 'partner' in the New York census of 1900. Whether or not they were married in Seattle is an open question as no record has been found. Elizabell fades out of sight until 1924 when she, or another wife or paramour, turned up in South Whitley one Sunday noon, an unexpected guest at The Hicks Tavern.

Bob's successful mail order business venture failed because of his drinking. Leaving Chicago, he went to St. Louis for a time, finally drifting back to New York City.

By June 21, 1911, he had a daughter, Helen Lois, by his wife, Lois Hawley, whom he had married about 1910, possibly in New York; however, no record of the marriage has been found. Lois had applied for a job as a stenographer at Bob's office and to use the old cliché, "the rest is history". Lois was 25 years younger than Bob and may have been entranced with his debonair sophistication and his ability to appreciate a good-looking young woman. Marriage did in no way cure Bob's appetite for whiskey, good whiskey when he could afford it and 'rot gut' when he couldn't.

On the 26th of June, 1912, Lois gave birth to their second daughter, Sarah Phoebe. Bob continued in the printing business and continued drinking as the mood took him. He never shared with Lois his mail fraud schemes, arrest, skipping bond and being a fugitive from the Federal government. The strain and stress began to build inside and alcohol eased the worry. In 1913 Lois gave birth to Robert Emmet, Jr., his third son. Bob continued to publish the odd jobs that came his way and to indulge in periodic bouts of drunkenness. He always returned home the penitent and Lois always forgave him. What else could she do? There was barely enough money to provide for the growing family. Divorce was out of the question. It had yet to become a socially accepted answer to an unhappy marriage. If she left her husband, where could she go with three infants? She could not return to live with her parents, people of modest means themselves. And Bob had a romantic streak in him that never failed to win a woman. He had a way with words of love few men could match and it worked every time. Lois was hooked for life.

Lois was not among the young married women who marched in the streets of New York City following Harriet Stanton Blatch's bid for women's suffrage. The ones who carried the banners were women with the time and means to leave their households in the care of family members or servants so they could work for better conditions for their less fortunate sisters. Lois would die too young to benefit from the women's movement that changed and continues to change the mores of American society.

A NEW BEGINNING

After Bob's release from prison, he pulled up stakes in New York and moved to the village of South Whitley, Indiana, where he had been offered a job. Years later, in 1922, Bob wrote his own version of why he made the decision to go to South Whitley, this time with his family.

When I was discharged from the penitentiary on July 20th, 1915, I at once commenced to lay plans to start the magazine. A few days after my discharge I received a letter from Frank E. Miner, then president of the Atoz Printing Company in South Whitley, Indiana, telling me that he was coming to New York to see me with reference to becoming a part of his organization. He came to New York where I told him of my plan to start a magazine. He wanted me to accept a salaried position with the Atoz Printing

Company. This I refused to do. Finally he agreed that his company would take over the proposed magazine and pay me a salary of $18.00 a week — the Atoz Company would absorb and own the magazine and I would be given from three to four thousand dollars worth of stock in his company.

A salary of $18.00 a week did not appeal to me; in fact, a salary of any kind did not appeal to me but I was determined to start a magazine for the purpose of making restitution. I did not have sufficient money to have printed the first issue of the magazine, so I decided to accept Mr. Miner's proposition. A salary of $18.00 a week was not what I would work for; the salary would tide me over and I would, I thought, possibly derive something from the interest in the Atoz Printing Company which I was to have.

I went to South Whitley with my family. When I arrived there I had $222.00 which I deposited in the Gandy State Bank·

Cleon Fleck wrote another version of Bob's return to South Whitley in an article entitled "The Amazing Robert E. Hicks":

He arrived in South Whitley in August with his family, $222.32 in money, credit for two printing presses and that was all. He gained an agreement with Frank Miner, owner of the Atoz Printing Company, that he might work there in his effort to start his 'dream' magazine, at a small wage. For a *place to live, he found two upstairs rooms in a house with kitchen privileges downstairs. How to feed his family was a daily problem.* J. E. Remington, a South Whitley bank clerk who later became an employee of Bob's, wrote a third story of the Hicks family arrival:

One hot – terribly hot – Sunday afternoon in August, 1916, five tired-looking, travel-stained human beings alighted from a day coach of the New York-Chicago train at South Whitley. I had been appraised of the time of their arrival and was present with my wife to greet them.

The little party consisted of Mr. and Mrs. Hicks and their babies, Phoebe, Helen and 'Bobby', the namesake of his dad. They had traveled in the sleeper over night, but at Buffalo, early in the morning, they had transferred to a day coach in order to save the extra expense of Pullman fares in the daytime.

If you ever have traveled four hundred miles in a dusty, smoky day coach on a hot Sunday in August with three little babies to look after, you may realize something of the appearance and feelings of this little family.

My wife and I had not seen Mr. Hicks for several years and then under conditions so different that we felt a distinct shock as we tried to welcome this gray-haired, tired-looking man and his weary wife and babies to their new home.

Quarters, an upstairs room and kitchen privileges

downstairs, had been secured for them at the home of a widow living near the printing plant which was to print Mr. Hicks' magazine that he had traveled a thousand miles to inaugurate. I might say here that the motherly heart of this woman immediately went out to the wife and her little babies and no objections were raised when the family overran their quarters. This widow's solicitude for their comfort and the treatment she accorded them was a bright spot in their drab existence.

Mr. Miner proved to be a shrewd businessman. Bob agreed to assume the indebtedness of $1,300.00 already spent in preparation for the first issue of the magazine, called *Canvassers Magazine,* and to turn over all advertising and subscription money as it came in to Frank Miner. Bob made a trip to Chicago to talk with prospective advertisers, believing that he could get at least $300.00 for the first issue. But it was not to be. Bob wrote, *I went to Chicago, but it was not as I had expected. I called on a large number of firms but did not secure a single advertisement. I know that I am a fairly good salesman; I knew that I had what every man engaged in direct selling should have, but I failed to close a sale. I did not present my proposition right. If I had, I would have secured a few advertisements, at least.*

In spite of Bob's disappointment in Chicago, he persuaded Miner to publish the first issue in

November, 1915. As that first issue of *The Canvassers Magazine* rolled off the press, Bob had the satisfaction of knowing his determination had brought it about. Thirty-eight articles were listed in the table of contents. Bob had written, under assumed names, twenty one of them. In his article on page 1, entitled "The Instability of Fallacious Advertising Methods", Bob wrote about a personal experience:

The "free sample" misleading statement has been worked for years - almost as long as I can remember. Forty years or more ago I answered advertisements that offered "something for nothing," but in reality they offered "nothing for something."

It has been so many years ago that I have forgotten how long-so many years since I answered an advertisement to sell twenty papers of needles for 10 cents each, send the two dollars received and get a shot gun worth four or five dollars. I sold about half the needles, but to help me get the coveted shot gun, my mother gave me the money for the unsold needles. I remember my joy when I mailed the letter with the money to the benevolent and generous firm that was to give me such a valuable premium. After waiting a reasonable time, the package arrived. I borrowed the money to pay the express charges and when I opened the package and examined the premium, joy disappeared, while disappointment— the kind that sinks deep—took possession of me.

Made of sheet iron, only a toy, the gun was not worth the express charges.

I wanted "something for nothing" and I received, as I should have expected, "nothing for something."

On page 29 of that first issue, Bob set forth the purpose of his magazine:

It is not our intention to injure the business of any honest man or firm, but it is our intention to expose dishonest advertisers who are robbing the public through misleading advertisements, circulars, letters, etc. We will investigate complaints from our subscribers who have been defrauded by dishonest advertisers. When making a complaint, it is necessary to send us all letters, circulars, etc., received from the advertiser and after we make a thorough investigation and find that dishonest methods are being used, we will expose the advertiser in these columns.

It is not my intention to expose an advertiser until I have positive proof of an act of dishonesty. The fact that I know the firms that are sending broadcast misleading circulars and letters is not enough. I must have proof. I have a number of letters from advertisers that I have asked for an explanation of their methods—their side. I am now waiting to hear from the readers of the Canvassers Magazine to learn how they have been separated from their money and then - I will do my duty.

The first issue had twelve pages of advertisements that netted about $175.00, only enough to bring out the December issue. It was touch and go. Mr. Miner refused to print the January, 1916, issue. Subscriptions and ads were increasing but, by no means, covered expenses. Miner agreed to print the February and March issues, skipped the April issue but got out May and June, then skipped July. By now advertisers and subscribers were taking notice and money began to trickle in. Miner decided the magazine held promise and offered to extend Bob's credit through the December issue.

In the October, 1916, issue Bob printed "A Conscience Unburdened—Cowardly Attacks Refuted". The article's preface follows:

"To my loyal friends – canvassing salesmen everywhere- I owe it to you to tell the truth-to refute the terrible blows that are being hurled at the Canvasser Magazine and at me personally in the hope of forcing the suspension of this publication. Underhand cowardly, treacherous attempts are being secretly made night and day to poison your minds and if possible, to destroy me. In this article I am telling you the whole truth – holding nothing back- revealing the darkest blots upon my life, that you may know and understand. It is for you to decide whether I am to be trusted or the mail-order pirates who are robbing you and your brothers of millions of

dollars every year." Many a politician, including President Clinton, might well have saved their reputations had they had the courage and integrity of Bob in confessing all. By revealing his mistakes of the past he completely disarmed blackmailers at one stroke of the pen.

In January, 1917, Miner said he would give Bob another $1,000.00 credit if he could have half ownership in the magazine. Bob refused and Mr. Miner quickly reminded him that he owed the Atoz Printing Company not less than $2,700.00. Bob was desperate. Where and how would he find the money to continue? Chicago might hold the answer.

5
THE CHICAGO YEARS

I packed my household furniture and when it was loaded for shipment I did not have enough money to pay the railroad fare for my wife and myself to Chicago. My three little children were under age so that it was not necessary to buy tickets for them. I may have had two or three dollars after paying freight on the furniture but I did not have enough to buy those two railroad tickets. I sold my cook stove to the junk dealer here for $15.00 so that I could buy our tickets and have enough to rent a furnished room when we reached Chicago.

As I look back, those were dark days but at the time I knew that I was going to make a success. Failure never entered my mind.

As he had failed to collect sufficient money in November, Bob failed to publish the Christmas, 1916 issue. Determined, he tramped through the heavy December snow from one possible client to another. He got enough money together to print the January, 1917 copy. He changed the name, hoping to change his luck, from "Canvassers" to "The Specialty Salesman

Magazine". *I got the copy ready for the February issue but I had no printer. Several printers in Chicago turned me down. I had about given up the idea of printing the February issue but I did not entertain for a moment the idea of discontinuing the publication.*

In the meantime I had moved from the little furnished room where I had taken my family when I first arrived in Chicago to a house on the south side where I was paying $25.00 a month rent. I could not get a printer to go ahead with the February issue and I did not have money to pay my rent. The landlord told me I would have to pay or get out.

Luck appeared in the form of Luther C. Rogers of the Rogers & Hall Company, one of the big printing establishments in Chicago. Rogers agreed to print the February issue in return for Bob's signing over all the advertising accounts then due and to become due. Bob made an agreement with the manager of the Western News Company to place 5000 copies a month of the newly named magazine on their newsstands, although the man frankly told Bob the magazine had small chance of success. Bob also promised Rogers to turn over any money that the news company owed Bob. Rogers ran a tight ship, yet Bob had only the highest praise for him:

Mr. Rogers was taking a big chance but as he afterwards told me, he believed in me and believed that if I received the money I would pay him. I continued to do business with the Rogers & Hall Company, except during the period when we were at war with Germany, up until I purchased the printing plant here in South Whitley. So long as I live I shall remember the credit extended to me by the Rogers & Hall Company and the manner in which they treated me. I shall remember with gratitude Mr. Rogers, not only for the courtesy extended in the way of credit but for his kindly advice. Bob brought his readers into his personal life. He wrote of the struggles to make the magazine a success, giving credit to his 'loyal readers, subscribers and advertisers'. In the February, 1917, issue his column ALL FOR ONE AND ONE FOR ALL he wrote:

"I have received ever so many letters from specialty salesmen telling me how much they appreciate my magazine. Now, boys, it's not my magazine – it's your magazine – has always been your magazine and will continue to be your magazine so long as Bob Hicks has a suspender over his shoulder."

An additional homey story about his oldest daughter, Helen Lois, appeared in the same issue re-assuring his readers that Bob was a 'family man' with good, American, Christian values:

Little Helen, my little Helen, she's my sweetheart, your sister – not quite six years old. I've got three sweethearts, Helen, Phoebe and their mother – their mother is my wife and then there's little Bob- he's my 'pal', and your brother. He's three years old and is the youngest member of the Specialty Salesman Magazine Family of Sellers. Already I am teaching little Bob how to sell things. He makes some good bargains when trading with his sisters. My ambition is that my 'pal' will grow up to be a great specialty salesman- one that every member of our family will be proud of.

Oh, yes, I started to tell you about Helen: It was last winter. The snow was falling fast—great, big flakes. Helen was in the yard, and as the flakes would fall she would catch them in her little hands, crush them into a small ball and then try to hit me. It was great fun. These flakes were powerless when only a few were together – a little child doing as she pleased with them, crushing them at will. Next morning, though, it was different – the snow flakes had combined – millions and billions were banded together. Great railroad engines weighing tons, with a speed of sixty miles an hour, were unable to move. They were helpless. So it is with us. Before we combined together in one great family, the mail order pirates – the junk sellers- the dishonest of every class robbed us right and left- laughed at us if we dared demand fair play. We are banded together – ten thousand of us- the engines of destruction –

they cannot move – truth, right and justice has come into its own. Powerful! I guess we are, and why? "All for one and one for all."

Oh, yes, I want to tell you this; After little Helen had played in the snow for some time, she paused for a moment in deep thought, and then she said to me, "Papa, do you know what I was doing?" "No, sweetheart." I said "what were you doing?" "Papa, I was praying the snow prayer." "Snow prayer, dear, what is that?" Don't you know, Papa? Mamma teached it to me- dear Jesus, make me as white as the snow."

Say, boys, let each and every one of us pray the snow prayer tonight before we go to bed and again in the morning before we start out to sell things. It will do us good – make us feel better all day."

Bob's personal approach reached out to the readers. They believed in him. He had that quality of a good preacher whose openness and simplicity draw the congregation to him. The sale of the magazine grew month by month. Bob held the position of editor, journalist, sales and advertising manager. He investigated fraudulent advertisers, exposing them through his editorials. He wrote articles for the magazine using fictitious names as there was no money to pay free lance writers. A small office, with two stenographers and an 'office boy', served as headquarters. More and more salesmen sent in their one dollar bills for a year's subscription. Every dime that came in was re-invested in the magazine. Then in March of 1917 disaster struck. He listened to a man he considered a friend:

A supposed friend came to me and said that he could organize a Company if I would incorporate for $10,000.00, that he was confident that he could sell to his friends and my friends 48% of the capital stock. The company was organized, a charter was secured from the State of Illinois, officers and directors were elected and I supposed that they were my friends. But, on the contrary, they were my most bitter enemies who had planned to destroy the magazine and if possible to destroy me with it. After the March issue was printed they notified me that a meeting of the Board of Directors was to be held. I now realized that these directors had deceived me. I refused to attend this meeting. Four against one and I knew that I could do nothing. The meeting was held and on the next morning I was informed that I was no longer the editor of any publications of the corporation.

They carried away everything of importance, discharged the two stenographers and the young man who was assisting me. For a few moments I sat at my desk. I was knocked out or I might say that I was down and out. I had but a few cents in my pockets and there was possibly one or two dollars at home. I went down in the elevator and walked up the street to the next corner, about a half-block away, with my hands behind me and my head down. I reached the corner and looked up and down the street. My hands that were clasped behind my back fell to my sides. I threw my shoulders back and the determination which came to me in a prison cell came to me again with greater force. I was no longer down and out and I said to myself, "This is just what I needed to inject real pep into me."

It was now time to go home. The little children needed shoes. My wife needed clothing. She had bought scarcely anything for herself for eighteen months. How was I to tell her that the magazine had been suspended and that I was discharged as its editor? She had struggled along with me since November, 1915. But home I went.

After the evening meal was over I called her to me and told her. I had expected tears but she came over to me, put her arms around me and said, "They don't know you. This is the turning point. I will go out and get a position as a stenographer. I will get someone to take care of our children and you can get a position and together we will print the magazine somehow."

The evening was not one of disappointment and discouragement but rather a renewal of determination to make even further sacrifices if *necessary.* Lois knew Bob. Bob's enemies didn't know him. April 5, 1917, the Board of Directors notified the printers, Rogers & Hall, the advertisers as well as the subscribers, that the magazine had been suspended. Bob had to make a new start but where could he find the financial backing? Why not be realistic, look for a good position in the publishing business? Bob had a ready answer:

The manager of a large corporation in Chicago came to me the morning of April 6th. I had less than $5.00 in money. He had heard that the magazine had been suspended and he supposed that I wanted a position. He knew that I must get something to do in order to support my family. He offered me $100.00 a week if I would join his organization. He offered me a very important position but I told him that I could not accept for the reason that I was going to publish my magazine.

"Why, that is impossible," he said, "You tell me you have no money, the magazine has never paid and you certainly are up against a stone wall."

"I may appear that way to you but somehow I shall continue this magazine as long as I live."

"Mr. Hicks, I have always had a suspicion that you were a little bit crazy but I never before knew that you were a fool."

He left the office apparently disgusted and sometimes when I look back, I feel that he had a right to be. At that time, apparently, there was no

chance, no possibility of getting a printer to print the magazine for me. I realized that I had a man's job before me but I never felt but that the magazine would eventually be printed and would ultimately be one of the great big magazines."

Bob did not list the names of the men who were on the Board of Directors in the July, 1917, issue. He had assumed them to be supporters. He had misread their intentions. Their intent had been to destroy the magazine that exposed mail-order fraud as they were behind such operations. One of them came to see Bob a few days after their victory.

"Mr. Hicks, you have a right to feel that we are not your friends, but we are. Several of us met last night and decided that as you are getting old and have a wife and three little children, we would each contribute $1.00 a week to help you support your family."

This was a slap in the face that stung. Seemingly, they were not satisfied with what they had done but apparently they wanted to 'trample on my face' after they had me down. I don't recall a greater insult – me to accept charity for the support of my family!

At the time I had practically nothing of value, but I had, perhaps, what they did not have – determination of the deep-rooted kind. I do not say this boastingly, but today no doubt I could support their families more abundantly than the four could support my family." With the magazine suspended, Bob took advantage of the time to call on potential advertisers, assuring them that the magazine would be published. Some believed him. Some even paid him in advance. Bob continued, "I think it was about June when the antagonistic Board of Directors resigned, returning to me the list of subscribers, the book of accounts, and the correspondence that had accumulated, but I want to say, what little money came in was not returned.—They also turned over five judgments against the Robert E. Hicks Corporation amounting to something like $1000.00 which was a fortune to me at that time. It was not a very encouraging start to say the least, but I was determined and judgments, debts, knock-out blows and things of that kind do not interfere to any great extent with deep rooted determination."

Bob gave a short explanation concerning the resignation of the Board of Directors in the July, 1917 issue:

At a meeting of the Board of Directors of the Robert E. Hicks Corporation on April 30, 1917, the four antagonistic directors resigned. Whether or not they thought their work of the destruction was complete or whether they thought that they were powerless to succeed in their undertaking, I do not know, but the fact remains that they resigned.

One of the men whose company had been exposed in *The Specialty Salesman* had sent out hundreds of circulars and letters to subscribers, advertisers and newspapers telling of the suspension of the magazine and the discharging of its editor. The result was not the anticipated one of ruining Bob's reputation but rather gave him beneficial publicity. No issue was published in April, May and June of 1917. Bob again went to see Mr. Rogers of Rogers & Hall Company who took the risk of printing the magazine for the remainder of 1917.

America formally entered World War I on 16 April 1917. 'War fever' against the 'Huns' ran high and droves of young men entered the U.S. military services. In the last issue of 1917 Bob wrote a sentimental account of 'Christmas past' recalling a romantized version of his childhood memories:

"– but our boys who have gone to the front – they will not go home for Christmas in the body – loved ones at home will not greet them in person – but they will be at home at Christmas time.

And I am going home at Christmas time – to the old house in Knox County, Missouri. I, too, cannot go in the body for the old home is now owned by strangers. The dear old log house in which I was born has given way to a modern structure. I do not now think of the changes two score years have wrought. I go back to the old house as it was in the long ago. *The revered father and mother have long since reached a "a fairer country" and with them two brothers and two sisters have also gone and the sister and two brothers who remain live in different parts of the country and their once glossy locks are silvered with gray.*

At Christmas time I will again be at the old home – the house long since left behind in the journey of life – but its memory hovers over me. My soul is hungry within me – crying for the happiness, the joy of Christmas in the long ago. Let me bask in the sunshine of the years of happy childhood in a Christian home. The hours of evening have come – the fire burning furiously in the fireplace gives both light and heat. My father takes down the well worn Bible and reads a chapter from its hallowed pages. Mother, my sainted mother, sits at his side with my sleepy head upon her knee, and brothers and sisters are grouped reverently around. I do not understand the words, but I have been told that they are the words of God and I believe it. The long chapter ends – we all kneel and Father prays. I fall asleep with my head on the chair. Mother wakes me – pulls from under the bed the trundle bed in which I sleep with my two older brothers. She tucks the heavy bedclothes close around me – whispers a prayer and kisses me good night.

The next morning after breakfast the Bible is taken

down again and Father prays again, and through all the days of my golden years the worship is repeated. How well do I remember the pleasant evenings by the fireside of the old home – the simple songs, the innocent games, - checkers and "fox and geese" – the words of encouragement as I bend over my school tasks, the kiss as I lie down to rest, the patient bearing with my restless nature, the gentle counsel mingled with reproofs and approvals, the sympathy that lessened every sorrow and sweetened every success. All these return to me now and I feel that I once lived in heaven, and straying had lost my way.

Strangers own it now, but that home is still mine and shall be forever until mind and memory fail. It wakens holy recollections and springs high hopes of the heavenly home of which it was a type. Backward across the space of nearly two score years I go to my childhood's home and from the faith born there I look forward to the glorious home above.

I thank God for the happy home behind me, which in childhood I had and the heavenly home before me, where I may soon overtake the loved ones who have gone, and await the loved ones who will follow.

Just a thought of the years to come – a thought of Christmas time when I have gone to my heavenly home. Will my little children, Helen, Phoebe and Bob – will they in thought go back to the home that now is? Will they remember a praying father and mother

– the evening and morning prayers? Will the recollections of their Christian home be the sweetest thoughts of their lives? It will if I so will it."\

Bob paints a pretty picture of Christian piety but there is little evidence that religion played a significant role in Bob's life. He acknowledged Christian principles as the basis for a civilized culture and preached the Golden Rule as the guide for mankind to follow. As for his children, their religious education rested entirely upon their mother and concerned him not at all.

The first issue of *The Specialty Salesman* in 1918 held the following editorial:

"Financial difficulties prevented me from getting out the February issue. We had entered the World war – the best blood of our country was called to arms and advertisers were of the opinion that it would not pay to advertise. The news-stand sales had dropped off to a very large extent but I succeeded in printing the March, April and May issues and then I was forced to print every other month instead of monthly. When the armistice was signed on November 11, 1918, I knew that my chance had come – that the uphill fight would not be so severe."

And Bob was right. The financial boom that followed the defeat of Germany in the World War spread throughout the Allied world. The Treaty of Versailles, signed by President Woodrow Wilson and other heads of state, officially ended the war in 1919. The 18th Amendment established Prohibition and the 19th Amendment in 1920 gave women the right to vote. America was coming of age among the economically progressive nations of the world. America prospered and so did Bob. By the close of 1919 the magazine had a national distribution. All debts had been paid and there was money in the bank. Bob's hard work and determination had paid off.

Bob had the money now to rent offices at 508 South Dearborn Street in Chicago's business district. Advertising, the life blood of any magazine, filled over 27 pages of the April, 1919, issue. Bob and his magazine were beginning to be taken seriously. No longer did Bob go, hat in hand, to solicit advertising; ads came unsolicited. Bob increased his staff; nevertheless, he continued to work a ten to twelve hour day, usually sending the office boy out to bring him a sauerkraut and sausage sandwich from the local deli for lunch. Success spurred his work.

One article written in the April issue is by G. M Walker, entitled "Is Robert E. Hicks Sincere?"

This is at once a confession and an apology.

When first I read The Specialty Salesman Magazine and read its broad challenge to unscrupulous operators, I smiled in a rather supercilious manner and from this standpoint considered the challenge and the so-called 'exposes' as a mighty good advertising stunt; however, I had later the pleasure of eating lunch with Mr. Hicks, the editor, and at his own suggestion I was invited to his own sanctum, shown the correspondence files and told to 'snoop around' to my heart's content, to ask for anything I wanted, and in short, to become perfectly familiar with the operations of the publication. This was more than I had expected - - -I am a stranger to Mr. Hicks. I came with no letter of introduction yet the editor gave me complete carte blanche and the results are to be set down here in the belief that some of the readers of this magazine may ask themselves the same question I use as a caption.

After reading a number of letters from salesmen across the country thanking Bob for investigating various companies in their behalf, Walker ends his article as follows: *To me, some of these letters, penned in a hand obviously unused to writing , written in perhaps poor grammatical form with their spirit of boundless hope for the future, were at once a spur and an inspiration . And in some of them, the confidence they place in this man, Robert E. Hicks, whom they have never met, was a tribute to a real 'personality'.*

And having broken bread and eaten salt with the gentleman, I can truly say to you who were as skeptical as myself, have no fear, your affairs are in reliable hands.

Not every commentary upon Bob's magazine and its business practices were quite as complimentary as Mr. Walker's. In 1919, a contributing writer for the magazine, a certain A. H. reported that Bob virtually tried to "stiff" him for a story he'd submitted. The following account appeared in the "Experience Exchange of the Editor" in a contemporary publication:

In the latter part of April, I sent Mr. Hicks a semi-humorous story containing 3000 words. While I was wondering when I was going to hear from the story, or expect its safe return, I happened to pick up a copy of The Specialty Salesman *for May, and glancing down the contents table saw that my story appeared on page 93....*

After a reasonable time I wrote this "silent" editor in regard to the story, but he failed to answer. Then I wrote again, enclosing stamp, and once again he refused my request to let me hear from him.

The third letter I sent Mr. Hicks must have shown my impatience rather strong, for I received a letter by return mail, and with it a check for my story, which nearly stilled my breath. For that literary effort of 3,000 words, covering over four pages of his magazine, Mr. Hicks paid me five dollars!

But hark ye! Mr. Hicks writes:

"...I was very short of copy when I received '_____ ' and for that reason I ran it. ...Had I not

been short of copy I assure you that I would not have run the article even though you paid me to do so."

How's that for an excuse? Because this editor was short of copy he cuts down the value of a manuscript by claiming it was not just what he wanted....

Short of copy! Is it any wonder?

In addition, A. H. mentions a previous contributor to the "Experience Exchange" who seems to have had the same complaint with Bob and his magazine. He refers to this contributor as "California":

..."California" squeals on Robert E. Hicks, the "silent" editor of The Specialty Salesman Magazine of Chicago.... As "California" stated, Mr. Hicks conducts a department in his magazine in which he exposes frauds and fraudulent methods, for which, no doubt, he is to be commended. However, this standard he sets for himself in his magazine, doesn't seem to apply to his contributors.

Bob saw himself as a reformed man after his release from prison, and he certainly promoted the principle of operating a business according to the golden rule, but he was obviously not above dealilg shabbily with his contributors. In the October, 1919, issue, Bob printed a letter from a W. S. Grant of Philadelphia, Pennsylvania who suggested an organization of specialty salesmen and women be formed. Bob enthusiastically endorsed the plan adding, "May I propose the name of National Association of Specialty

Salesmen of America?"

By December Bob had outlined his plan of organizing a nation-wide association and requested interested readers to send $2.00 for charter membership. In the 1919 issue of the magazine, Bob published a number of letters sent by readers heartily endorsing the idea of an organization protecting the rights of sellers. Bob had expected not less than 500 salesmen to share his enthusiasm but the number proved to be far less. In the February, 1920, issue Bob wrote an article entitled "A National Association of Specialty Salesmen": *This is a message to specialty salesmen. Are you one? If you are this message is of vital importance to you. It is with reference to organizing a national organization of specialty salesmen....Lest many may misunderstand me, I want to say the only interest I have in an organization of this kind is to be of service. A great many who have written me have suggested that if the organization is completed that our magazine be made its official organ. I want to say that this magazine will never be the organ of anything except honest business methods. It will have no connection with the association in any way except to boost the association and do everything within its power to enlarge the membership. So long as the association is conducted on absolutely clean, straight lines this magazine will stand for what it stands for and will work hand in hand with the association for the best interests of specialty selling...*

I said in the December issue that if 500 specialty salesmen would send me $2.00 before January 1st that we would go ahead and complete the organization. Not more than one-fourth of this number have responded with $2.00. I am surprised. Can hardly believe that the thousands of my readers who are a thousand times more interested in this organization than I am will refuse to come forward and do their part. I have made up my mind to complete this organization – to get it started and I am not going to quit. When it is started, then, and only then, I will quit. I want no active part in the organization. I am not eligible for membership. If I can get the co-operation of 500 real sellers there is no doubt in my mind but what we will have 100,000 before the close of the year.

Do you know what 100,000 active, real seller members mean? It means that hundreds of the largest and best manufacturers in the country will offer our members selling propositions of the very highest class. It means that specialty salesmen and saleswomen will not have to search for something worthwhile to sell.

Why not be one of the original starters – a charter member – one of the men who made the organization possible? Do it today – let's get going without further delay.

Bob had a vision and, like a pit bull-dog, once he got his teeth in a project, he saw it through.

Lois was not well. She had borne three children in just over four years. Life had not been easy. Just as Bob's venture turned toward success, she became ill, spending more and more time in bed. A doctor told her she had a serious heart condition and recommended rest, hot baths and a cold pack around the heart. "Breathe in spirits of ammonia," the doctor advised her, "and take these pills. They may help."

But they didn't. Lois died the night of February 23, 1920, at their house at 8924 Malta, in Wilmette, Illinois. She would have been 34 years old on the first of April. The death certificate gave the cause of death as mylocarditis, an inflammation of the muscular wall of the heart. Would an easier life have given her a few more years? Bob wrote the following memorial for her:

February 25th – your editor's birthday- sixty-two years ago in a log cabin in Missouri, God gave me to loving, Christian, praying parents. I have never known a greater sorrow than is mine today – Mrs. Hicks, the brave, true, faithful wife and mother, was suddenly called to her eternal home on Monday evening, February 23rd at eleven o'clock.

To grieve is only human, but when I recall that "in the beginning God created the heavens and the earth," and heaven was created for such as she, there is joy in my heart as I grieve. Because of her, my life was made better. At times I faltered – the way was dark- but she never faltered. God gave her to me for more than eleven years – to her father and mother- Mr. and Mrs. Lewis M. Hawley of Schenectady, New York- for more than thirty-three years. She gave to me three little children- Helen, nine years old, Phoebe, eight years old and little Bob, six years old.

I have something else to live for and that is, to go on with our magazine and the principles for which it stands, and the principles for which she encouraged me never to give up. She deprived herself of much that the magazine might live, and the brave fight she made with me encourages me more than ever to accomplish that which she always believed would be accomplished. It is a great consolation to me to know that our family of sellers will appreciate what she was to our magazine.

The days will come and go-may be only days, may be weeks or years, but it will not be long until I will rest by her side and join her in the heaven that God created for such as she."

Despite his personal loss, Bob lost no time in promoting his new idea. Forty-two charter members from 14 states held the first meeting of the National Association of Specialty Salesmen at Bob's office, 443 S. Dearborn Street, Chicago. Not surprisingly, Bob was nominated and unanimously elected as first president in spite of his weak protests. Preparations for the first annual convention to be held in Kansas City began.

In March, 1921, Warren G. Harding became the 29th president of the United States with Calvin Coolidge as his vice-president. Harding's campaign mantra had been "less government in business and more business in government." Congress passed the first national quota on immigration, drastically reducing the number of immigrants from Eastern Europe. Race riots in Tulsa, Oklahoma, left 43 dead. In July Harding signed a document formally ending America's involvement in World War I against Germany, Austria and Hungary. And, on a lighter note, the first Miss America Beauty Contest took place in Atlantic City, New Jersey. The magazine's circulation increased steadily. Manufacters signed contracts for advertising and small ads filled six to seven pages. Readers wrote letters personally addressed to Bob, such as those that follow:

Dear Bob, Yours is the cleanest reading of anything outside the Bible. You are not only helping others to find themselves in a business career, but (although many may not realize it) you are giving them wonderful lessons in Christianity, which I am sure is appreciated by all right-thinking men. Your readers are of an intelligent class, and know that

Specialty Salesman is divinely authorized. -Elbert Searles, Baraboo, Wisconsin.

Dear Mr. Hicks, I beg to thank you for the sample copy of your Specialty Salesman Magazine which reached me some time ago. After careful perusal of same I wish to congratulate you on your meritorious work in editing and publishing so wonderful a book; moreover, I tell you frankly and without any adulation whatsoever, that it is the most inspiring, interesting and fearless Magazine I have ever read and I shall also add that it should be in the hands of every salesman. Find enclosed my $2.50 for a year's subscription. -Chester H. Young, Pensacola, Florida

Dear Mr. Hicks, After reading and re-reading your December (1921) issue, which is the first magazine of its kind I have ever obtained, I feel I must express my enthusiasm over its contents and those who are influential in its publication. Mr. Hicks, for nearly three years I have had the nerve to go from town to town calling myself a salesman, even being successful in some lines but now, after thoroughly digesting a few of the many wonderful tips regarding salesmanship, etc., in the December issue, I wonder how I did it. If every edition has been, and continues to be, as good in comparison as the copy I obtained, there is no doubt that the time is not so far off when every man who carries a grip will eventually refer to Specialty Salesman Magazine as his individual guide.

– *W. Jack Hall, Ligonier, Indiana*

"*A man is never thoroughly reformed till a new principle governs his thoughts.*" Bob. a one- time mail order swindler, a fugitive from the FBI had changed. The concept of the Golden Rule replaced his 'do them before they do you' philosophy. Bob was not an intellectual, but he wrote plainly and honestly his thoughts about life:

I don't believe you can find any bigger fool anywhere than the man who tries to get ahead by wholly selfish and ruthless methods, by trampling on everybody beneath him and trying to pull down everybody above him. It can't be done. Maybe it seems to be successful now and then, but take it from me, it never is in the long run. If you could know all the facts you would always see that it didn't pay – that even when Mr. "Practical" Man seemed to be making money hand over fist he was sowing the dragon's teeth of future failure, and unhappiness, and the enmity of those he had wronged – often the fatal enmity of the law itself.- - - The Golden Rule works – it pays and pays big- it means lower costs and prices, a better product, a smaller labor turnover, more contented and loyal employees and salesmen, a better served and better satisfied public.

Bob's article "Eliminating the Rule of Gold in Business" brought the following reply from Mr. H. T. Clark, vice-president of the F. E. Royston & Co., Inc.

Wholesale Grocers of Aurora, Illinois:

...I want to express to you my gratitude for the loving spirit that seems to permeate your Magazine. I have longed for the era when the Golden Rule would be applied to business generally. I know it has to come, but during the war period selfishness seemed to come to the surface to such a degree that the long hoped-for era seemed afar off.

Two years ago we decided to pass from the Rule of Gold to the Golden Rule in our business, and we worked out a plan of profit-sharing very similar of that adopted by Mr. Arthur Nash. ....This plan was worked out by the writer, about the time the inspiration came to Mr. Nash, which would again lead us to believe that the one great Mind governs.

We have found that the plan works out splendidly. It has increased production, and multiplied harmony and good will by eliminating selfishness which, as the writer sees it, is the cause of nearly all the suffering and discord in this world. I sincerely believe that the solution of our labor troubles and many of our financial difficulties is to be found in the application of the Golden Rule in business.

I wish you success in your work and hope the dawn of a new era is near at hand.

THE DOMESTIC SITUATION

With Lois gone, what to do with the children? Bob was

at a loss. A neighbor volunteered to take the children to school but there was no one to look after them when they returned home. Bob worked long days and the children ran wild. Neighbors complained. Bob got in touch with his older sister's daughter, Mary 'Mollie' Belle Doran, who agreed to take them if he would pay for their maintenance. So little Helen, Phoebe and Bobbie were put on the train to Des Moines, Iowa.

A letter written in 1962 by Mercelia Hicks Chino, Bob's niece, gives an account of what happened:

According to Uncle Will, Robert E. sent his three children to live with the Dorans in Des Moines after his wife died. Pete and Mary Belle were fanatically religious and spent so much time on church work that they were very poor. Also Pete never had much ambition. So Robert E. felt that the money he paid them would be a help and of course Mollie Belle was a teacher. All went well for a while until one of the children wrote Robert E. that Mollie Belle was beating them. Being a Hicks, he could not stand for anyone to mistreat his children, so he took them away and advertised in the Chicago newspapers for a mature, unencumbered woman to look after the children and be his housekeeper.

From the applicants, he chose a 38 year old attractive widow, Margaret Mae Davis Joy. He made a good choice. She brought order out of chaos in the home and the children grew to love her. She also exerted a good influence over Bob. It had been his habit when he came home Saturday evening to lock himself in his room with a bottle or two of whiskey and not surface until Sunday. The second time this happened Mae told him his behavior was not acceptable. He should think of the bad influence his drinking had on the children. If he continued to drink so heavily, she could not stay. He begged her not to leave. What would he do without her? The children were being well cared-for, the house clean and neat, and the meals tastefully prepared. Furthermore, Mae had a good figure, a winsome smile, provocative hazel eyes and a pleasant manner. She wore her dark brown hair in a chignon at the nape of her neck. When the tortoise shell hairpins were loosened, her hair cascaded to her waist. Hidden from view under modest ankle-length skirts, Mae had a pair of shapely legs worthy of a screen star. She made Bob feel young again. No, he couldn't let her go. He gave up the weekend binges, but continued to down a modest glass or two of whiskey before dinner each evening. Bob had never learned to drive a car although cars fascinated him. Looking to the future, he hired a driving instructor to teach Mae. They started on the quiet streets of Wilmette but soon progressed to Michigan Avenue. Mae had the skills of the natural born driver and soon drove the children to school and Bob to his office. Testosterone aside, Bob began to appreciate Mae as an indispensable woman of quality.

On May 21, 1921, Mae and Bob married in a civil ceremony in Chicago. The new Mrs. Hicks was 24 years younger than her husband. Was it a good match? Happily for both it satisfied a pressing need. Bob needed a woman in his life, especially as he found himself alone with three young children to rear. Mae came along at the opportune time and, as shown by his letters, he truly loved her. As for Mae, she had been struggling to make a living since her husband, Michael Joy, had died, leaving her nothing but two teenage children to support. If the marriage failed to meet the requirements of a match made in heaven, it suited them both. Prior to the ceremony, Bob had his attorney, Pearly Bishop, draw up a pre-nuptial agreement, in essence providing for Mae and guaranteeing any child born to their union an inheritance equal with his three older children by his third wife, Lois Hawley. The document made no mention of Elmer Elisha, the eldest surviving son by Bob's first marriage. Shortly after the marriage, a brief society news item appeared in the local paper:

Friends of Robert E. Hicks, a former resident of Vanderpoel Avenue, were interested and pleased when they read of his marriage to Mrs. Margaret Joy on May 16. Mr. Hicks publishes the Salesman's Specialty magazine, a monthly magazine exposing fraudulent advertising and having a tremendous circulation. Mr. and Mrs. Hicks are living in Wilmette. Their Ridge friends are sending them sincerest congratulations."

Thanksgiving, South Whitley, IN, 1923. Bob's family and employees.

Bob dictating to his secretary in his office, Couth Whitley, IN, 1924

1923 state-of-the art Lincoln with Mae, Bob and baby Margaret

Eight year old Margaret, Queen of the American Legion,
DeFuniak Springs, FL

St. Margaret's Roman Catholic Church, DeFuniak Springs, FL, 1930

Family wedding of Phoebe Hicks and Henry Hughes 1931, Alpine Heights

Mae and Helen Hicks at Alpine Heights –
'Beautiful Florida Homes' publication

Bob and Mae in front of gates to Alpine Heights' Gates. 1929

Margaret, Black Billygoat and Peggy Pony, Alpine Heights, 1929

George Peabody, Bob, L. R. Beane at Alpine Heights, 1931. Last known photo of Bob.

Passenger ship Bob, Mae, and Margaret sailed from
Los Angeles to Hawaii 1927

'House of a 130 Windows', Hicks' family home, South Whitley, IN, 1923

Rear of the home, South Whitley, IN photo taken 2014

Barney and Queen with Bob. South Whitley, IN 1924.

Four of the five Hicks brothers. Circa 1879 Cambridge, KS

Mrs. Rob't. E. Hicks, DeFuniak Sptings and her new
mustard-colored Lincoln. 1929

1927 photo of the Hicks Tavern –South Whitley, IN

1993 photo of the Hicks Tavern –South Whitley, IN

1925 cover Specialty Salesman Magazine –
painting of little Margaret Hicks.

Nursemaid Etta with little Margaret 1924

U. S. Governors Convention, Cheyenne, WY 1926,
Indiana Governor guest of Hicks family

Lois Hawley Hicks, third wife of Bob, circa 1912, New York City.

Mae Davis Joy, fourth wife and widow of Bob. 1921, Chicago, IL

Robert E. Hicks, 1903, NYC

6
THE ASSOCIATION

Determined to see the Association flourish, in every issue of the magazine Bob wrote articles encouraging his readers to join the new organization. Thirteen months after that first meeting in Chicago, Bob was able to announce that Kansas City would be the site of the NASS's national convention. In his editorials he outlined the benefits that would accrue to the members as the membership grew into the thousands. He rallied his readers by reminding them that conventions combined a 'good time' with 'good business,' the 'old boys club' mantra:

Don't go to bed tonight until you have satisfied yourself that you have done everything possible today to put yourself just a little bit closer to Kansas City. Go at it just as you used to go after dad when you were a kid, to get him to buy that toy engine you saw in the window. Concentrate. Be a boy again – get excited over this Kansas City proposition. There will be two thousand (possibly five thousand) other 'boys' to meet you in Kansas City. It will be the most worthwhile combination pleasure and business trip you ever made.

Organizing a national convention takes vision, energy, dedication and money. Bob wasted no time since that meeting in 1920. Once the executive board, formed at that first meeting in Bob's office, decided on the site, the hotels had been contacted for space, successful salesmen enticed to speak and the railways contacted for reduced rates.

A staff member of the magazine wrote an article detailing the arrangements made with the Burlington Railway: *As announced in the June issue of The Specialty Salesman Magazine, the Burlington Railway will operate a special train between Chicago and Kansas City to be known as 'The Trail Blazers Special'. They have promised that this train will consist of the very best equipment they have. This 'Trail Blazers Special' will leave Chicago at six P. M., Wednesday, August third, and will arrive at Kansas City around eight A. M. the next day. Arrangements are being made for special cars from several Eastern cities. These cars will arrive in Chicago the afternoon of August Third and will be attached to the 'Trail Blazers' special. Reservations for accommodations on this train should be made through your Association's president, Robert E. Hicks. Address him at South Whitley, Indiana. The fare and one-half fare holds good on the 'Trail Blazers Special' as well as on all other trains from every section of the country and* on all railroads."

Bob's address needed no postal code, no street number, only the town and state. The world of 1921 was a less complicated one than today's world.

The effectiveness of the new NASS had its first test when a member, Mr. J. G. Smith, wired the headquarters informing Bob he needed help. Bob handled the case as follows:

Just as we went to press with this issue of our Magazine a telegram was received from J. G. Smith of Libby, Mont., which I pass on to our readers. "I have been arrested for taking orders for goods that are in Spokane, Wash., to be shipped and collected for a later date. I am going to jail. Trial set for Monday, 2 P.M. You arrange for bond. Handle case and instruct me."

Immediately upon receipt of this telegram your editor, the president of the National Association of Specialty Salesmen, wired Rowland & Grey, lawyers in Libby, Mont. the following:

"J. G. Smith in jail claims was arrested for taking orders for goods to be shipped from another state delivered later. If true, wire me Monday. Have case put off. I will arrange bond, will want you to defend and sue city for damages if he was within the law."

I also sent the following telegram to J. G. Smith care of the city prison, Libby, Mont. "Will arrange for bond and lawyer for Monday."

Following the telegram to Rowland and Gray, I wrote the following letter:

"Have just sent you a night telegram that should reach you Monday morning with reference to J. G. Smith who is in jail in your city..Not necessary, gentlemen, to call your attention to the fact of the Interstate Commerce Law with reference to taking orders for goods to be shipped from another state..If he has been wrongfully imprisoned – arrested and imprisoned – while in lawful pursuit of his business we will sue everyone connected with his arrest and also the city of Libby. We want you to defend this man and defend him in such a way that you will have the right kind of a case to carry to the highest court of the United States if necessary. I trust that you will give this case your very best attention. Mr. Smith is a member of the National Association of Specialty Salesmen." (signed) Robert E. Hicks, president of the National Association of Specialty Salesmen.

"Just as soon as the telegram reached the attorney and Mr. Smith in Libby, the authorities did not lose any time in opening the jail doors and tell Mr. Smith to go his way. Here is the telegram received from Mr.Smith:

"Unconditionally released 11 A.M. Will write you full particulars."

Readers were left in no doubt that the NASS would and could protect the interests of salesmen. More applications for membership rolled in as preparations for the first annual convention continued. Bob's personal touch in his editorials brought his readers into his extended family. He wrote of his failures, his successes and his burning ambition to make the *Specialty Salesman* and the NASS a success. His article entitled "My Life's Ambition" in the June, 1921 issue is a prime example:

Ordinarily when I hear someone tell me he is not interested in making money, but is carrying on his work merely for 'humanity's sake", I am frank to tell you I'm afraid of that type and always feel that when they're around it's time to put my hand on my pocketbook and run.

I want to make money – and lots of it – but not for money's sake alone, but for the sake of what I can accomplish with money. As far as my personal needs are concerned I couldn't spend a penny more than I am now able to spend, and enjoy life any more. My family and I have a good home, good clothes, three square meals a day, an automobile and we can take in a picture show occasionally without straining our pocket-book. If someone were to give me a million dollars to make Specialty Salesman Magazine bigger and better, and of more service to salesmen, then I would accept it if I could find a place to spend it wisely, but only with the understanding that it be a straight forward business loan. I wouldn't want to continue Specialty Salesman Magazine one more issue if it were to be dependent upon charity. A magazine of real service should be a money-maker for its owner.

But what I want to get at is the fact that never during the early history of our Magazine did I have the making of money in my mind. True, I always expected that the Magazine would eventually make a good living, but as a straight out and out money-making proposition, I never had that in mind....When I once made up my mind that I was going to establish a real salesman's publication – something that hadn't been done before – I simply determined so far ahead that nothing could turn me from the path which I had chosen to follow. I said to myself, "This one thing will I do." In the following issue, one month prior to the convention, Bob informed his readers that the August issue would be suspended. He explained as follows:

The NASS is a much bigger proposition than any publication in the United States...After all, then, the suspension of the August issue of our Magazine is a mighty little thing...There is much to be done before we meet in Kansas City. As president of your Association I owe it more than I will ever be able to pay. It is my duty to devote every minute of my time from now on until we meet in Kansas City to the various interests of this most important Convention.

I feel that it is my duty to enlist in this great cause

the services of those associated with me to the end that our First Annual Convention will be a wonderful success. In doing this I am simply 'answering the call.' I do hope that every salesman in the country will take it upon himself to answer the call regardless of the cost. Keep uppermost in your mind that to salesmen there is nothing quite so important as the future of our Association.

The Convention Bureau of the Chamber of Commerce of Kansas City is soon to commence a publicity campaign inviting salesmen everywhere to visit Kansas City during our Convention...Local Assemblies of the NASS everywhere will be organizing in various cities throughout the country. They are rightfully demanding my co-operation and I must help. I must do all this and more, not because I am the editor of your Magazine, but because I have been honored as the first president of your Association – the World's Mightiest Selling Organization.

My financial interests are in Specialty Salesman Magazine. I have no financial interest in the NASS. Neither has any other man...I will not again accept the honor of being president of this great organization. I make this announcement so as to set aside any thought that might be created in the mind of anyone that I am taking so much interest in the Convention in the hope that I will again be elected its president...I am taking this great interest in the Convention because I know that the association will live on and on – will live for all time – and will always be a mighty power for good.

Men, the call has been sounded. It is your duty to be in Kansas City August 4 to 7. Are you going to respond? Are you going to sacrifice just a little and be there? Remember, all things really worth while come only through sacrifice. I'm answering the call – how about you?" It all came together on August 4th to the 7th of 1921. The first annual convention of NASS, with members attending from 28 states, gathered at the Baltimore Hotel, Kansas City, Missouri. There had been a large exhibition of manufacturers' products, workshops on selling techniques, committee meetings, and banquets as well as tours provided by the Chamber of Commerce. Bob could congratulate himself on a job well done. The December issue carried photographs of the delegates. Bob sits at a front table. Directly behind him was Mae, his bride of two months, wearing dark horn-rimmed glasses. She was beginning to reap the rewards of Bob's struggles, which had been denied to Lois.

At the closing session Bob turned the president's gravel over to the newly elected president, Arthur Nash of the A. Nash Corporation, the largest manufacturers of men's clothing, based in Cincinnati,

Ohio. Nash accepted, paying the usual tribute to his predecessor, saying, "Do *any of you realize what an honor you have bestowed upon me and at the same time, what a responsibility you have laid on me?...A great national organization that is going to be known from coast to coast, from the Lakes to the Gulf, has elected me president. All I can say is, I'll do my best – I must have your prayers and you must hold up my hands. I thank you.*"

Nash, tall and slender, with a shock of silver hair, wore expensive tailored suits that emphasized his trim physique. A close friendship had quickly developed between Bob and Art, both men having the determination and energy a capitalistic society admires. They had met several years previously and Nash had written a number of articles published in the *Specialty Salesman*. There is a photograph of the two men. Though differing in physique, they could be brothers with their silvery hair and purposeful demeanor. They sit side by side, looking directly into the camera. Nash is the younger of the two. He has the look of a man who works out at his health club after a busy day at his office. Bob's years of heavy drinking left their mark. Overweight, his fleshy jowls gently droop and his eyelids sag, but both men have a presence, a look of self confidence that mark the winner. The second annual convention would be held at Cedar Point, Ohio, from July 5th to the 10th, 1922.

The National Association of Specialty Salesman was up and running. The name of Albert J. Burns of Oakland, California, had been bandied about in Kansas City. He had offered to serve a two year term as a Director on the Board of the NASS and had been accepted. To stir up a little enthusiasm for the second annual convention, he had challenged Harold Marshall of Boston, Massachusetts, as to which of them could bring in the most members within the coming year – West versus East, so to speak. In the December, 1921, issue Bob reported that Burns had organized the first chapter of the NASS in California. 300 prospective members had gathered for a banquet at the Oakland Hotel. The governor of the State and the mayor of Oakland, both former salesmen, honored the Association with their presence. A. J. Burns was proving to be of considerable worth to the new organization.

A month later Bob ran a photo of Burns in an article entitled "Activities of the NASS on the Pacific Coast'. Other 'go-getters' were mentioned but it became clear that Burns had become the rising star of NASS. Bob had a purpose in promoting him.

In the same issue, Bob, normally given to hyperbole, reached new heights in comparing the Fourth of July in Kansas City with the Founding Fathers in Philadelphia, in 1776. He wrote:

The 'New Fourth' – August 4, 1921 – has come and

gone – passed into history. Needless to say, I was not present at the Continental Congress, 1776 but my determined forefathers were. They were in earnest. They believed in the great cause for which they were ready to fight and die. The men and women who met in Kansas City August 4, 1921, from twenty-eight states were there for a great cause – to make the Association a great success."

He continued to predict with fulsome terms that the NASS *'would revolutionize the cumbersome method of merchandising', 'the greatest organization of salesmen the world has ever known', 'the most remarkable Convention that has ever been held at any time or any place since the beginning of time.'* It was Bob's 'brain child' and he was determined to make it a success.

BACK IN SOUTH WHITLEY

Back in South Whitley the Atoz Printing Company had run into difficulty. The new owner, Mr. George Lee, came to Chicago to see if Bob would buy the plant, but they could not agree on the price. That was the autumn of 1920. By March of 1921, Lee, now desperate, offered Bob a price he accepted— $36,250.00. Bob paid in cash, which resulted in some hardships for him and his family.

In June, 1922, Bob wrote the following editorial: *"Speaking of money, the plant cost me $36,250.00* *but that is not what I paid for it. Let me tell you what I paid. One evening after I went to Chicago I went home. It was a Saturday. Mrs. Hicks (Lois Hawley) had laid out the children's clothes all ready for Sunday school the next day. When I reached home, she said to me, "I have washed and ironed the children's clothes for Sunday school but I find that Helen has no shoes to wear. Bob and Phoebe can go but Helen can't." Time after time I have gone into Child's restaurant in Chicago and ordered beans and coffee which cost 15 cents. Often my appetite was not satisfied and often I would want to finish my lunch with a piece of pie or dessert of some kind that would cost five cents and I had to keep the five cents for car fare home. There were times when Mrs. Hicks told me "we have no milk for the evening meal. I owe the milkman $1.80 and he refused to leave milk this morning until I could pay him."*

The sole of my shoe on the left foot had worn through. For four days I put cardboard in my shoe so that my foot would not come in contact with the hot stone sidewalk. At that time it cost 90 cents to get a pair of shoes half-soled, but for the want of 90 cents I went four days before I could afford to get my shoes half-soled.

I could tell you a hundred and one other things which entered into the price paid for the printing plant at South Whitley. The lack of proper food for myself did not matter – that did not hurt. When I was compelled to go four days for the want of 90 cents to get my shoes half-soled, that did not hurt, but I tell you it did hurt when my little children could not go to Sunday school for the want of shoes – could not go out and play with other children for the want of proper clothing.

As of June 10, 1921 the family still lived at 1230 Gregory Avenue, Wilmette, near Chicago. Bob hurried back and forth by train from Chicago to South Whitley organizing his business and buying a house for his new bride and his three children. He wrote the following letter from South Whitley:

Sweetheart – the bestest little wife in the world –

Just a line to tell you a secret – I love you – idolize you – worship you – so lonesome for my precious baby – counting minutes until 7.45 Sunday morning – yes, would be pleased to have you meet me at La Salle St. station.

Train arrives at 7:45 RR Time – or 8:45 Chicago time. Don't you think you had better bring children along to watch car – or if you don't bring children, you will have to remain in car, and I will find you.

Received letter and shirt. Love kisses and hugs from your faithfulHusband

Gandy sent check for $500. – it's a start – big press today.

The family celebrated Christmas of 1921 in

Wilmette as the house in South Whitley was not ready. Turning his thoughts to his childhood prior to the Civil War, Bob ran a sentimental editorial that he had previously written for the 1918 Christmas edition. A few changes brought it up-to-date:

...And I am going home for Christmas – to the old home in Knox County, Missouri. I, too, cannot go in the body for the old home is now owned by strangers. The dear old log house in which I was born has now given way to a modern structure. I do not now think of the changes two score years have wrought. I go back to the old home as it was in the long ago. The revered father and mother have long since reached a 'fairer country', and with them two brothers and two sisters also have gone, and the sister and two brothers who remain live in different parts of the country and their once glossy locks are now silvered with gray. –Let me bask in the sunshine of the years of happy childhood in a Christian home.

The hours of evening have come- the fire burning furiously in the fireplace gives both heat and light. My father takes down the well-worn Bible and reads a chapter from its hallowed pages. Mother – my sainted Mother – sits at his side with my sleepy head upon her knee, and brothers and sisters are grouped reverently around. I do not understand the words but I have been told they are the words of God, and I believe it. The long chapter ends – we all kneel and

Father prays. I fall asleep with my head on the chair. Mother wakes me! Pulls from under the bed the trundle bed in which I sleep with my two older brothers. She tucks the heavy bed clothes around me – whispers a prayer and kisses me good night.

How well do I remember the pleasant evenings at the fireside of the old home- the simple songs, the innocent games- checkers and 'fox and geese'- The words of encouragement as I bend over my school tasks, the kiss as I lie down to rest, the patient bearing with my restless nature, the gentle counsel mingled with reproofs and approvals, the sympathy that lessened every sorrows and sweetened every success,- all these return to me now and I feel I once lived in Heaven and straying, lost my way....

In that same issue the first Woman's Page, edited by Mrs. Edith C. Fraser, appeared. Times were changing. Slowly women began to enter the workplace, generally due to financial need, but the stigma of working outside the home had also lessened to a degree. Mrs. Fraser, somewhat obsequiously, introduced her 'page' as follows:

Beginning with the January number Mr. Hicks is going to let us take part in, or become a part of, his wonderful magazine, and we are to have a whole page to begin with, all to ourselves, entitled "The Woman's Page" and edited by Mrs. Edith C. Fraser. I feel certain that it will not be long before we will need another page, especially if you all feel as enthusiastic about it as I do. ...I would like to hear from every woman who is interested in Specialty Salesman Magazine and all the good things for which it stands, that we may come to know one another and become friends through its pages. I have found in my own experience that some of the truest and best friends I have ever had are among those whom I have never seen, so let us just get together and boost as we never did before to help make the "Woman's Page" a huge success, that Mr. Hicks may never need to regret that he has given us this opportunity of expressing ourselves through the pages of his magazine.

Address all communications to Mrs. Edith C. Fraser, R.R.5, Fremont, Michigan.

There will also be a "Lonesome Folks" column conducted by Jane Lee who loves "lonesome folks" and will be glad to hear from them anywhere and everywhere. So, dear lonesome people, don't forget to write. Women did read the magazine and the readers were ready with their words of praise and their recipes and their poems. In the next issue, Mrs. Fraser filled two pages. The Women's Page became a standard feature of each issue. Short stories written by free lance women writers began to appear. *The Specialty Salesman* thus reflected that times were changing. The long skirts of 1918 had been cut almost to the knees, hair bobbed, and more and more young women joined the work force. Teachers who married were permitted to keep their positions until they became pregnant, when they 'retired'. In August, 1921, Bob was in South Whitley overseeing the installation of new equipment for the publishing plant. He took time to write his bride, addressing the letter to "Mrs. Robert E. Hicks, 1230 Gregory Ave., Wilmette, Ills:"

Thursday, 10/2am

Mother sweetheart wife,

Just talked with you over phone. It done me so much good to hear your sweet voice. Everything going fine. The machine operator arrived last night with his wife- looks good to me. Lots to tell you about return of underwear and jokes. Start to printing magazine in the morning (Friday). So lonesome for you. Love you with all my heart and soul. You are my other self, a part of me. A committee of S. Whitley business men called to see me today. I can have anything I want. Will tell my baby girl all about it Sunday.

Call up Mrs. Hoffman and arrange for her son to be at our house Sunday. I want to see him. Oh, how I wish you were here with me. Love you – that don't express it. Wait until Sunday. I'll show my sweetheart if I love her. Good night precious angel, darling, lover wife. (Here the handwriting spreads across the small page) *Longing for you. So lonesome. Kisses and hugs-millions of them.*

Your own devoted, true, faithful and worshiping, loving Husband- Your Sugar Husband.

The following morning he added a footnote:

Will leave on 3.30 a.m. train Sunday morning. Arrive in Chicago 7.45 RR time or 8.45 Chicago time. So glad you will meet me at La Salle St. Station.

Your Sugar Husband

Say, but don't we love each other?

The last line was underlined with a bold stroke. Mae had become not only his wife, but a partner.

After his move to South Whitley Bob wrote Mae an undated letter on new *Specialty Salesman Magazine* stationary:

Sweetheart – Wife – My Own Love, Put off writing until train time. How I do miss my own precious darling.

A letter to you sure to-morrow. I love you-I love you-miss you-my own precious one – my life – my other self.

Your own – all your own- your true devoted Husband."

Bob had not shared with his readers his marriage to the new Mrs. Hicks or the fact that in the summer of 1922 she became pregnant. Bob had not only bought the Atoz Printing plant but sixteen acres of land at the end of South Whitley's main street. When Bob's business ventures finally succeeded, the family moved from Wilmette to a comfortable four bedroom, two storey house on the new property.

*I am now building two residences on this land –
one for our superintendent and the other for my little
children, who, for the want of shoes could not go to
Sunday school five years ago. The house will cost me
$24,000.00 and every dollar will be paid as the work
progresses....Please don't think I am boasting. It is
not that. I want to help you. If I can, you can.*

*Men, you can have anything you want if you will
pay the price. I paid the price and would have paid
more if it had been exacted.*

*Don't say to yourself "I'll try," or "I'll do my best,"
or make excuses of that kind, but if you will set out to
do a certain thing, let it permeate your entire system,
live with it, eat with it, sleep with it, dream of it by
night and think of it by day and just have that one
thought coupled with a deep-rooted determination to
carry it out. Then, nothing can stop you. But you
must pay the price. Hunger, kicks and jolts must
mean nothing to you and the harder the knocks the
tighter you must hold."* Dale Carnegie, 40 years later,
could add nothing to Bob's inspirational writing. The
family moved from the house in Wilmette into the
two-storey home in South Whitley on the acreage Bob
bought. Close by, construction began on the 'big
house' that would be the family home. Bob was
putting down firm roots.

In the June, 1922, issue seven full pages in the

magazine were devoted to encouraging salesmen to attend the second annual NASS convention to be held at Cedar Point, Ohio, from July 5th to the 10th. The July issue, on the newsstands by July 2nd, carried Bob's 'Last Call for Cedar Point' as well as an article entitled "Activities of the NASS" spotlighting the organizational ability of Burns.

Bob praised Burns as follows: *The activities of Mr. Burns on the Pacific coast are phenomenal. We owe to Mr. Burns a debt of gratitude that possibly we will never be able to pay. He has proved to each member of the association that powerful local assemblies can be organized and maintained. We have often said in our magazine that what Mr. Burns has done on the Pacific Coast can be done in every section of the country and after Cedar Point, I am convinced that it will be done.*

It's no surprise to learn of Albert G. Burns' being elected as president of the IASS – the name being changed to the International Association of Specialty Salesmen during the convention. Burns agreed to devote his entire energy to the running of the Association with a salary of $7,200.00 underwritten by the Robert E. Hicks Corporation. It is worth noting that the equivalent purchasing power of that amount in 2015 would be $101,000. Neither Bob, the first president, nor Arthur Nash, who followed him as president, had accepted one cent from the organization for their time nor for their travel expenses. Nash had 'volunteered' his executive secretary as the secretary of the IASS paying her full salary. Furthermore, H. S. Alexander, director and treasurer, would be relieved of his duties at the magazine to be Burns' 'right hand man,' his salary being paid by Bob.

Burns, a native of California, had urged the Board of Directors of the IASS to hold the 1923 national convention in his home town, Oakland; however, from a geographic perspective it made no sense. The Board wisely chose Chicago, centrally located between the east and west coasts. As a compromise, because the membership had proliferated in the western states, a district convention was to be held in Oakland from February 20th to the 24th.

The headquarters at 509 Wabash Avenue, Chicago, would continue to be the center of operations so it was deemed necessary for Burns to give up all business connections, which did not seem extensive, in California and move his family to the IASS headquarters.

Two months after the convention a staff writer wrote a short biography of Burns. His background seemed sketchy although the author tried manfully to make his subject appear a dynamo of leadership. Burns had dropped out of school by seventeen and ran a small coffee and tea shop in Alameda, California, his birthplace. Then he sold scales and other equipment to stores in the area. Leaving the sales field, he became associated with a sanatorium owned by the Order of Foresters for an indefinite period. Next he styled himself a 'business engineer'. What does that title mean? According to the article, the answer was "in the case of Burns, he has developed many business enterprises, floated bond issues, erected factories, obtained distribution of products."

By October, 1922, any number of new assemblies had been formed in Iowa, California, Oregon, Washington, Nevada and Toronto, Canada. Each issue of the magazine had articles promoting the IASS and praising the enthusiasm of members organizing local assemblies. Bob had reason to feel he had picked a 'winner' with Burns.

Burns received as much support from Bob in furthering the growth of the IASS as Bob's time would permit. From November 11 to the 19, the two men traveled together to ten cities in five states and Canada delivering charters and encouraging new members to promote the Association. Bob met Burns in Chicago where they boarded the train for meetings in Detroit, Toledo, Cleveland, Youngstown and Columbus. There they arranged to drive to Pittsburg with R. D. Palmer, a member of the Association and president of a large wholesale supply company. Bob never learned to drive but automobiles fascinated him. Born in the 'horse and buggy days', his enthusiasm knew no bounds for the speed and ease of riding in a car over paved roads. In a long article praising R. D. Palmer's rise from a specialty salesman selling receipt books to the president of a large corporation, Bob's enthusiasm spilled over when describing the 209 mile journey from Columbus to Pittsburg with Mr. Palmer:

The road was paved every foot of the way. I do not believe we went ten miles of the trip under forty miles an hour. Mr. Palmer is an expert driver. I never occupied a seat beside a driver who so perfectly handled his car. There are many winding roads and hills through the coal fields of West Virginia. Down these winding hills we would go at the rate of 45 to 50 miles an hour – up the hills at 65 to 70 miles an hour. We ate lunch at Wheeling, West Virginia – were there an hour and thirty minutes. When we arrived at Pittsburg we stopped at the hotel, gave our luggage to the porter, drove to a garage and returned to the hotel. As we started up the elevator I looked at my watch and to my surprise, it was fifteen minutes past four'o clock. A wonderful drive with a wonderful driver in a wonderful car."

It would be of interest had Bob informed his readers of the make and model of Mr. Palmer's 'wonderful car'.

From Pittsburg Burns and Bob continued to Buffalo

and Toronto, Canada, returning to Chicago. On trains
between cities, Bob had vetted and polished Burns'
speeches, drank Scotch (bootleg when crossing a 'dry
state' and first rate whiskey when legal), and got as
much sleep in a Pullman berth as possible. Bob, in
1922, an overweight, silver-haired, cigar-smoking,
brash man of 62, had the energy and ambition of a
twenty-five year old. When a considerable percentage
of men at his age were looking forward to retirement,
why was Bob fully dedicated to publishing and editing
an international magazine as well as promoting and
financially backing an international organization? At
the age of 45 he had been a pathetic alcoholic,
stumbling from one low-life bar to the next in the
Bowery of New York City. He had neglected his young
wife and three small children. Federal agents looked
for him for defrauding the public through the U. S.
postal system. What was the secret of his phenomenal
turnabout?

In 1910 a man by the name of W. D. Wattles
published The *Science of Getting Rich*, outlining the
law of attraction – concentrate on what you want and
it will come to you, in other words, 'Think rich and
you become rich'...Wattles offered this piece of
satirical advice to his readers, "Get rich; that is the
best way to help the poor." It is doubtful Bob took the
time in those years to read Wattles' book. He moved
his printing press from one New York City address to

another to escape the law. But when he decided to play it 'straight', Bob summed up his philosophy in words that could have been written by Wattles:

"It's just the way we think – if we think big things – and have confidence in ourselves to do big things, we can do them. We can have what we want if we want it bad enough and will pay the price and make the effort which means 'hard work.'

And Bob, past middle age, continued 'thinking big' about the IASS. Why not build a Temple of the Square Deal in South Whitley? The building could serve as administrative headquarters and be a retirement home for specialty salesmen as well as needy widows and children. It was a grand idea. It took no time for Bob to convince the executive board in Detroit to pass a resolution approving his idea. In the November issue of the magazine Bob announced he had donated $5,000.00 to the IASS for that purpose. Members and manufacturers were asked to "buy a brick for $1.00." The article ended, "How many bricks do you want?"

An entire page with a projected drawing of the Temple appeared in the last issue of 1922. Several architectural firms submitted plans to the Board of Directors. The average cost ran about $40,000.00.

The business community of South Whitley enthusiastically supported the project, Bob's readers learned:

The members of South Whitley Assembly immediately ordered the erection of a forty foot sign board near the junction of the railroads and at a point where it will be read by practically all tourists passing through the town. The sign will announce South Whitley as the future home of The Square Deal Temple of the IASS."

Construction of the Temple began in January, 1923, on land donated by Bob; however, hard frosts and snow made construction difficult. Contractors suggested that a cornerstone ceremony be delayed until May. Another architectural drawing showed the front of the building with a life-sized sculpture of Robert E. Hicks on a pedestal in the center of the entrance. Did Bob's ego over-reach Napoleon's? Both men were small in stature but big in ambition. Modestly he told the architect to eliminate the sculpture.

THE BIRTH OF MARGARET

As the birth of the baby approached, Mae wanted to return to Chicago in order to give birth in a proper obstetrical hospital, but Bob would have none of it. Only a few months previously newspapers had carried the story of two babies mislabeled in the delivery room in one of Chicago's finest hospitals. Bob comforted his wife by arranging for the local doctor, Eberhaart, and a nurse to be at their home at the first signs of labor. A little after midnight on February 8, 1923 Bob telephoned Dr. Eberhaartt telling him the time had come and to bring the nurse with him. The baby, a girl, arrived as the wintry sun crawled over the horizon. Bob named her 'Margaret May' in honor of her mother. It had not been a particularly difficult labor even though Mae was approaching 42. She had given birth to two children as the young wife of Michael Joy. Her son, 21-year-old Edmond Patrick, at that time served in the U. S. Coast Guard and would soon come to work for his step-father in the publishing plant. Edmond's 19-year-old sister, Helen Joy, had already joined her mother in South Whitley. Helen, beautiful, willful, sharp-tongued, resented her step-father and argued about him with her mother once too often so that Bob finally ordered her out of their house. She returned to Chicago to stay with relatives and soon married Gilbert Keebler, a prominent, wealthy real estate broker.

In a "baby book" Mae made for their new daughter, Bob wrote under a photograph of himself the following: "My life is sweeter, richer and fuller because of my baby girl, Margarette."

Unbeknownst to Mae, Bob ordered a special gift, a surprise, for his wife—a state-of-the-art black Lincoln sedan.

DISTRICT CONVENTION IN CALIFORNIA

Seven days after the baby's birth, on the afternoon of February 15, Bob and a group of delegates left Chicago at 6:10 P. M. on the Chicago, Milwaukee and St. Paul railway, making a grand 'progress' through Des Moines, Ogden and Sacramento. At each stop welcoming members met them at the station, some joining them for the convention. On Saturday morning, the 17th of February, Bob wrote a short letter to Mae on Pacific Limited pale blue stationary that was posted at Omaha:

Dear Darling Wife and my sweet little Margarette, We are just crossing the line into Colorado – feeling fine – miss my mother, oh, so much – and Margarette – arrive Ogden in the morning – train running on time. Albert feeling much better – Mr. Hull & rest of party in best of spirits. Kiss our little Margarette for me – Love to all.

A million kisses for my sweet darling wife.

Your own loving true Husband The group arrived in Oakland on the evening of February 19th. The Municipal Auditorium was crowded with delegates from ten western states, outnumbering the delegates who had attended the National Convention at Cedar Point. It was with pride that Bob addressed the opening session. He was a natural born story teller with the gift of a deep resonant voice that needed little amplification. Once at the podium he glanced at his notes, and put them aside. He knew what he wanted to say and he knew how to capture his audience. Journalists referred to him as 'silver-tongued' and he warranted the accolade. In Chicago, prior to leaving for the Oakland District Convention, Bob had ordered a special gift for his wife. On his return home he presented Mae with her Lincoln sedan. The $5000.00 payment-in-full check Bob had written, May carefully pasted in little Margaret's baby book. As a contrast in value, a teacher in Illinois at that time drew an annual salary of $1,239.00. A stenographer working at the New York Times made $25.00 to $30.00 per week. A Willis touring car sold for $690.00. An extant photo shows a beaming Mae, wearing a chic hat, sitting behind the steering wheel while an over-weight Bob, one foot on the running board, holds tiny Baby Margaret in his arms. Life was good. Tentative work on the building site of the Temple began early in the spring of 1923. It was to be financed entirely by members of the IASS and manufacturers buying 'as many bricks as they wished'. To encourage participation, a scroll with the names of donors would be hung in the entrance hall, once the Temple opened its doors. Burns and Bob and three other members would be responsible for keeping track of the donations. Members would not be asked for future contributions as the Temple would be maintained from dues as the membership grew into the hundreds of thousands. Cottages were to be built for retired elderly salesmen 'down on their luck,' and their widows and orphans would be welcomed as well. Such humanitarian projects had been successful in the past and Bob saw no possibility that his dream could fade; however, he could not envision the great changes taking place in merchandising with the advent of advanced communication systems and the shift of the populations from rural farming communities to urban centers. But that was all in the future.

Readers were assured as follows:

The Temple of the Square Deal will become a Mecca of all who are interested in the perpetuation of the Golden Rule in selling, and in this quiet little Hoosier village will stand forever the splendid memorial to the fulfillment of the cherished dream of Bob Hicks, the beloved founder of the Association – a movement which he founded purely on the basis of lasting service to his fellowmen, and from which he has not received, nor can he ever hope to receive, any material reward. It is a movement rather to which he has given freely his time, money and splendid effort and for which, as he has so often expressed himself, he feels more than rewarded by having lived to see his dream fulfilled and to know that the association is now so firmly established that it cannot possibly languish, but rather go forward in its great purpose to still greater achievement. Always ready to promote better business concepts, Bob spoke at the North Manchester Kiwanis Club luncheon on March 19, 1923, encouraging the members to welcome and cooperate with new businesses that come to their community. The local newspaper, *North Manchester News-Journal*, covered the meeting. The final paragraph of the news article noted that "Mr. Hicks was accompanied to North Manchester Wednesday by Mrs. Hicks and their five weeks old daughter, Margaret."

The South Whitley Tribune, April 19, 1923, carried the story of the contractor, A. M. Strauss of Ft. Wayne, conferring with Albert Burns about the preliminary plans for The Temple of the Square Deal. Burns hired Strauss to supervise the construction of the building. The article noted that Burns was the Chairman of the Board of the Building Fund. Strauss promised to have the detailed plans and the specifications for the foundation work ready by the 25th of April. On May 15, 1923, the first shovel full of earth had been ceremonially dug by Albert Burns. The July issue of *The Specialty Salesman* carried the story:

The ceremony of removing the first shovelful of dirt for The Temple of the Square Deal was in the nature of a local holiday and celebration. Most of the grading and preparation of the site had been done last fall, but the formal opening of building activity occurred on the afternoon of May 15 that marked the beginning of the realization of a dream that has for so long inspired the founder and officers of the IASS.

Shortly before 4 o'clock the business houses of the little town of South Whitley closed their doors, the schools were dismissed and all industrial activities ceased. The school children marched in procession to the grounds where the Temple is to be erected and were joined there by throngs of local citizens headed by the South Whitley band.

...Despite the fact that a light rain was falling, the crowd waited in respectful silence until the ceremonies were completed , and because of this disagreeable feature of the weather, they repaired to the spacious but uncompleted home of President Emeritus Robert E. Hicks where inspiring talks were given by Mr. Hicks, Mr. Burns and Mr. Mokstad (officers of the IASS). In his remarks Mr. Hicks spoke feelingly of his heart interest in the Association which is very much that of a father toward his favorite child. He expressed his appreciation of the support being given him and his undertakings by the citizens of South Whitley, as well as the part they are taking in the activities of the association.

President Burns described the wonderful work that is being accomplished by the association and its plans for the future. He told of the homes that will be built for aged members and their widows and orphans. He pictured the benefits that will come to those who are faithful in their adherence to the organization and its ideals....

Mr. Burns further spoke of the plans for the laying of the cornerstone on June 17th...It can be said that there will be present notable public men from all parts of the country and hundreds of visiting members and friends. The expected guests will be entertained by the townspeople who have generously opened their homes for the occasion. Efficient committees have prepared plans for the day and arranged interesting and inspiring programs."

As predicted, the laying of the cornerstone took place on Sunday, June 17, 1923. The deputy state fire-marshall of Indiana, a resident of South Whitley, gave the welcoming address. The local band played patriotic music and the crowd sang The Star Spangled Banner. Board members came from Chicago and Detroit. The Rev. Stith, pastor of the First Baptist Church, gave the invocation. The actual ceremony of laying the cornerstone was performed by The Rev. Arthur J. Folsom, pastor of the Plymouth Congregational Church, Ft. Wayne, Indiana, who then delivered the address of the day.

If programs had been arranged for out-of-town guests, no mention was made about them. Bob's elaborate plans for the expansion of his dreams may well be summed up in the paragraph following:

It is not difficult to conceive of the Temple of the Square Deal growing into a community comprising of other administrative quarters, homes for the aged and indigent members of the Association, their widows and orphans, schools for the education of the children living in these homes and even factories where they may maintain themselves and learn trades that will enable them to become useful and productive members of society. But the city fathers were not cooperating.

In the first week of October, 1923, Bob gave a dinner for the leading business men of the town held at the Baptist Church, the only building large enough to accommodate them. The good ladies of the parish supplied the 'combustibles' for the occasion. Bob outlined his proposals for bringing more business enterprises to South Whitley and his own plans for expanding the land holdings of the IASS. Although some men responded enthusiastically, the majority gave a cool response.

The following Wednesday, October 11, the South Whitley Tribune printed the following news item:

SOUTH WHITLEY MAY LOSE HICKS CORP.
Lack of Cooperation May Cause Town
to Lose Big Magazine
Robert E. Hicks, head of the Hicks Corporation, and Albert J. Burns, president of the IAS announced Wednesday forenoon that they are considering

moving away from South Whitley in the immediate future. Dissatisfaction over the attitude of the public towards them is ascribed as the reason for this unexpected action. . . .

Since a conference of business men held Wednesday evening, it is thought that a mutual understanding between the Hicks interests and the citizens may soon be realized.

Mr. Hicks has an investment of over a quarter of million dollars in South Whitley and does a printing business of over $200,000 per year, which no town, large or small, would want to lose.

Messrs. Hicks and Burns state they have not received the cooperation of the general public which they expected in their various enterprises. On the contrary, in some cases obstacles have been strewn along their pathway.

It would seem to any fair minded person that when all that the Hicks interests ask of South Whitley is their cooperation, it should surely be accorded them forthwith.

Mr. Hicks' achievements of the past few years are too well known to need any summary.

Five months later on March 27, 1924, the tide had turned in favor of Bob. References to Albert Burns and the Temple of the Square Deal had disappeared by that time, but Bob was still pursuing a building project to serve the community of South Whitley. The local newspaper printed a supportive article, as follows:

COMMUNITY BUILDING PROJECT
DISCUSSED AT PUBLIC MEETING

About 150 interested citizens were present, discussing ways & means by which this much needed building could be erected. The meeting was called by the women's Civic League, which organization has undertaken to sponsor this movement. ....

Rev. Stith called attention to some things that should be avoided if a community building were to be successfully operated. He said that if it were conducted on a moral plane it would have the support of the churches. Robert E. Hicks, among others, called to the attention of the meeting the fact that no concrete working plan for achieving the ends toward which they were directing their efforts had been outlined. He suggested that some way be devised for securing the building before too much emphasis was laid on how it was to be conducted. At the close of his talk, Mr. Hicks announced that he would probably give not less than $5,000.00 to the building fund.

It was the practically unanimous sentiment of the meeting that South Whitley was in dire need of such a building, it being pointed that the town and country around it were without a suitable place for public gatherings of any kind other than the churches.....

...Such a condition is reflected in the attitude of the

people. Community activities are stagnated; mass gatherings being impossible, there is a dearth of co-operation and the entire community breaks up into little cliques of a size suitable for such gathering places as are at their command. This creates a vast number of conflicting or selfish interests, while it atrophies the interest in the common welfare through the very inability to cultivate and nourish it....

Folks, we must have it. Let everyone give the matter careful and serious thought, so that when a definite plan is offered there may be no contention or discord, but a hearty co-operation that will put across in a big way. We owe it to ourselves, to the community we call home, and to our children.

Can Bob's voice be heard in the background dictating to the editor? Bob dreamed big and if a particular dream did not come to fruition, there was another vision to take its place. The Temple of the Square Deal had obviously metamorphosed into something else by March of 1924, for reasons that shall soon become apparent.

The third annual convention of the IASS opened at the Coliseum in Chicago July 11th and ended on the 14th , 1923. Several presidents of large corporations and a member of Congress were featured speakers. Automatically the members re-elected Burns as president. The Board of Directors announced that "a plan has been devised and will immediately be put into effect whereby members of the Association may obtain life and total disability insurance at a minimum cost, in amounts ranging from "$1,000.00 to $5,000.00".

For the first time a special event for the ladies, a tour of Marshall Fields, followed by a luncheon in the Walnut Room, was hosted by Mrs. Robert E. Hicks, Mrs. Albert Burns and other wives of the Association's Board. The Chicago Assembly honored the ladies at yet another luncheon at the Lexington Hotel. A photograph of the event showed Mrs. Hicks as the only woman present without a hat. She sat at the head table, wearing dark rimmed glasses, smiling broadly.

Bob wrote the editorial about the convention for the September issue of the magazine with studied precision. The fourth convention was scheduled to take place in Des Moines, Iowa, from August 13th to the 16th.

Meanwhile, the *South Whitley Tribune's* August 9, 1923 issue commented on the progress of the new family home:

Work on the interior of Robert E. Hicks' palatial new residence is progressing rapidly. When you stop to think that there are over 130 windows in the building you begin to realize the immensity of the work of interior finishing. The mansion is reputed to cost $40,000.00.

A nursemaid, Etta Ridenbaugh, had been found to

take care of little Margaret. Auntie, as she would be called by her charge, was a tall, thin, gray-haired widow who came from a neighboring town. Unencumbered, she came with excellent character references. She and little Margaret slept in a bedroom directly opposite her parent's bedroom. It was Bob's idea, the nursemaid. He wanted Mae to have more time to devote to him, more time for running the household and for caring for his other three children by his deceased wife Lois—Helen, Phoebe and Bobbie—when they were home from boarding schools. Mae, a devoted mother, took great pride in this healthy, new baby. The nursemaid freed Mae of any of the tiresome chores of having a new baby—preparing bottles, changing and washing diapers, getting up in the middle of the night at the first sound of a whimper. Little Margaret's first introduction to the readers of *The Specialty Salesman Magazine* appeared in the October, 1923 issue. The previous month Bob and Albert Burns arranged an exhausting seven day speaking tour promoting the IASS, and Bob wanted Mae and the baby with him. The party left South Whitley early the morning of August 16, in Burns' 'big Nash'. They stayed the first night in Kalamazoo, followed in quick succession by Grand Rapids, Muskegon, Ionia, Flint, Bay City, Port Huron, Detroit, Michigan, and then Toledo, Ohio, returning to South Whitley Wednesday night of the 23rd. One might think caring for a six-month-old baby in those conditions would have ended Mae's enthusiasm for traveling with Bob on business, but such was not the case. That first trip had delighted Mae even when the '*big Nash slipped and slithered over clay and ruts between Port Huron and Detroit*'.

At Flint, Mae and Bob posed for photos, each taking a turn holding little Margaret. Mae pasted the pictures in the baby book with the date and place.

From then on when Bob traveled by train to business meetings, Mae, with little Margaret and Auntie Ridenbaugh, usually accompanied him. Mae carefully saved postcards of each hotel where they stayed, pasting them into a 'memory book', noting the date as well as the room numbers, e.g. "Rm.309 our room, Little Margaret & Etta, Rm. 311". Bob and Burns planned a whirlwind trip through Iowa to visit IASS Assemblies. When Bob realized Sioux City would be a stop-over, he made yet another attempt to contact his beloved sister of his boyhood, Mary Ann. She had stopped answering his notes as he became more and more involved in his frantic life style and some twenty years had slipped by since he had heard from her. Somehow Bob made contact with her and informed her of the date he would be in Sioux City, asking her to bring her family to the hotel because he looked forward with great pleasure to seeing her and meeting her family. Bob and Burns left for Des

Moines, their first stop, on November 16th, where Bob had received an invitation to speak at the Central Presbyterian Church on Sunday evening. One account of his address follows: *Mr. Hicks filled the pulpit of this church for the 7:30 evening service which was in charge of Dr. McKean. Mr. Hicks took for his text 10th verse of the 3rd chapter of Malachi: "Bring ye all the tithes into the storehouse, that there may be meat in mine house, and prove me now, saith the Lord, if I will not open the windows of heaven and pour you out a blessing that there shall not be room enough to receive it.*

The church was crowded and all present listened with rapt attention to Bob's eloquent address. He stressed the fact that it is not possible to discharge our obligation to the Master by making gifts of money and taking no personal or active part in the work to be done and that only by rendering unselfish personal service can we receive the great blessings promised.

The Malachi text had obviously continued to inspire Bob since his first few days in prison on Blackwell Island, especially the key phrases about opening the windows of heaven and blessings so large that there shall not be room to receive it.

It is difficult to discern Bob's attitude toward religion. Bob himself wrote and encouraged his staff to write articles on religious themes and teachings, but in terms of his own personal religious commitment, he and his family did not attend church services often, nor did prayer become part of family rituals. As he became more financially successful, however, he donated more and more money to various Protestant churches. Further, he took pride in quoting passages from the Bible now and then, urged his readers to attend church and, above all, to practice The Golden Rule. At Sioux City the anticipated meeting with his sister, Mary Ann Doran, took place. Her husband, daughter and grandson, Harold, accompanied her. Mary Ann would out-live her younger brother and would be remembered by him with a monthly stipend in his will. Harold, a tall, gangly, lackadaisical young man with no ambition and no goals, gave Bob an opportunity to help his sister as well as change the future of his great-nephew.

At his first meeting with Harold, Bob said, "I hear you're not working, my boy. That's not good. What about coming to work for me?" Quickly pushed in the ribs by his Grandfather Doran, Harold agreed.

"That's settled then. I'll send you a railroad ticket later."

In December, 1923, Harold arrived in South Whitley and never left. Sixty three years later a woman from The Columbus Historical Society interviewed Harold with a tape-recorder about the life of his great-uncle, Bob. Unfortunately the tape began to deteriorate by the time a librarian transcribed it, but revealing portions of the interview remain. In part Harold spoke of Uncle Bob as follows:

When I was a kid I wished I had a rich uncle and when I did have a rich uncle, I had a different opinion. Guess 'cause Uncle Bob said I was family I was on duty anytime he needed me. I didn't work a ten hour day. I was on call night and day. I'd get up at five in the morning to take him to the station to catch a train for Elkhart or some other place where he'd talk at some church or somethin'. That 'ud be a Sunday, a day of rest, but not fer me. No sirree. Then he'd send me to Chicago to pick up some papers or somethin'.

The interviewer said, "I heard from somebody that neither he nor Mrs. Hicks ever patronized the local butcher shops here. Is that true?"

Ooh, yeah – the beef. He'd not permit me to buy a piece of steak locally. This country meat was not to go in his house at all under no circumstances. His meat had to be shipped out of Chicago. Normally he'd call up and he'd have it delivered to the head waiter of the dining car on the train and he'd send me down to the station to get it. He'd give me $5.00 to give the head waiter. Can sound cheap today but it sure wasn't then. Harold also remembered the first time he went to the commercial butcher in the Chicago stock yards. The butcher, Gordy McDee, invited Harold to see the carcass hanging in a long hall with temperature set at 40 degrees F. Harold became traumatized when he saw the hairy, headless animal hanging from a swinging hook. He could only refer to the carcass as a 'thing'. Harold continued answering the interviewer's questions:

The butcher told me, "Mr. Hicks wants that one right there. Yeah, wait 'til I clean that hair and green mold off it."

The butcher cleaned the carcass while explaining to Harold that it had been hanging there for nine months. Harold admitted that when Gordy finished his work, the steaks looked just as they did in meat markets. Harold brought 47 pounds of aged beef to South Whitley that evening.

The interviewer asked Harold about the financial status of the Hicks family when Bob retired in Florida. It is doubtful Harold could peek into family finances, but he estimated his uncle had at least a million dollars, property, investments and cash, after he sold the magazine.

No, they sure weren't broke, and that's a fact. When they went to Florida, he thought he was going to go in the real estate business, bought a few thousand acres but the Depression stopped folks buying - who'd buy that piney woods, sandy flat land? They build that big house on the Old Spanish Trail with no view but the railroad track. Hobos would drop off the freight cars at the watering station down the way and come to the back door to ask for food. Aunt Mae told the cook to give them somethin', but to be sure they left the property. Aunt Mae had a good heart. She got two sons of a widow cousin in the WPA and sent one girl cousin to a fancy summer camp in North Carolina – the same camp Margaret went to.

I didn't know 'til Uncle Bob died that after I came to live with them he sent a check every month to my grandma. After he passed away it kept comin' 'cause he put it in his Will. They had funny ways – Aunt Mae liked to help draw up plans for a new house and Uncle Bob loved expensive cars but he never learned to drive. So they were sort'ta like fabulous people when you think about them. They weren't normal. Burns and Bob returned to Chicago eight days later after visiting Waterloo, Mason City, Fort Dodge, Sioux City and Des Moines. It would be the last trip they would ever make together. Thanksgiving of 1923, Bob, Mae and the children celebrated with the employees and their families at the printing plant in South Whitley. An article published in the magazine gave the following account:

So it was that at seven thirty about 60 people sat down to a dinner which consisted of the following menu – celery, pickles, roast chicken, dressing, gravy, creamed peas, pumpkin pie, bread and butter, coffee, salted nuts, mints. Following the dinner a short program of readings by Mrs. E. F. Eberhard and heads of various departments and the Old Man Himself and impromptu remarks by each employee present. Bob spoke feelingly of the pleasant relations existing between him and his associates and expressed a devout wish to become a still more worthy exemplar of the Golden Rule in his attitude toward them. It was at a late hour that a tired though happy crowd returned to their homes, voting the occasion a wonderful success and Bob a wonderful entertainer and a lavish provider. In the December, 1923 issue Albert Burns' article "Business Is Good" appeared. It would be the last time he would ever write for *The Specialty Salesman Magazine*. The readers would soon learn the reason.

7

A Change of Direction

On December 18, Bob's secretary answered the telephone and after a minute or two in order to verify the message, said, "Mr. Hicks, you have a long distance call from Cincinnati. I believe it is Mr. Nash."

"Did you say Mr. Nash, Arthur Nash?"

Bob took the telephone and motioned to the secretary to leave the room.

When the long conversation ended, Bob sat at his desk staring at the wall, his face drained of color. Bob had not heard from Arthur Nash since that Sunday morning, July 9th, 1922, at the closing of the Cedar Point Convention when Nash had suggested Burns might be a risky choice for president of the IASS. Now his old friend had dropped the bombshell, and Bob reeled from the impact.

Bob learned that two days previously Albert Burns had traveled to Cincinnati to beg Arthur Nash for a loan. He confided in Nash that the IASS was financially bankrupt and asked Nash to cover Burns' personal expenses. Because of their friendship, Nash telephoned Bob. Ruefully Bob remembered all too well his friend's warning at Cedar Point. The time had come to let the members of the Association know the facts. The following day Bob telephoned his attorney, Pearly Bishop, in Chicago who agreed with him. Write the facts and publish them. Bob knew that his dream for the Association had ended. Now he faced the task of writing its epitaph.

Desperate to find the best way of handling the demise of the Association as well as running the magazine, Bob spent long hours at the plant, telephoning, conferring, writing, planning. Fortunately, he had no need to be concerned for his domestic life. Mae had taken charge of all family affairs. That December she supervised the move of the family into the new "house of 130 windows" recently completed, hired a farmer to take care of the twenty-acre farm and his wife as cook and housekeeper. Mae also made all the preparations for their first Christmas in their new home. Many years later Mae confided the following to her daughter:

I appreciated how hard your father worked and when he came home in the evening, I always saw to it that everything was ready for him. I knew he had a number of attractive women working in his office. I never met him at the door with curlers in my hair or worried him with tales of woe about my day. Granted, he wasn't an easy man to live with, but I knew he loved me and took care of me. He was the most important man in my life and I certainly let him know it. Some distance behind the house stood the traditional bright, red barn, the home of the fine, black Belgian dray horses, Queen and Barney. A photo shows Bob, standing between them, holding each by its bridle. The horses are looking benignly down on their master, Bob, a short man, dwarfed by their size.

Mae did magic with pancakes, which she prepared on demand, but with the new cook installed in the kitchen, Bob took time to instruct her how to prepare his breakfast of Porterhouse steak: heat adequate butter until hot, sear steak quickly on each side, cook until juices run pink. Serve immediately on a warm plate with German fried potatoes, buttered toast and scrambled eggs.

Neither the December or January issues of the magazine gave a hint of the problems facing the IASS. The magazine continued to attract more and more advertisers paying for full page ads. More stories by women free-lance writers were being printed and the issues ran from 110 to 125 pages. The price continued to be a quarter. Sales at newsstands across the United States and Canada increased as well as subscriptions. The *Specialty Salesman* had come of age.

Bob had written many speeches and editorials with considerable ease but, because he realized he had shirked responsibility for the IASS's finances, he spent hours writing "In the Shoals" for the February, 1924, issue:

Cedar Point. I shudder when I think of Cedar Point. I recall my last meeting with Arthur Nash. We met in the lobby of the great hotel there. I remember, word for word, many of the things he said to me when we were seated face to face. Arthur Nash was the first to speak and in substance, he said:

"Bob, I have the hardest task of my life but I cannot shirk it. I cannot go with you along the road you are starting to travel."

"Arthur," I replied, "I do not understand your meaning."

"No, you will not understand now. But, Bob, I cannot help but be impressed with the tragedy of the thing by the fact that the current issue of your magazine now on the newsstands tells the story of your tieing [sic] up with a bunch of directors who turned you out of your own office, and of the terrible struggle you and your family had getting the magazine started again. The same result will come from the action taken here at Cedar Point." "Arthur, I still am at a loss to understand what you mean."

"Well, Bob, it is not possible for me to make my meaning clear now but I do want to say this to you, that the group that came here with their slate made up and determined to put it through, no matter what methods were required, were in the minority of this convention but neither I nor those counseling with

me were willing to enter into a disgraceful fight, so the whole thing has gone through as scheduled; and, now, as Harold (Dr. Harold Marshall of Boston), *John* (Dr.John Smith Lowe of Providence, R. I.) *and I talked the matter over, we decided that there was nothing that we could do except to wait for the inevitable result. Harold's own words were 'perhaps when the whole thing goes to smash, we can help him gather up the pieces'....Bob, in a very real sense you are going into a burning building. I can't make it clear to you now, and perhaps I haven't done all I could but I have done all that I knew how to do to stop this thing, and now, I say 'good-bye' to you. I cannot go through this thing with you but I will be waiting with the same love that I have always had for you when it is over."*

I do not recall what reply I made, if any, but we said 'good-bye'. I started to my room. I began to realize the terrible sacrifice I had made for Albert Burns. I went down the hall only a short distance and stopped. I wanted to go back to Arthur and plead with him not to leave me and, if possible, go with me in the great work we both had undertaken...

It may have been an unusual response, but Bob continued: *My heart and soul were in the Association. I failed to consult with the friends who were very near and dear to me. They were scattered in different parts of the country, and when Burns came on to South Whitley I made up my mind that it was to the interest of the association that he give all his time to its up-building. It was a monstrous mistake. I turned my back to men who I knew were heart and soul in accord with the great ideals of the association and who stood firmly for the application of the Golden Rule in all human relationships. I accepted a man whom I knew but little about, but in whom I sincerely believed. I have made mistake after mistake; I have traveled the wrong road many times and I have jumped at conclusions; but I now see that one of the most vital mistakes of my life was when I turned my back to those dear, sincere souls who loved me as a brother. It is not pleasant for me to make this confession. It is not pleasant for me to confess I was deceived....Under the management and dictatorship of Albert Burns, The International Association of Salesmen is in the shoals – financially it is on the rocks. Albert G. Burns has made a miserable failure.* Reading Bob's emotional confession, some 90 odd years after the event, it is difficult to understand Bob's lack of normal business sense in regard to the IASS. Bob held the title of Chairman of the Building Committee. He had the responsibility of overseeing the conduct of the members of that committee and he neglected to do so. How could he be unaware that Burns had mingled the Association's membership fees with monies for the building fund? How was he to solve the problem? What could he do to maintain credibility with the members?

On 30 January 1924, Bob, by registered mail requesting a signed receipt, sent out to each director, including Burns, a list of twenty reasons Burns must be forced to resign as president of the IASS. As soon as Burns read the February article "In the Shoals", he sued Bob for libel in the amount of $100,000.00. With cavalier distain, Bob tossed the news aside, writing, "The case may come to trial and it may not. I may get my day in court and I may not, but if I do, I will be ready." The twenty charges Bob made against Burns, the Directors initially rejected. Bob, down but not defeated, wrote a scathing article with the unusually long title: "Emulating Tom Sawyer, Board of Directors of the International Association of Salesmen Aspire to Duplicate Feat of Mark Twain's Famous Character – Kalsomine Applied to President Burns – Some Spots that were Overlooked".

The article's title, substantiated by eleven pages written by Bob, convinced the Board of Directors Burns was not qualified to be a member. He had mingled funds, misrepresented the number of the membership, failed to pay Association bills, and padded his expense account with personal debts. The Board of Directors took another look. Another meeting, held in Chicago, turned the tide. *FOUND*

GUILTY AS CHARGED: Tried by Assembly #7, Albert G. Burns was Unanimously Voted Unworthy of Membership in the International Association of Salesmen. The Next Step is to insure that he cannot longer Use the Association for Personal Purposes.

Burns became a persona non grata; however and unhappily, the IAS vanished as well. By September, 1924, the IASS had a number of supporters who wished to reorganize. Bob opposed it. The IASS was finished. He wrote the following: *I am not in favor of reorganizing the association thus debauched and wrecked by Albert G. Burns, but I will support with the very best that is in me any organization founded upon the solid rock of the squarest kind of a square deal in every human relationship...I realize it will take some time to come for the cleansing winds to blow away the stench left by Burns and his gross, if not criminal mismanagement. And I realize, too, that no man can be accepted on his own statements, but must be, as Burns should have been, if I had not been so grossly careless, rigidly investigated as to both his private and business life before he can be accepted as the leader of any movement along the lines of the original principles of the IAS.* Rereading the early articles about the initial attempts to found the association, one can understand Bob's despair over its demise. However, many questions remain unanswered to this day. How was restitution made to those who had contributed to the building fund of The Temple of the Square Deal? Recent membership dues? Monies paid by local assemblies to the IASS headquarters? Bob urged the treasurer and Board members involved with the finances of the organization to return the money to the subscribers, but was there money to return? Bob owned the land on which the Temple was to have been built, the cornerstone laid but the reason for its erection had dissolved with the demise of the IASS. The only record of the 117 donations made appeared in the August, 1923 issue. The majority were of $1.00. Bob topped the list with a donation of $5000.00. Bob would have made restitution quietly and quickly to those 116 donors to maintain his reputation as a man of his word. However, the actual answers regarding the reimbursement of funds have disappeared within the files tossed into trash cans along with Bob's dream of an international association of house-to-house salesmen.

With the death of the Temple of the Square Deal, Bob cast about for another opportunity to leave his stamp on the village of South Whitley. The chance came when the Women's Civic League called a meeting on March 22, 1924. Approximately 150 citizens attended. The topic of discussion focused on the need for a community hall. Bob made his presence known by loudly voicing his opinion. The town needed a meeting place open to all organizations. To add emphasis, he volunteered a donation of $5,000.00 to the cause.

Nothing developed from that initial conference but it planted a seed in Bob's imagination. He didn't need the Women's Civic League to sponsor a building. He would build a 'community hall' to suit himself.

Years later Mae told her own version of the history of The Hicks Tavern. She had said to her husband, "The closest hotel is in Ft. Wayne. Who calls that boarding house over by the bank a hotel? And where do your business men stay when they come to South Whitley? At our house! Sometimes I feel I'm running a hotel."

Never mind whether or not that family legend is true. The Hicks Tavern became a reality.

Such an idea excited Bob, as new business concepts always did. Bob selected T. R. Strauss, an architect from Fort Wayne, to draw the plans. The hotel would be small but elegant with twenty bedrooms, large banquet and dining rooms with a state-of-the art kitchen. The design had to include a 'comfort station' accessible from the outside at each end of the building. Bob understood the need of farm families coming into town to shop. Bob also instructed the architect to hire as many local contractors and workmen as possible. The *South Whitley Tribune's* article of April 29, 1926 made public Bob's intentions:

THE HICKS TAVERN

Robert E. Hicks to Build Fine Hostelry for South Whitley

REH assured us that a new hotel will be erected on the site formerly occupied by the tie barn, just west of the Norris drug store....Mr. Hicks had advanced money for the lot and he now proposes to carry out an ambition that has been his for a number of years, the erection of a hotel. His plans are not to make it over-sized, but to have it the finest and best equipped of any small hotel in the country.

...At the northwest corner, with an outside entrance, will be placed a ladies rest room, which will be entirely cut off from the other part of the building. Nr. Hicks wants to provide a real comfort station here, one that will be a credit to the town. At the northeast corner will be located a men's toilet. He will ask the town, and rightfully so, to maintain these comfort stations.

...The furnishings will be equal to those found in the exclusive hotels in the large cities and every comfort will be provided for guests.

Excavation work for the basement is to start at once.

Mr. Hicks informs us that his long cherished ambition to provide South Whitley with the best small town hotel in the country is to at last be realized in the erection of the Hicks Tavern. He says nothing can prevent his going ahead with the proposed improvement.

We hear some pessimistic talk, but we are pinning our faith to Mr. Hicks in this hotel matter.

There is some skepticism in the article, but thirteen months later the hotel became a reality. However, the gala opening scheduled to take place on April 16, 1927, had to be postponed.

The *Speciality Salesman* appeared on the national and Canadian newsstands the first days of each month; therefore, all articles and ads were ready for the type setters at least ten days before publishing. In the April issue a two page story entitled "Hicks Tavern Opens May 16th" indicated that there could be a delay.

Of course at the time of writing this announcement plans for the opening day are tentative. It is even possible that the opening may be set for a later date, although every effort is being made to have the Tavern completed and ready for guests at that time....

The article describes the interior of the building, pointing out that Bob has spared no expense to make The Tavern one of the best small hotels in the country. Each guest room is furnished with Baker Furniture of Michigan and each has a bathroom, telephone, desk, over-stuffed chair and a large closet. A handsome walnut stairway, heavily carpeted, leads to the second floor. There is no elevator. The main floor dining room seats one hundred while the banquet room in the semi-basement can hold two hundred guests. The lower level was described thus:

A broad easy stairway leads to the banquet room. A fireplace at the east end adds to the cheeriness of this room. In the rear is the furnace room, the kitchen, the laundry and a huge electric refrigerated room large enough to hold food for a garrison for a long siege. Every labor saving contrivance is to be found in these rooms, such as electric dishwashers, washing machines, mangles, hot plates, steam tables, Food is sent to the dining room on a dumb waiter. No odors of cooking can reach either the dining room. or the banquet room."

In the same article readers are informed that those who cannot attend the opening can tune in to WOWO radio station, Ft. Wayne, Ind., if they have a radio or "perhaps can induce their neighbors to let them listen in at 8 P.M. central standard time and you will at least hear the music from Hicks Tavern. Please write and tell us how you enjoyed the program and don't forget the Mandolin Club founded by Mrs. Hicks for girls."

The article,"Friday the Thirteenth" in the May, 1927 issue, announced the Tavern would open on that inauspicious date. The formal opening scheduled for April had been postponed because, try as they did, the decorators were not able to finish their work on time. In the May, 1927 issue of *The Specialty Salesman*

Magazine, a staff writer extolled in detail the interior:

No hotel in the country can possibly have better furniture in its rooms, or surround the guests with so many aesthetic delights. From the antique style furniture in the dining room to the four poster beds in the bedrooms the furniture is the best that money can buy without going into hand carved and genuine antiques. The dining room tables are even worn on the sides as if by the coat sleeves of a multitude of former habitués, and some of the natives of our little town were very much excited and dismayed when they found worm holes in the chairs. (I might add parenthetically that the worm holes are so placed that they do not make the chairs at all insecure. The worms who ate the holes were well trained and bored holes only where they were directed to do so).

On the inauspicious day of Friday, May 13, 1927, the grand opening of The Hicks Tavern took place. Another lengthy article, with half-page photographs, appeared in *The Specialty Salesman* issue of July, 1927:

The opening exercise began with the raising of the flag. Little Margaret Hicks, Bob's curly locked youngest, all dressed up in her little red dress, pulled the rope that raised the Stars and Stripes over the building while the South Whitley school band played.

Bob Hicks briefly welcomed the audience of more than 2000 and introduced U. S. Senator Arthur

Robinson of Indiana who paid many compliments to Bob Hicks for his enterprise and his generosity in building so outstanding a hostelry and asserted that the Tavern was not merely a South Whitley enterprise but was something the State of Indiana could be proud to claim.... Arthur Nash of Cincinnati told of the time Bob Hicks had to sell his cook stove to get enough money to leave South Whitley some eleven years previously. U. S. Senator Arthur Capper of Kansas, Governor Ed Jackson of Indiana, Governor A. V. Donahey of Ohio sent congratulatory telegrams. 257 guests dined at the banquet held that evening at 6:30....

Two days earlier on Wednesday evening, May eleventh, the employees of Bob Hicks and their families were guests of Mr. and Mrs. Bob Hicks at a banquet served in the banquet room of the Tavern. There were approximately ninety who sat down to the kind of dinner only a chef of real ability could prepare. ...

The Hicks Tavern is open. There seems to be no jinx on it because it was opened on an unlucky day. The tavern did not burn down.... Such are the words that tempt Fate—"did not burn down".

It became somewhat of a family custom of the South Whitlians, after Sunday church services, to have dinner at The Tavern . Fred Fox, the manager, reported that approximately 150 meals were served each Sunday. The Hicks family rarely missed a Sunday lunch. One Sunday Mae noticed that melted ice cream was being served to the disgruntled early diners. She immediately went down to the kitchen to find the chef, with his toque askew, leaning against the refrigerator, drunk. Mae, normally a soft-spoken, even- tempered, shy woman, became overwhelmed with anger: *I don't know what happened to me. I told him to take his apron off and get out of the kitchen. At that, he stood up straight, telling me to mind my own business. He added that Mr. Hicks has hired him and he was staying. I literally hissed, "And Mrs. Hicks is firing you. Get out." I picked up the apron he'd thrown on the floor, put it on and finished the cooking.*

The following day one of the waitresses told the manager, Fred Fox, "We were so glad Mrs. Hicks fired that man. Fern and I stood right behind her because we didn't know what he might do. None of us liked him."

Mae showed herself to be a woman of spirit who could hold her own when the situation called for it.

When Margaret became a young woman, Mae told her of a family incident that also occurred at a Sunday dinner at The Tavern. The family was having their meal when an attractive, middle-aged woman walked into the dining room with the manager who pointed to the Hicks' table. As soon as Bob saw her, he pushed his chair back and stood up. Without any preliminaries, he pointed to an empty table, saying to the woman, "You sit over there." He sat down and continued eating. Later he told Mae that the woman had been a former wife. Wife? Mistress? Even his explanation to Mae raises questions. Which wife? Which mistress?

Rosa E., the French girl and mother of his first two sons, had dropped out of Bob's life years before. Lois Hawley Hicks, the mother of Helen, Phoebe and Robert Jr., died in 1921. But what about Elizabell Smith, the Irish singer, listed on the 1900 census with Bob as his 'partner'? Or could it have been Viola Colepaugh, his bride of two days? And there was Jeannette Wren who divorced him in New York City in 1902. Whoever she might have been, she remains the 'mystery woman'.

When Bob retired at the end of 1928 and the family moved to Florida, The Tavern remained open. Guests were few. Some travelers passed by on their way to Fort Wayne or Indianapolis, but seldom stopped overnight. South Whitley had little to attract the tourist.

After Bob's death in 1932, The Tavern became part of his estate. Mae, as widow, with their young daughter, returned to South Whitley to settle business matters. She hired Bob's grandnephew, Harold Doran, as manager of the hotel. Doran, in an attempt to revive business, set up an advertising campaign. He printed 'flyers' distributed throughout the village and bought ads in the newspaper with the heading "Hicks Tavern Under New Management". The ads explained that Sunday, November 20 through Tuesday, November 22, 1932 were to be set aside for special events— chicken and turkey dinners, card parties with prizes, refreshments, even dances with music by a live orchestra. Prices were 50 cents per person for the dance nights and $1.50 per couple for dinner. The reasonable prices attracted only a limited number of diners and dancers, for the Great Depression left few families with adequate means to splurge on a night out.

Predictably the Tavern failed to make a profit in spite of the advertising campaign. The Hicks Estate sold it to the Kaadt Diabetic Institute. When the Institute failed to prosper, the building became the South Whitley Rest Home and then the Christian Manor. In 1989 Peter and Rusty Beauchamp became the owners and, with a sense of community history, renamed it The Hicks Tavern Apartments. Only remnants of The Tavern's former glory remained—the neo-classical façade, the walnut staircase, the impressive coach lights at the entrance and in the manager's office, the Baker Fine Furniture mahogany desk. Finally, at two A. M. June 10, 1993, a volunteer of the fire department awoke to learn that the apartment building was aflame. The volunteer fire brigade did their best, but to little avail. The headline in *The Journal-Gazette* the next morning reported as follows:

1 Dead, 34 Homeless in Whitley Fire

South Whitley – A blaze killed a 35 year-old man and left 34 people homeless when fire destroyed the 70 year-old Hicks Tavern Apartments building. Firefighters rescued a man and a child from an upper-floor apartment. Damage was estimated at $500,000.00.

The former residents, when interviewed, pointed fingers at 60-year- old John Crawford who lived in a basement apartment next to Jeffery Zombor who died in the blaze. Crawford, after several interviews with the police, confessed his guilt. He told officers that he had meant to set himself on fire, but once his chair began to burn, he changed his mind and left the building. Eight months later, February 8, 1994, Crawford received a sentence of four years. The victim, Zombor, had emigrated with his family from Hungary. He had been hired temporarily to make repairs on the building. His parents, his widow and five small children survived him."

In the numerous newspaper accounts of the disaster, not one journalist suggested that Crawford might be suffering from a mental disorder. No account was recorded of his being examined by a doctor. One journalist suggested that had Zombor been a native-born American, Crawford might have received a longer sentence. In an article entitled "Would a Jinx Stop You", published on the opening of the Hicks Tavern, Friday, May 13, 1927, the journalist wrote, "Bob Hicks pays no attention to black cats crossing his path nor to other superstitions. The Hicks Tavern is now open and, see, it didn't burn down...." In those intervening years, between the end Bob's 'association dream' and the realization of the Hicks Tavern, the *Specialty Salesman Magazine,* flourished, with issues running from 140 to 170 pages,. Bob's prestige had grown in the publishing world. Politicians sought his favor and he readily responded. Always the extrovert, Bob took pride in his climb to financial success and basked in the praise received for his charitable donations. In the June, 1923, issue he wrote an editorial entitled "Bob's Philosophy":

Men, we can have what we want if we want it bad enough and if we will pay the price. "Prosperity's Price" is not money. "Prosperity's Price" is service first and then effort. Service means giving to get. Effort means "Hard Work". Yes, sir, we can accomplish anything within human possibilities if we will put our souls into our efforts to get what we want.... There are men that love their work, the kind that build permanently and eventually sign their names as presidents of big manufacturing institutions; but they worked, and they worked with their hands and their heads and they put their souls into their work.

Bob had a simple philosophy: Set goals, work earnestly and achievement follows. With complete frankness he boasted of his 'rags to riches' legend assuring his readers that "luck" is an elusive goddess, but "hard work" produces results.

Keynote Speaker for *Americana Encyclopedia*, 1926

At one of the annual conventions of the *Americana Encylopedia* held in New York City, the directors asked Bob to be the keynote speaker. At that period in time house to house salesmen sold encyclopedias. Those volumes of knowledge were the computers of today. The district managers choose bright, educated, poised young people generally, but older retired teachers often applied for positions.

Bob, Mae, little Margaret and Etta Ridenbaugh took the Pullman from Chicago to New York City and checked in at the Waldorf Astoria. In one of Mae's 'Memory Books' she pasted a postcard of the grand old hotel and carefully wrote beneath, "Daddy & I had Rm. 438 Little Margaret & Etta Rm. 410"

The following evening Mae accompanied Bob to the auditorium where approximately 1000 salesmen gathered. When Bob, a short man, stood on a small stool behind the podium, he shuffled his notes a few seconds and surveyed the audience, "I see you have a pretty big poster hanging on that back wall saying 'We Do Our Best'. I tell you it's a lie. Yes, it's a lie. Not one of us truly, honestly does his best." He immediately captured his listeners. Later his speech appeared in a book entitled *Noteworthy Speeches by American Orators*.

8

TRAVEL

THE GOVERNORS' CONVENTION

Bob's reputation as an entertaining, lively speaker continued to grow. In January of 1926 Bob addressed the annual meeting of the Women's Press Club of Indiana in Indianapolis. Mrs. Ed Jackson, wife of the Governor of Indiana, sat next to Bob at the head table. Bob liked women and they knew it. He appraised them with his smiling blue eyes in an intimate and flattering manner that aroused the feminine anima. Although in his sixties, he radiated a puckish, masculine charm quite appealing to women. Mrs. Jackson would not forget him.

A few months later Bob became the speaker at a dinner for the directors of the Wheeler Mission Home also held in Indianapolis. The Republican Governor Jackson, as one of the directors, attended. It was a serendipitous meeting for both men. Politicians need a favorable press and Bob took delight in associating with the "high and mighty" who also made good press.

For whatever reason the men became friendly. Bob, Mae and little Margaret visited the Governor's

Mansion where Margaret played with the Jackson's young son. In the Hicks family memorabilia there are photos of the two families sitting together on the veranda. The Jacksons motored north to stay with Bob and Mae at their home in South Whitley. A less violent age, no body guards accompanied the Governor's family. Little snippets in the local newspapers announced that the Jacksons were the houseguests of Bob and Mae.

In the March, 1926 issue of *The Speciality Salesman*, a six page article appeared, written by Bob, lauding the Jacksons for their simplicity and humility, their willingness to work among the poor. Work among the poor? Perhaps that is not the correct phrase. Mrs. Jackson read stories to a few carefully selected and chaperoned waifs now and then. The Governor occasionally read the Gospels to a few homeless men in the basement of one of the churches. It made good copy and tightened the friendship between the two men.

The Wheeler Rescue Mission directors invited Bob to join them as a director. He accepted with pleasure. The Indianapolis News July 12, 1926, duly noted that the Jacksons and the Hicks would attend the Board of Directors meeting and dinner on July 12, 1926.

A few days later newspapers announced that Bob had made an offer of a gift of $10,000.00 to the Mission if the people of Indianapolis would match it.

The annual convention of the U. S. Governors would be held in Wyoming that year. Bob approached Jackson. Would it be convenient for him and his family to attend? Bob would be pleased to be his host and to make all the arrangements. Yes, indeed, the Governor could set aside the time. Indiana needed to be represented at the National Convention.

Bob's staff quickly began making arrangements. They chartered a private railway car, The Philadelphia, with a chef and steward. The route mapped from Indianapolis to Cheyenne included stops at cities along the way so that the Governor and party could be welcomed by local dignitaries. Good publicity for the home-town newspapers.

When Bob assured Mae the 'Grand Tour' would take place, Mae drove to Ft. Wayne to buy clothes for the children and herself. Bob, who practiced strict economy at his office, instructed Mae to buy the best and put it on their charge account at Wolf & Dessaer Department Store. For their own formal apparel, they took the train to Chicago where Bob's new tailor measured him for two suits and a tuxedo. He accompanied Mae to Marshall Fields. An older saleswoman with an assistant led them to a room paneled with mirrors and furnished with comfortable armchairs. Bob instructed the saleswoman to show his wife only the latest fashion in dinner gowns. Finally Mae, with Bob's approval, selected two pastel chiffon dresses festooned with flashing stones. Mae, when told the price, blanched, but Bob grandly instructed the assistant to wrap them properly. The smiling saleswoman accompanied them to the door, assuring Mae it had been a pleasure to wait on her.

With all plans completed, *The Indianapolis Times* carried the following story on Thursday, July 22, 1925:

JACKSON TO START TRIP, Executive Plans include Governors' Convention, Park Tour

Governor Ed Jackson and his family will leave early Friday morning for an extended trip to the west in which he will attend the convention of Governors at Cheyenne, Wyo. July 29 to August 4. They will be the guests on the trip of Robert E. Hicks, South Whitley, and will travel in a special car, The Philadelphia. An all day stop will be made in Omaha Saturday and a four hour stop in Denver Sunday. The Governor will be entertained in Wyoming by special trips. An automobile tour of Yellowstone Park will begin July 31, requiring four days.

The private car will be detached at Yellowstone Park and the Governor and Mr. Hicks will return by way of Salt Lake City, Pueblo, Colorado Springs, Topeka, Kansas City and St. Louis.

The party consisted of the Governor and Mrs. Jackson, their four year old son, Eddie, Bob, Mae, their four children and Mrs. Ridenbaugh, little Margaret's nursemaid – ten persons total.

The stop in Omaha proved disappointing. The person in charge of the welcoming committee failed to receive the notice that the Indiana party traveled by private railway car and not with the group coming from the east. The newspaper reporter hurriedly wrote a disjointed article with the headline:

GOVERNORS FROM EAST to STOP HERE TODAY
Hoosier Executive, First to Visit on Way West,
Spends Pleasant Day Sightseeing

The twenty governors expected arrived the following day so the banquet the Jackson party had expected never took place. Instead a convoy of cars, hastily assembled, took them around the small city with several local dignitaries as guides. Bob had been prepared for a flag flying, band playing and an official welcome.

Departing Omaha late afternoon, they passed through Denver, arriving in Cheyenne on Sunday. At the station Governor Nellie Tayloe Ross, with a contingent of Cheyenne warriors, greeted them. The Governor invited them to join the party at The Plains Hotel that evening. The children and Mrs. Ridenbaugh stayed aboard The Philadelphia.

Mae wore one of her chiffon gowns for the occasion. As they left their stateroom, Bob gave her a little hug. "Nobody's got a prettier wife than I've got," he told her. The following two days the Governors met in conferences while the wives, children and other guests shopped at Indian Trading Posts and went sightseeing. In the evening of Tuesday, July 28, the special train of four Pullmans and two baggage cars provided by the Wyoming State Transportation Department left for the overnight trip to Casper. It is worthy of notice that only the Governor of Wyoming and the Governor of Indiana traveled in private railway cars.

Upon their arrival in Casper, chauffeured automobiles awaited to drive the guests to the Teapot Dome oil fields and Buffalo. The next stop was Sheridan, then on to Thermapolis to see the Hot Springs. Another night on the train brought them to Cody, then on to Yellowstone National Park. There is a photo in Mae's Memory Book of the journey – a bear stands on its hind legs, its head almost inside the car window while Mae feeds it a tasty morsel. It took the killing of many 'friendly" bears before the Park Rangers learned that wild bears are not always so friendly. There are pictures of Mae and Bob with Margaret standing between them in front of Old Faithful, photos of the entire group nestled in & around a stage coach with three-year-old Margaret in the lap of Governor Ross, and one of the cook, steward, Etta Ridenbaugh and Margaret standing on the rear platform of The Philadelphia. Unfortunately there is no picture of Mae and Bob at the formal banquet held at the Old Faithful Inn.

August 3, the Governors took the trains to Victor, Idaho, and back to Cheyenne. The Hicks/Jackson party reluctantly bid farewell to The Philadelphia's staff who had served them so well. They boarded a scheduled train for Indiana and home. When the photos were developed, Mae wrote a note to Mrs. Jackson including a set of the pictures. In due course, a polite 'thank you' note arrived from Mrs. Jackson which Mae enclosed in her 'memory book'. Not long after the Convention, Jackson became involved in a scandal dealing with the Ku Klux Klan and then was brought to court on a charge of bribing the former governor, McCray. Herbert Hoover later pardoned Jackson.

No real friendship had been formed between the two families and never again did Bob attempt to maintain the relationship. Jackson's cloudy term ended and he died in 1954 having suffered a stroke that left him bed-ridden the last five years of his life.

HAWAIIAN ISLANDS, 1927

Bob's life revolved around his magazine. Gardening was his only hobby. That rich Missouri soil had seeped into his veins as a boy and he never denied the pull of Mother Earth. But his magazine dominated his life. On the other hand, Mae, in mid-life, had married a wealthy man and her vision extended beyond a comfortable domestic life style. She wanted to see something of this world. No doubt it took some gentle yet persistent persuasion for her to convince Bob that his magazine would not shatter into shreds if he took his first vacation in eleven years. Mae dreamed of going to Hawaii and her tactics proved successful. The complicated travel arrangements proved too difficult for Bob's secretary, so four men on the executive staff volunteered to help. In October, after the November issue went to press, Bob, Mae and little Margaret motored to Chicago. As they passed through the gates of their home, Bob took out his pocket watch, saying, "What time did you say we'd be back?" His heart never left his office.

In Chicago they boarded 'The Chief' at the Dearborn Street Railway Station. The daily service from Chicago to Los Angeles had only recently been inaugurated. The train was advertised as "extra fine, extra fast, extra fare" and "only two business days on the way". The services included a barber shop, valet, ladies' maid, cigar store plus a shower bath in each private compartment. After leaving Chicago the train stopped at Kansas City, Albuquerque and Winslow to reach Los Angeles 63 hours later. Average speed was estimated at 43 miles per hour. Fred Harvey's Service provided all the meals. Bob, a man from a Horatio Alger novel, kept an eye on his checkbook—there was no need to have a 'drawing room' when a private compartment cost $25.00 less. Probably Bob spent considerable time in the men's smoking lounge, leaving Mae and four year old Margaret to find their own amusements.

Many years later Mae told her daughter an incident that happened on that trip:

You were lying in the top bunk when your father and I had a little tiff. For the life of me I can't remember what it was all about but he became annoyed, slamming the door as he left the compartment. I muttered, "Silly old man." You poked your head over the edge of the bunk and piped up, "And you're a silly old woman." Well, it taught me a lesson. Mae had the endearing quality of never denying her mistakes.

Upon arriving in Los Angeles they made their way to the Port where their ship, the *SS City of Honolulu*, berthed. Bob, a fugitive from justice back in 1903, had crossed the Atlantic to Southampton, but Mae had never been aboard an ocean liner in her life. Their steamer trunk, Bob's personal suitcase and Mae's hat boxes were hustled aboard. At the Purser's office a steward escorted them to their first class cabin. The *SS City of Honolulu* had been built in Germany in 1899 for the German American Line. By 1904 it had been purchased by the North German Lloyd Steamship Company. Sometime in 1917, during the First World War, the U. S. Navy seized the ship as a war prize. By 1921 the United States Steamship Co.

renamed her *Princess Matoika*. In 1926 she sailed
through the Panama Canal to Los Angeles, becoming
the property of the Los Angeles Steamship Co. and
was renamed *City of Honolulu*. Half as large as a 21st
century cruise ship, the *City of Honolulu* had all of the
amenities—breakfast, lunch and dinner interspersed
with ten-o'clock coffee with hot croissants and
cinnamon buns, four-o'clock tea time when dainty
watercress and cucumber sandwiches were served
and, after the floor show, a midnight supper, buffet
style. Bob, up early, ate breakfast in the dining room
while Mae elected to have Margaret's and hers served
in the stateroom. At ten AM Mae would take Margaret
to the children's playroom where two aspiring
teachers entertained the youngsters until lunch time.
The second evening out the captain invited Bob and
Mae to dine at his table. Mae wore a pale cream-
colored, ankle-length, sleeveless, chiffon gown
studded with fake pearls. Bob, a short, over-weight
man, took pride in his attractive, hazel-eyed wife,
twenty years his junior. On the other hand, Mae could
be embarrassed by Bob's brash manner; however, he
knew the art of story- telling, captivating his audience
with remembrances of early days in Kansas and
Oklahoma. On a calm day Mae sat in her assigned
deck chair, often reading stories to Margaret who
liked to snuggle against her. A deck steward carefully
tucked a blanket over them. If Mae began to doze, her

voice faltering, Margaret would nudge her mother in the ribs impatiently. "Read, Mama, read."

Margaret never forgot the voice of her mother reading fairy tales for her.

As the ship docked in Honolulu, the U.S. Navy Band played a raucous greeting and single engine Navy planes flew over. Mysteriously, the ship caught on fire while docked in Honolulu. Not long after, the stock market crash of 1929 brought a halt to luxury travel. The days of wine and roses gave way to soup kitchens for the jobless. The insurance company settled the owners' claim three years later when the burned out 'old lady' was towed to Japan for scrap. A chauffeur held high a sign for The Royal Hawaiian. The 'Pink Lady,' as the hotel is often called, remains one of the finest five star hotels in the Pacific, along with the Peninsular in Hong Kong and the Stamford in Singapore. The Royal Hawaiian had opened in February, 1927, only eight months prior to the Hicks' arrival. There is no record of the amount Bob paid for their three week stay. In 2013 the prices ranged from $375.00 to $1500.00 per night, no extras included.

When the limousine pulled up to the curb at the entrance, two doormen hurried to open the doors. Bob sat in the front seat by the driver as he always liked to do. Two dark eyed Hawaiian girls in hula skirts put leis of hibiscus and fragapani round their necks. They were escorted to their bungalow in the tropical gardens as soon as Bob gave his name. For Mae it was magical.

In 1927 the rich sailed to the Islands for holidays. In his magazine Bob took great pleasure writing of his own financial prosperity, but the purpose was to impress upon his readers the concept "if I can do it, you can do it." He boasted of the long hours of work that brought him success, but felt a little sheepish spending those hard-earned dollars on frivolities, as he considered holidays to be. Consequently only one reluctant allusion to the trip found its way into *The Specialty Salesman.*

The W. J. Thompson family, learning of Bob's arrival, soon contacted him. The Rev. W. J. Thompson, D. D., pastor of the First Foreign Church, Hilo, held a position of some importance in the local, as well as the foreign, community. Perhaps through church newsletters he had heard of Bob's charity; however it came about, the Thompsons became the tour guides for the Hicks family. They saw the volcanoes, Hale Maumau and Kilauea, sugarcane and pineapple plantations, and they dined at the parsonage at 506 Puueo Avenue, Hilo. No doubt Bob made a suitable donation to the church. On the 16th of November the Thompsons escorted the family to the pier where Bob, Mae, and Margaret boarded the Matson liner, the SS Manoa. The Thompsons presented Mae with a small album of postcards of Hilo and photographs of the church and a sentimental poem written by the good Reverend. The memento remains with the family.

Mae focused her 16mm Kodak movie camera, catching the excitement, but not the cacophonous energy. As the great engines of the ship began to throb, men struggled with the heavy ropes looped over the bollards, passengers threw colored streamers into the crowd ashore, the band played "Good Night, Ladies, It's Time to Say Goodbye", the ship's sonorous horn boomed and Bob held Margaret high as she waved enthusiastically to everyone. It was a final grand finale to Hawaii as none of the three ever returned to the Islands.

The ship sailed for seven days, crossing 2400 miles of the Pacific to reach San Francisco—days of leisure and pleasure for Mae. Given Bob's dedication to his work, he may have been pleased to see the shoreline of California come into view. The ship docked the morning of November 23.

Ashore they took a taxi to the Palace Hotel. Let Bob narrate what happened: *My friend, Arthur Nash, was in my mind that day in the lobby of the The Palace Hotel in San Francisco, when a stranger introduced himself to me and a moment later told me Arthur Nash was dead.*

I could not speak. I could not think. I grew suddenly weak and found a chair. What was this man telling me? It seemed it could not be true. Arthur Nash – my friend - closer than any brother could be –dead? The enormity of it overcame me, dulled and stupefied me, as the full sense of my great loss and the world's loss began to creep into my comprehension....In Arthur Nash the world saw a vigorous man holding firmly to certain high ideals and making them function in his business. The world called him astute, wise, able and gave him credit for sincerity. But I saw more. I saw a man whose heart was always filled with sympathy, who felt the worries, fears and griefs of his fellow men touching his own life, who used his ideals not as a policy but because they were right. I saw a man so moved by his desire to help that many a time I have seen him borrow large sums of money in order to help some worthy person or cause. I saw a man willing and anxious to give, not only of his substance but also of himself, his time, his thoughts, his labor. He was generous, not because he could be but because what he gave was needed; his philosophy of life made generosity an obligation if he were to be true to himself. Perhaps the true worth of a man can be measured by the respect given at his funeral. The following report by R. A. Dunkelberg appeared in the December, 1927, issue of *The Specialty Salesman: I attended the funeral held at the Walnut Hills Masonic Temple, Cinncanati. A number of thousand men &*

women passed before the casket where the body of Arthur Nash lay in state. At the funeral services it was impossible for more than part of the throng to crowd into the hall. Hundreds were crowded at the entrance and more stood on the lawn in front of the Temple.... In the 21st century, one can find at least eight references to Arthur Nash on the Internet.

In general, men differ dramatically from women where friendship is concerned. Women confide in their female friends—their joys, their disappointments, their dreams, their fears. Men have business associates with whom they discuss business, their golfing partners with whom they play golf, and their fishing buddies with whom they fish, but conversations stay on an unemotional level. Men do not readily make new friends as women will. Bob was the exception to the rule. Bob and Arthur met in middle age but they saw in each other a kindred spirit and became close friends. They shared their ideas, ideals, and plans for the future. They were true friends.

A Foray into Politics

In his magazine, Bob shied away from politics. The *Specialty Salesman* educated and supported salesmen. Though Bob felt strongly about the candidates in the 1928 election, he expressed his opinion elsewhere.

In that year, Democrat Alfred Smith ran against Republican Herbert Hoover for the Presidency of the United Sates—Hoover, a dour, conservative candidate, against an ebullient, gregarious Smith. Both had held important political positions—Smith as Governor of New York and Hoover as Secretary of Commerce under President Calvin Coolidge.

Hoover's campaign posters suggested that the current prosperity of America rested on the good foresight of Hoover to maintain the status quo. Smith wanted to repeal the 18th Amendment—Prohibition. He backed the Progressive Movement promoting better protection of rights for the Negro in the South. (When the November election came, five Southern States, normally Democratic, voted Republican—To keep the status quo.)

Most damning of all in the minds of conservative Protestant Americans, Smith was a practicing Roman Catholic of Catholic immigrants. Newspapers and magazines around the country published cartoons of Smith seated in the Oval Office, with the Pope whispering in his ear, another Rasputin to Alexander ll. Ministers, from their pulpits of various faiths, encouraged the fear of 'foreign influence' among their parishioners. Bob ranked 'bigotry' foremost among the Seven Deadly Sins. For the first time, Bob, a Republican, wholeheartedly supported the Democratic platform. For Bob a man could not be judged by his religion or the color of his skin. One does not preach hatred from a Christian church.

To support Smith, Bob wrote and published a political broad-sheet, "The Hornet," advocating for Smith. All to no avail—Hoover won by a landslide. Nowadays, a few copies of "The Hornet" are to be found in the stacks of the Whitley County Public Library, South Whitley, Indiana.

Sometime during Bob's busy year of 1927, U. S. Representative Hogg of Indiana arranged an interview for Bob with President Calvin Coolidge. Bob immediately made reservations at the Mayflower Hotel in Washington, D.C. and left by train for the Capital. Bob arrived at the White House at the specified time and was escorted to the door of the Oval Office. When introduced to the President, one may assume Bob was respectful and subdued. When exiting the santum santorum two reporters questioned Bob:

"Mr. Hicks, what did you and the President discuss?" Bob answered immediately, "We stared at each other for four minutes."

Apparently, Coolidge deserved his pseudonym of "Silent Cal":

In the Christmas issue of his magazine, 1928, Bob wrote an article entitled "God Speed You." He had sold the *Specialty Salesman*. To dedicated readers the news came as a surprise because to them he seemed indestructible. The word 'retirement' still did not exist in Bob's vocabulary even though he would celebrate his 71st birthday within a few weeks. It had been a word Bob used only when referring to others, not himself.

Bob, reluctant to face the facts, had finally submitted to Mae's gentle urging to admit the truth—his lack of energy betrayed him. No longer did he spring out of bed ready for a day full of decisions. Some of his habits had not changed to any degree. When he arrived at the plant, he made the rounds of the various departments, stopping to exchange a few words with various employees, calling each by his first name. He had made a point of establishing personal relationships with his workers just as he had with his readers. Yet the time had come to sell. He reminded himself he would find other challenges in due course.

Pearly Bishop, Bob's long-time attorney in Chicago, put out 'feelers' for prospective buyers. Soon the sale had been made and the legal papers signed. No longer would the cover of the magazine carry 'Edited by Robert E. Hicks.' That line had been replaced, through temporary courtesy, by 'Founded by Robert E. Hicks.' Soon his name would not be mentioned at all.

Bob moved his office to the Hicks Tavern. Prior to the official announcement of the sale in December, a banquet honoring Bob's long career as a publisher and editor took place at the Tavern. Some 26 gentlemen of the Fourth Estate gathered to confer the distinction of Editor Emeritus upon the retiree.

Charles L. Benjamin, keynote speaker for the evening, the publisher and editor of Printer's Ink and Beardslee Speaks, gave a fitting tribute to Bob's courageous fight against those who use fallacious advertising methods to rob the innocent. Several more distinguished speakers followed, each praising Bob for his sterling business practices and his foremost ability as an editor.

Only E. P. Joy, Bob's step-son, cast light on Bob's domestic life:

I am sure that all of us are more or less familiar with the stories which appear in the press at frequent intervals about this or that celebrity or well known personage. It seems that some of these people live a sort of Dr. Jekyll and Mr. Hyde live.. ... I have had occasion to be out front as well as back stage, during the last few years, in the life of Mr. Hicks, because my mother is Mrs. Hicks and I have made his home my home; and I want you gentlemen to know that Mr. Hicks is just the same back stage as he is out front. True, he rears and tears and raves occasionally but he does that out front so that's all even.

Perhaps Mr. Hicks does not realize it but ever since I have known him, he has been a constant source of inspiration to me.

Some ten years ago I was connected with a branch

of our naval service called the Coast Guard. One day near the end of my enlistment I received a letter from Mr. Hicks , which was written in his usual inspirational style, and shortly after my discharge, I came here to South Whitley to work in his printing plant and to learn the trade. Personally, I feel as some of the other gentlemen present here must feel, a great deal of responsibility resting on my shoulders.

A few days ago Mr. Hicks sent me a wire engaging me as plant manager of the new organization. As I said, I feel that I have quite a responsibility resting upon my shoulders – not only am I confronted not only with the task of improving our publication from a printing standpoint, but I have the added duty imposed upon me of carrying into the new organization some of the ideals which were instilled in me by Mr. Hicks. I feel as though I am one of the abutments on this bridge that runs between the old and the new. Mr. Hicks, I will not fail you. I will do my utmost to carry into the new organization under Mr. Bligh's management some of the ideals which you have instilled in me.

Mr. Bligh, I look toward the future with a great deal of anticipation as I feel that under your able direction we will carry on and on.

After the extravagant four course dinner, the guests mellowed by aged Scotch and French aperitifs, the female entertainer made her appearance as reported in *Specialty Salesman:*

It was fitting that the cap sheaf of entertainment be added. Little Margaret Hicks, daughter of the guest of the evening, entertained with a number of solo dances. As her dancing showed considerable versatility, along with a technique equal to that of many older dancers on the operatic stage, the company called her back again and again. Mr. B. C. Bean, a distinguished editor of some forty years, presented Bob with the certificate of Editor Emeritus trusting that Bob would enjoy the fruits of his achievements with pleasure for many years to come. The gentlemen raised their glasses to toast the honoree. Bob rose slowly to his feet to thank his colleagues for the accolades bestowed upon him; however he could not refrain from telling a little story of how a Cincannati church had recently offered to place a bronze bust of him in front of the building after he had donated 50,000.00 to the building fund. He modestly had declined the honor.

Why did Bob's ego need bolstering? He had won considerable respect and esteem for his work in defending the innocent from mail order swindlers. He had defeated his blackmailers by publicly admitting his crime. There are American presidents who might have profited by his example. Through hard work, determination and skill he had built a national publication from a bankroll of $200.00. He had proved himself to be a man among men. Bob waxed sentimental in the last part of his speech:

In accepting this honor, I also feel that it will be an honor for my little Margaret for in the days to come, when I sit on the porch of my home here and look out over the lawn and see the flowers and my little girl playing around, and I can say ,"Margaret, your father has known despair and tragedy, but look at this honor that has been conferred upon him; for all that is past he has paid in full."

I appreciate your coming down here, gentlemen, to be present at the dinner given in my honor. It will be one of the pleasant recollections of my life and I thank you.

Over Bob's desk hung a sign: *More Men Are Buried in Ruts than in Cemeteries.* He did not plan to sit on his porch watching the grass grow.

9

RETIREMENT

With the magazine sold, Bob looked for new worlds to conquer. Mae provided the answer. "Why should we stay in South Whitley? You don't like the winters any more than I do. What about taking a look at Florida?" she asked. She had no wish to spend the remainder of her life in a small village in Indiana isolated from the big world she had begun to know.

For Bob Florida was new territory, and for Mae, the place of her birth and girlhood. De Funiak Springs in northwest Florida lies approximately fifteen miles south of the Alabama border. Many of Mae's cousins continued to live on the family farms they had occupied since Andrew Jackson had herded the Native Americans off this land. Bob's reputation as a Northerner with gold coins lining his pockets quickly brought him to the attention of Realtor Robert E. Lee McCaskill who chauffeured him through the "piney woods" of Walton County. In spite of the monotony of the landscape—mile after mile of scrub oak and pine trees occasionally enlivened by a few dogwood and redbud trees—Bob bought 5,500 acres. In his mind's eye he envisioned commercial investments in housing projects, reforestation of timber and canning factories.

R.E. L. McCaskill then drove Bob and Mae to Bay County near Sunnyside Beach where he showed them a 188-acre tract overlooking Lake Powell to the south and the Gulf of Mexico to the west. Mae immediately responded to the natural beauty—the oaks festooned with Spanish moss, a native American midden, the broad white sand beach and the pristine solitude of nature.

Bob, seeing her delight, took her by the hand saying, "This is your land, your place, with no strings attached." The old lion had not forgotten how to please a woman.

Returning to De Funiak, McCaskill had Flournoy draw up the bills of sale and without further ado, Bob signed the papers. The Feb. 28, 1929 issue of *The Breeze* weekly carried a three-column article announcing the incorporation of the Hicks-McCaskill Development Company. Bob, as financial backer, automatically became president and McCaskill the administrative head in charge of sales. Once again Bob had accepted at face value a 'friend' for a business colleague. Considering the amount of land they now owned, Mae and Bob selected an uninspiring twenty-acre parcel on which to build their new home. The house faced the Old Spanish Trail as well as the railroad tracks running from Jacksonville to Mobile,

Alabama. To be honest, Walton County is flat, bleak land; however, an article in *The Breeze* gave an explanation:

...Mr. Robert E. Hicks of North Whitley, Indiana, a banker and capitalist of very large resources and president of the Hicks-McCaskill Development Co. has himself purchased 20 acres facing the Old Spanish Trail on which development has begun. On this he is about to erect a costly Spanish style bungalow which will be an ornament to the county and a most attractive advertisement to tourists who cannot avoid seeing it as they pass.

Returning to De Funiak from a short trip, Bob asked McCaskill to recommend a contractor. McCaskill and Bob selected the site. Mae studied the plans with the builder, explaining in detail what type of house she wanted. Bob happily turned the project over to her. She had a talent, a native talent, for house design. Mae envisioned no colonial plantation mansion of the 'old South'. She wanted a house that hugged the earth, a modern house. She and the contractor finally settled on a rectangle shape with a room at each end running the width of the short end of the rectangle. The one to the west became Bob's office with a desk for himself and one for his secretary. The other end of the room had a sofa, coffee table and comfortable armchairs flanked by reading lamps, At the opposite end of the house, the same size room held three beds (more could be added if the occasion demanded) to serve as a dormitory for weekend house guests. Both of these rooms had the appearance of sun rooms with eight windows.

The front door opened into a hallway that led to the living room and continued to the four bedrooms and dormitory. Each bedroom was separated from the other by a bathroom with a bathtub, shower, lavatory, toilet and bidet—a European bath accessory Mae had admired a trip to Havana. The living room's fireplace shared a chimney with the dining room's fireplace. The wall separating the rooms had an archway giving access. The kitchen off the dining room held a commercial sized refrigerator, two stoves—one electric and one wood-burning with a large oven—a double sink, a long row of shelves, cabinets and counter space and a table with chairs for the cook. At the rear of the kitchen a door led to the paved parking area and the two-car garage, quite inadequate for the five cars the family owned. Next to the steps leading into the kitchen, were steps leading down to the cellar, housing the furnace that heated the 3,864 square-feet of living quarters (smaller than the South Whitley home, but still spacious).

Some distance behind the main house was a two-room frame house, the home of some prior owners. Now it served as a servant house. The primitive bathroom for the Negro help was located in the pump room directly behind the garage. The former owners had planted the now mature pecan trees that had survived years of neglect and were scattered over the grounds. Mae immediately set about reviving them. The entrance to the grounds was guarded by two fourteen-foot tall brick columns crowned by electric coach lanterns supporting twelve-foot high wrought iron gates. The driveway curved around the side of the house. By the end of 1929 the entire family moved in, including Etta Ridenbaugh, who slept in a bedroom with Margaret. Helen and Phoebe shared a large bedroom and young Bob had the bedroom next to his parents. The little black and white pony, Peggy, had been brought south by trailer and had her stall in the big red barn along with two registered Jersey cows and a pair of handsome dark brown mules. The tack room, with a strong lockable door, housed the various plows, harnesses, pony cart, farm tractor and other farm implements. Bob hired an overseer, instructing him to hire other white men as necessary. A certain number of acres were set aside for truck farming— corn, beans, black-eyed pea, peanuts, soybeans and sugarcane. The aroma of the freshly turned earth brought a lump to Bob's throat as he reminisced about his boyhood on the little farm in Missouri.

Helen, a graduate of St. Mary of Notre Dame Academy, enrolled in Florida State College for Women, Tallahassee, while Phoebe and Bob and

Margaret attended the private school misleadingly named Palmer College because the curriculum included first through sophomore class of college. Mae shuttled the students the six miles from Alpine Heights to De Funiak.

The lawyer, Colonel Flournoy, seemed anxious to integrate his family of three daughters and three sons into the Hicks family, often arranging a picnic at the lake or a croquet game at his home. It is likely he and Miss Alice, his wife, hoped for a closer connection between one of their sons and Helen or Phoebe; however, Eleanor, the youngest of the Flournoys, and Margaret became devoted friends.

A few remarks upon the character of the Colonel would be pertinent to mention as the story of his relationship with the Hicks family unfolds. He always dressed the part of proper Southern gentleman, carried himself well and attended the Presbyterian church regularly. On the other hand, the colonel had a saying that six-year-old Margaret didn't understand but knew wasn't true. Why would a grown-up tell a lie? *You can tell an honest' negrow' because he'll have hair growing in his palms'.*

HAVANA, CUBA 1929

Mae had a cousin, John Wilford, who had taken up residence in Havana, married a Cuban woman and founded and edited the largest English written newspaper on the island, *The Havana Morning Post*. What better excuse did Mae have to persuade Bob to visit Havana?

Bob had been tinkering with the idea of having his life story written. His executive secretary, George Peabody, had worked for Bob for two years. Peabody encouraged his boss's idea and put himself forward as the best man to do the best job. Havana, removed from all distractions of other business, seemed a perfect spot to start the biography.

"George, what do you think about going down to Cuba? I'm not much on leaving the good old USA but Mrs. Hicks has a cousin down there and she wants to meet him again. So, if it makes her happy I'm glad to do it."

"That sounds good to me, sir. Never been out of the States but I'm game."

"All right, George. Let's see. You got a wife and, is it, two children?

"Yes, sir, my girl's twelve and my son's nine."

"All right, George. Ask your wife if she would like to go with us – the children as well. Give Mrs. Hicks a call or drop by the house. Get the name of that cousin of hers. He publishes a newspaper down there so he must know something about the place. Ask him to help you make reservations and anything else you think of. I think we take a boat out of Tampa, but you find out."

George went home that evening to tell his family the news. His son, Rodney, thirty years later, remembered that evening and wrote the following: *In 1929 when Mr. Bob Hicks my dad's boss, decided to go to Cuba & asked my dad to go along & help him in some of his business deal's in Cuba & outline his life's story, we didn't know he included our whole family – Dad and Mom & Janice & me. Janice & I were jumping for joy. Dad was going to drive the 1928 Whippet sedan clear to Key West & take it to Cuba, too, so he could drive Mr. Hicks here & there. We left South Whitley, Indiana, toward the end of February. After 4 days of getting lost most of the time, we finally came to the last Key where the road ended. We met and joined up with the Hicks' there. We boarded a small ocean liner along with the Whippet that went in the hold & we took off for the 90 mile cruise. The Hicks' had their little daughter, Margaret, and she & I had the run of the ship. We were all over that ship & no one ever said a word to us unless we were in a dangerous area. I think Mr. Hicks knew the captain or something like that He knew everybody every place we went. His wife, Mae, told me to watch out for Margaret so I did. I was nine years old and she was six & full of fun & energy & being Bob Hicks' daughter was a huge plus. With Margaret & I running hither & yon all over that ship nobody said a word to us. They must have known who her father was. I made sure nothing happened to her & no two kids ever had so much fun. Margaret was used to important people and a Captain's uniform didn't impress her one bit. But everyone just loved her and she really was a sweet little girl & was nice to everybody. Mr. Hicks rented a house for us in Havana and all the people around us were so nice. Janice and I even learned a few words of Spanish...*

In the 1920's Havana had become the playground for American 'rum runners,' gangsters, the 'idle rich' and business men who had a hand in commercial dealings. Cuba had vast sugarcane plantations and did a thriving export business with the States. The U.S. exported to Cuba machinery, steel, and electrical wiring. It proved economically serendipitous for both countries.

Bob and Mae's cousin Wilford, with a common interest, liked one another, to Mae's delight. Wilford took them to his home in the Vedado to meet his wife, Teresa Maria, and his son, Heriberto. They became frequent dinner guests, although it was somewhat awkward as Teresa spoke no English and the Hickses no Spanish.

They went to the Havana American Jockey Club on Sundays to watch the horses run and to dine. They visited Morro Castillo, built by the Spaniards in 1589. As always Mae recorded their visit with her camera as well as her new state-of-the-art 16 mm. Bell & Howell movie camera. The photos were later pasted in the Memory Book. One particular evening Wilford escorted them to the San Souci Night Club for a performance by the famous Josephine Baker, a mulato dancer who had become the 'rage' in France. On stage Ms. Baker, wrapped in a flowing cape of scarlet satin trimmed in white fur, descended a broad staircase. At the foot of the stairs she flung the cape aside to reveal her naked body.

Margaret, wide-eyed, leaned against her mother to exclaim in a stage whisper, "She forgot to put her dress on". Mae admitted later that she was as shocked as her daughter.

Wilford had arranged for them to stay at the Royal Palms Hotel as Mae did not intend to 'keep house' while on holiday. They ate their meals at the roof garden restaurant with a view of Morro Fortress and the azure sea that stretched to the shores of Florida. Many years later, at a picnic on the beach near La Jolla, Margaret remarked that the steak had the same flavor as the meat she had eaten those many years ago in Havana.

"Is that right?" her host inquired, "Well, it's horse meat."

Wilford suggested that Margaret be enrolled in the first grade at the convent of La Imaculada Conception so she would have an early indoctrination in Spanish. Mae pasted the registration papers in the Memory

Book, writing on the edge of the page "A school Margaret attended for a short time." The budding student lasted five days.

"I don't know what they say," Margaret explained to her mother.

The day before their departure aboard the *S/S Cuba.* the March 15 issue of the *Havana Morning Post* carried a two column article with an impressive photo of Bob entitled "Robert E. Hicks, Internationally Known Writer,Philanthropist, Expresses Pleasure with Havana"

The article quoted Mae as being absolutely enchanted with the people, the architecture and the beauty of Havana, promising that the family would return. Bob told of his new land purchase in Florida and his extensive plans to build a housing project for writers where they could pursue their craft. The newspaper article noted that Bob was editor emeritus of *Specialty Salesman* Magazine. "Mr. Hicks solicited no advertising; he held that the publication was interested first in the welfare of its readers and he insisted upon exposing fraudulent concerns no matter whom they might be or how powerful they were."

'No doubt,' Mr. Hicks said, 'this unusual policy had something to do with the magazine's success. Others said I would fail, but I thought I knew my public.

That he did is proved by the phenomenal success of his publication.... It returned him well over a million dollars and was sold last fall for nearly half a million more.

Now, ably assisted by Mrs. Hicks, he is planning an even greater service to his people. He has purchased over five thousand acres of land in NW Florida, near DeFuniak Springs, and is proposing to develop it. But this is to be a unique development. He is not conducting it as a money making scheme, but as a matter of building homes for people who need them. He will not sell the bare land to anyone. Each purchaser will get a complete home with roads built, house built, land planted, everything prepared for immediate success and no one who does not furnish evidence of ability to make good will be permitted to undertake to settle there. In a word, Mr. Hicks will attempt to come as close to guaranteeing the success of the venture as is humanly possible.

'I am not interested in profits,' Mr. Hicks said, "I have enough & if in ten years I can drive through that section & see a happy community of home owners prosperous and contented that will be reward enough.

The Peabodys with the four cylinder Whippet and the Hickses boarded the ship the morning of March 16. At Key West George and family disembarked. The Hickses sailed on to Tampa where their Lincoln had been stored.

The Retreat from Havana

Rodney Peabody wrote his version of their return to De Funiak Springs:

Dad had to make telephone calls and send telegrams to set up meetings for Mr. Hicks with some business men in De Funiak. The main road skirted the spooky Everglades. Every place looked the same. We traveled 2 or 3 hundred miles along those swamps & De Funiak still looked a long way away on Dad's map....

We finally got on the last leg from Tallahassee when one of those storms hit & I never saw such a downpour. In half an hour there was water everywhere. Dad couldn't see to drive so he pulled over to wait it out but that didn't happen. So Dad said, "I'm going to try to make it to the next town". Luckily we did. Dad found a telegraph station and started sending wires all over trying to find the Hicks', but he couldn't locate them any place. He was quite worried as it just kept raining.

Mom and Dad talked it over & decided to keep going as far as we could and at least locate the Hicks'. He had his head out the window so he could see & was soaking wet. In fact, we all were. It was still early in the afternoon.

Suddenly up ahead we could see men with lanterns. A man jumped out in front of us and told us to stop. We had come to the Apalatchicola River although now it was water gushing as far as you could see. Big logs and whole trees came tearing along with the current and banging into the bridge abutments. A gang of men with poles and ropes kept trying to push the logs and trees & chicken houses& roofs of houses & all other kinds of stuff that floats. It was a terrible sight. On a sudden thought Dad asked a fellow if a yellow Lincoln with an old man and his wife and six year old daughter had crossed the bridge. The fellow said, "I remember the car and the people but we didn't have the bridge fixed up then. They got in a rowboat with an outboard motor and went across that way and there is the car back in town in a parking lot. It was very dangerous to go out in that mess in a rowboat as a log could bang a hole in the boat at any time or the motor could conk out. They had to go almost directly upstream because of the current and took most of an hour, but the word came back that they made it. The lady was a nervous wreck but the little girl thought it was a lot of fun. The old man was O.K. too.

With the help of the men, the Whippet and its family crossed the bridge and arrived into De Funiak about midnight. *Dad started calling hotels to find the Hicks' & finally did. We were so relieved to learn they were safe & sound. Margaret was conked out in bed but Bob & Mrs. Hicks stayed up to wait for word about us. They were so thankful that we had made it*

O.K. And then we all went to bed.

Next day we got together at dinner & told our stories. Margaret was still pretty groggy but she still thought that it was real fun. Mrs. Hicks said that logs bumped into their boat several times but by luck & prayer it didn't turn over.

Next day Dad & Mr. Hicks met with two men (Robert E. Lee McCaskill & Col. Wm. Flourney)& talked business or whatever. I was put in charge of Margaret which made me very proud.

Mr. Hicks had already rented us a nice house and they stayed at the Walton Hotel. We stayed in the "Springs" about a month. Mr. Hicks finally got the yellow Lincoln back when the river subsided and we drove all over the countryside looking at land - mostly piney woods & sand, I thought. Anyway he bought a couple thousands of acres & got the deal all settled. Dad had been taking notes on Mr. Hicks' life story every chance he could & had it pretty well outlined. The trip home was boring & monotonous after all we had seen & done. We all agreed that Cuba was a great place but Home is a lot better.

There is no explanation why Bob made the decision to hire a motorized rowboat to take them across the Apalachicola River in flood. They could have found some type of lodgings in the town, possibly Marianna, where they left their car. Mae undoubtedly was frightened but not enough to prevent her from filming the tops of houses and the expanse of turgid water surging past. The event made little impression on Margaret but she enjoyed watching the home movie later.

Mae thoroughly enjoyed Cuba and her cousin, John Wilford. After Bob died, she and Margaret returned often to Havana where they were always welcomed by their kin.

LIFE AT THE SPANISH TRAIL HOUSE

Bob's office on the northwest end of the house had two large desks, one for Bob and another for his secretary. Beside standard office equipment, there were comfortable chairs, sofa, coffee table, reading lamps and practical rugs on the hardwood parquet floor. The office had its own outside door thus ensuring family privacy, as not only local businessmen but also his field hands occasionally dropped by to see Bob, usually to ask for an advance on their pay. Bob, sitting in the seat of power, lectured the supplicant on the value of thrift, and gave him the money. From the office, a door led into the living room with its handsome Spanish tiled fireplace, flanked by recessed ceiling high bookcases. An impressive five-tiered Bohemian crystal chandelier hung from the ceiling. Two sofas, one backed by a teak refectory table, a radio housed in a cabinet with carved legs, a reading lamp by Bob's outsized comfortable armchair did not overwhelm the large room. In one corner stood a brightly hand-painted Chinese cabinet that opened into a desk with many small cubicles and drawers. Mae kept the household accounts there. A twenty-six-foot Persian carpet covered the floor's center, with smaller carpets scattered about. A non-pretensious, comfortable room, it suited the family.

The living room opened into the dining room through an archway. The rooms, identical in size with their fireplaces sharing the same chimney, differed only in furnishings. Another crystal chandelier hung over the banquet-sized mahogany table that, when extended by its four leaves, seated twelve diners.. Bob had ordered the hand-crafted furniture suite for the South Whitley home in 1923, from The Royal Furniture Co. of Grand Rapids, Michigan, one of the premier furniture companies of the time. Not counting the twelve dining-table chairs (four stored in the garage) there were five pieces in total—china cabinet, large sideboard, small buffet, fireplace bench and the table. It is believed that an artisan, perhaps German, and his three sons, working for the Royal Company, built three of these labor-intensive suites. A bell to summon the cook had been put in the floor at the head of the table. The family regularly ate dinner in the dining room, and now and then when she was not being observed or being ignored, Margaret would slip under the table to press the bell and quickly regain her seat. When the cook came into the dining room, Mae would gently scold Margaret, saying, "It is not nice to call Mary when we don't need her. Be a good girl."

Breakfast and lunch came on demand, unless Bob or Mae had visitors. Occasionally Margaret and Auntie ate at Mary's table in the kitchen. Dinner time in the evening brought the family together. Mary, the Negro cook, would place the platter of roast beef or pork loin in front of Bob, who carved it. The other dishes passed from hand to hand around the table. Bob thoughtfully sipped his double whiskey and water. By the time Mary cleared the table and brought the dessert, Bob began to eat. The main door, entered through an open vestibule, led into a hall. On the left side an archway opened into the living room. At the end of the hallway stood a fine Grandfather clock with Westminster chimes. The hall made a sharp turn to lead to the kitchen and the bedrooms and dormitory at the east end of the house.

Bob and Mae had the Master bedroom, Phoebe and Helen shared another, Bob had his own room and Margaret and "Auntie" Etta slept in the fourth. The dormitory with eight windows served a number of purposes other than as a sleeping room for weekend guests. Three single beds stood in a row with bedside tables and reading lamps by each. "Auntie" used the space for her quilting. Mae sorted her photographs and postcards to paste in family albums. Margaret had her own desk for homework as well as book shelves for her 'library.'

A simple two room frame house stood on the property when Bob bought the land. It served as a servant house when the family moved into their new home. Bathroom facilities for the cook were in the pump room behind the garage that also served as a laundry room.

A considerable distance behind the servant house stood a typical mid-western, red barn with great doors giving access to a hay wagon and heavy farm equipment. It housed three Jersey milk cows with soft brown eyes, two handsome mules and Peggy the pony. A tack room had space for the pony cart, the small farm tractor, and tools. The hen house, with Rhode Island Reds and a magnificent rooster, leaned against the outside back wall of the barn. Every week Mary would slaughter one of the chickens behind the kitchen. Once and only once Margaret heard the squawking of a hen and went round the corner of the house just in time to see the cook wring the chicken's neck and drop it on the grass. The hen desperately flapped its wide-spread wings, its head lolling this way and that, in its death agony. Margaret, aghast at the ebbing of life, did not wait to see Mary plunge the body into boiling water.

Whoever had lived in the frame house in the past

had planted a few pecan trees, now fully mature in spite of neglect. Mae set about landscaping the grounds. Within a few months flowers and shrubs bloomed, trees put out new leaves and the carpet of grass took on an Irish green. Rather than a watch dog, Mae purchased guinea fowl. Sprinkled black and white with garnet red combs and an alarming screech, the flock gave a new energy to the landscape.

Bob would be the head of this household for two years seven months.

Life had changed drastically for Bob. He continued to dream big dreams but no longer did he have the stimulation of being asked to be the keynote speaker at the general assembly of a national company. No longer did he fraternize with men running the government of America, legislators, senators and governors. No longer did he travel to Chicago, Indianapolis, New York or Philadelphia to meet with prominent men of commerce. Being the 'big fish' in the small pond of DeFuniak Springs, isolated from the hurley-burley of cities where 'progress' took place, he knew he was slipping away from the life that had made him the man he had become.

THE LAST YEARS

Bob's high hopes for a land development project that served the hard-working, 'salt of the earth' farmers did not materialize. Bob did build a service station cum grocerystore with living quarters a half-mile from his home, and a German-Swiss couple took over its operation; however, his extensive acreage along the Old Spanish Trail remained unsettled and forlorn.

Regarding the Hicks-McCaskill Development Corporation, with Bob as president and McCaskill the man in charge of development, nothing happened. The Great Depression had spread a black cloud over the land, and idealistic fresh adventures fell by the wayside. Not only America but all her neighbors felt the repercussions of the stock market crash. On the home front Mae, curious about her family, contacted cousins, most of whom she had never met. They continued to live on depleted farms that had belonged to great-grandparents and would be inherited by their semi-educated heirs. One, Jeff Davis, had the good fortune to graduate from high school and worked at the post office in De Funiak Springs. Mae, respecting ambition and learning, was appalled by the general apathy of her Davis clan. They had their unproductive land in Walton County and that suited them; better to stay with what they knew rather than venture into the unknown.

Bob loved the land and set about making his 180-acre farm the most productive in the area. He had his farm hands plant corn, watermelons, sweet potatoes, and a variety of grains for livestock, and the crops thrived. Behind the cook's house a small plot of ground, highly fertilized, became a vegetable garden with string beans, English peas, cabbages, onions and tomatoes for the family kitchen. Bob also re-forested many acres of his large holdings with Aleppo pine as turpentine tapping had destroyed hundreds of trees. During the summer of 1930 all the children were home—Helen, Phoebe, Robert and Margaret. Each of the three older children, all teenagers, had a car. Bob, who never drove, admired cars. The speed, the soft leather upholstery, the shiny hubcaps, the sleek lines of the design appealed to him. For Mae he bought a special model Lincoln in mustard yellow – the only one of its kind in all of northwest Florida. Helen had a black LaSalle, Phoebe a two door Chrysler, and young Bob a sporty Ford roadster with a rumble seat. Margaret had her pony, Peggy, and a two-wheeled pony cart. Phoebe became the first to leave the nest. She met a nice young man, Henry Hughes, from the neighboring town of Florala, Alabama. They celebrated their marriage on October 16, 1930, at "Alpine Heights," the family home. The local newspapers carried the obligatory press releases:

The beautiful suburban home of Mr. & Mrs. Robert E. Hicks formed the setting for the quiet but beautiful wedding of their daughter, Phoebe, when she became the bride of Mr. Henry A. Hughes of Florala, Alabama. The impressive ring ceremony was performed by Rev. Carlton of Florala in the presence of the immediate members of both families, etc.

In a post-wedding photo, Bob, looking old and teary-eyed, holds a handkerchief in his hand while Mae smiles broadly. The Hughes clan came with their ladies wearing fur stoles, high heels, hats and gloves and their men in three piece suits. Only Bob, Mae and the children represented the bride's family. None of Mae's Davis cousins attended, even if they had been invited.

A RETURN TO HAVANA

In the bigger world times changed. In Cuba after the stock market crashed in 1929, the exports of sugar and tobacco to the United States plummeted. The island faced the greatest economic crisis of its existence. The democratically elected president, Geraldo Machado, metamorphosing into a strong-armed dictator, changed the Cuban constitution in order to increase his power. Those leaders who opposed him vaporized. Rumor had it that schools of man-eating sharks began to congregate in the deep waters surrounding Moro Castle, guarding Havana's harbor. Demonstrations took place as opposition to his rule increased. Soldiers began to reinforce policemen in keeping order at the first signs of protest.

Shortly after Christmas of 1930 Bob, Mae and Margaret went to Havana and were welcomed, as always, by Cousin John Wilford. The two families celebrated New Year's Eve at the roof-top restaurant of the Royal Palm Hotel. John danced with Mae, and Bob, light on his feet in spite of his weight, danced with John's wife. Across the Malecon esplanade, ships rode at anchor, lit from stern to prow, and as the cannon on Morro Castle boomed at midnight, the cathedral bells rang, horns blared, and fireworks brightened the sky. Cuba welcomed 1931 as if it were to be a productive, peaceful year. It was not to be.

A long-time Cuban friend of Wilford was publishing and editing the liberal paper *La Voz*. The government ordered the suspention of *La Voz* that same week, and the publisher asked Wilford to print the paper, quite illegally, on Wilford's presses. Wilford agreed, knowing that when government operatives learned of his actions, his deportation or imprisonment would be assured. He conferred with Bob who heartily agreed with Wilford: "Print his damn paper, John, no matter what the price. We Americans stand for a free press," Bob said, always ready for a good fight. "I'll back you to the hilt."

A few days later, the Hicks family returned to Florida.

In Havana the arrest of eighty-two university professors brought rioting students out on the streets in protest. A number of them were taken to jail, Wilford's son, Herberto, among them. In the same-time frame, police raided the offices of the *Havana*

American Post, damaging the presses. Wilford took the next flight to Miami, leaving his wife to deal with their son's imprisonment.

Events moved rapidly. On February 7, the Associated Press's news desk in Havana released the following: . . . *Guiding the Havana American Post editorial policy – in place of John T. Wilford, who was expelled from Cuba by the government January 16 after many years of newspaper work here – will be J. A. Steverding, likewise well known in publishing circles in Havana.*

Robert E. Hicks, president of the American Publishing Co., returned to Havana today. Almost simultaneously arrived the government's official order lifting suspension imposed upon the newspaper January 8 when nine Havana publications were closed.... A few days later, on February 11, the *Tampa Tribune,* the *Washington, D.C. Star,* the *Birmingham Evening Standard* and other papers printed the following Associated Press dispatch:

HAVANA PAPER TO BE KEPT CLOSED UNTIL EDITOR CAN RETURN

Robert E. Hicks, publisher of the Havana American, stated tonight in a message from Florida that the paper would remain closed until John T. Wilford, its deported editor, returned to guide its destinies. Publication of the Havana American was suspended by the Cuba government more than a month ago, and an order was issued for the deportation of Wilford.

Simultaneously with the arrival of Hicks in Cuba last Saturday, permission was granted through presidential decree for the re-opening of the Havana American, with the restriction that Wilford's name was not to appear in the masthead.

"The Havana American was illegally closed," Hicks said in his message. "Wilford was charged with being a menace to Cuba in his effort to establish a free press there. To reopen and publish the Havana American under restrictions of any kind would be a direct admission of guilt on his part and would mean the destruction of the ideal of free speech for which he fought."

Hicks returned to Florida from Havana yesterday.

Bob's home town newspaper, *The Breeze*, chimed in on the on-going saga on March 12:

MACHADO LIFTS BAN ON
HICKS' HAVANA PAPER

The Havana American , the Cuban daily which R. E. Hicks of this place, purchased some months ago, and later suspended under order of President Machado, of Cuba, may now resume publication if Col. Hicks so wishes, the ban having been lifted by presidential decree by Machado, on March 6. Eight other Cuban dailies and magazines, the publication of which was stopped on the same day that Mr. Hicks found himself afoul of Machado, are also allowed to resume publication.

John T. Wilford, a former West Floridian, and who was publisher of the Havana American at the time that Colonel Hicks became interested in that publication, had the doubtful honor of being the first American to be expelled by presidential decree from Cuba. It isn't exactly right, either, to say that he was expelled, since he left the republic, mucho pronto, when he learned that a decree for his expulsion had been made, thus beating the Cuban officials to it. Wilford, who is said to have been a resident of DeFuniak in bygone years, is the nephew of Mrs. R. E. Hicks, and has been for a time at the Hicks home, following his flight from Cuba which he made in a Havana-Miami airplane. John Wilford, with his wife and son, returned to Havana when it was clear that the ban on the Cuban publications had been lifted.

One might wonder why the suspension of a relatively insignificant newspaper printed in English in a Spanish-speaking country, would be worthy of notice by the Associated Press. Could the hint of the rise of Communism in Cuba be the answer? The dictatorial powers of Machado did not sit well with the American government. A Communistic backed rising of the dissatisfied would not be welcome. Cuba lies only a day's sail off the coast of south Florida. A free press is the foundation of a free society.

It may well be that Bob had been in contact with American officials in the Consulate in Havana who had encouraged him to 'fight' for the re-publication of the *Havana American*. It is not known whether any money exchanged hands when Bob "bought' the newspaper. Bob's ownership may have been a bluff, but he was an American citizen fairly well-known in the publishing business, financially responsible and a fire-brand by nature – just what the American officials might want to stir up a little fuss about the Machado high-handed policies. Certainly Bob would have been sworn to secrecy. The undercover machinations of politics seldom see the light of day. Although the battle was won, the war was lost.

As the Great Depression tightened its grip on world economies, American tourism all but ceased in Cuba. The Royal Palm Hotel managed to keep its doors open but many hotels went bankrupt. The luxurious Sans Souci nightclub closed. Restaurants along the Malecon became a memory. And the *Havana American* presses no longer rolled at midnight for the morning editions. Wilford's paper had become reduced to printing ads, bulletins and whatever job came its way.

It is of interest to note that Machado, driven from Cuba by an angry populace in 1933, was given sanctuary by the U. S. government. He and his family lived a life of ease in a mansion in Miami Beach. Not given to writing, he left no memoir but died on March 29, 1939, peacefully surrounded by loved ones. His body lies in an impressive tomb in the prestigious Woodlawn Park Cemetery and Mausoleum. Sic transit gloria mundi.

Bob returned to the tranquil boredom of life at "Alpine Heights". It would be his last fight.

St. Margaret Roman Catholic Church

Northwest Florida, bordering Alabama, had been settled by Scotch -Irish colonials who had migrated south from Virginia and the Carolinas in the early 19th century. They brought their prejudices of race and religion with them; therefore, no Roman Catholic Church existed in all of Walton County even as late as 1929. Mae, a native of Walton County, had married in 1900 in Chicago an Irishman, Michael Joy. He quickly had his seventeen-year-old bride baptized a Catholic. It was of little importance to Mae. She dutifully attended the ritualistic services sung by priests in an unknown language. She was overwhelmed by the music of a formidable choir and awed by the statues of saints surrounded with candles. As for dogma, she knew none of it. She held a simple faith in God.

Widowed in 1916, Mae had met and married Bob Hicks five years later.

Occasionally a Roman Catholic priest would stop by the new house on the Old Spanish Trail for a visit with

Mae. If six-year-old Margaret were visible, she would be called into the living room to speak with him. Other than his long, black cassock and his strange accent, he was of no interest to her, and she would run out of the room as soon as her mother permitted. She knew her mother enjoyed his visits because she smiled and laughed and insisted he have another cup of tea. The jolly French priest's motive soon became clear. De Funiak Springs needed a Catholic church. Surely Mae's husband, known for his philanthropy, would build a church for the small community? Mae offered the proposition to Bob and he, for whatever personal reasons, agreed with one proviso—the church must be named 'Margaret' in honor of his wife and daughter. It interested him not which St. Margaret of the panoply of the church saints was chosen. The priest agreed that his request would be honored. They shook hands, the priest blessed Bob and the deal was finalized.

On Sunday, June 14, 1931, the dedication of St. Margaret, with the Bishop of Mobile and Father August Hoyne officiating, took place. Catholics from northwest Florida drove many miles to be present at the first mass and to honor their bishop. When Mae and little Margaret arrived, a newly appointed acolyte escorted them to the front pew roped with ribbons in their honor. When the mass began, the jolly black cassocked priest became the very image of a child's concept of God as he emerged from a cloud of incense in robes of scarlet and gold. Bob did not attend. He had requested the newspaper editor of the *De Funiak Breeze* omit his name as the donor in the articles written about the church at its consecration. For a man who enjoyed the limelight, Bob exhibited rare modesty on that occasion.

For many years St. Margaret served the Roman Catholic communities of Walton County, Florida, until the 1970's when it became too small to serve the increasing congregation. The little red brick church with its miniature steeple was deconsecrated and sold. A new church, built on twenty acres of land on the outskirts of the town, better served the needs of its parish. It was consecrated in 1981, exactly fifty years later than its namesake. As tradition demanded, the name remained 'St. Margaret'. At some point in time a priest asked the elderly parishioners to collaborate in writing a brief history of the origins of the church. The result, a hodgepodge of jumbled data, fact and fiction, neatly typed, hung on the wall of the new Parish Hall. In part, it read as follows:

Businesses and Real Estate Companies donated land and gave their time and talents to see the first Catholic Church built in 1931. A non-Catholic business man donated the land for the church and suggested that his disabled daughter be remembered in the naming of the church. His daughter had been named "Margaret" and the church was dedicated to

St. Margaret of Scotland. It was also coincidental that many Scottish people had settled in this area as homesteaders coming from the Carolinas before and after the Civil War.

Considering the fact that 1931 saw the heavy hand of the Great Depression descend on America, it is surprising that Bob would and could donate money for a religious faith in which he had no interest. Had he been spurred by hopes of a cure for a 'disabled daughter' named Margaret, his generosity might be readily understood, but young Margaret, his daughter, showed no impairments. Furthermore, he sought no publicity for his philanthropy, most unusual for a man of his temperament. Twenty four years and five months after the dedication ceremony of St. Margaret's, the funeral service for Mae took place in the sanctuary, where she and her six year old daughter had been escorted to the front pew. The eulogy was not recorded, but had the little French priest, August Hoyne, been alive, he would have recalled that the church was truly Mae's gift to the Catholic community.

The small church remained vacant and neglected until May 24, 2010, when the City Council of De Funiak Springs passed a motion, at the request of the current owner, George Miller, that the building be removed and relocated until the construction plans of the new owners, the Adkinsons brothers, were completed.

Jerry Evans, a grandson of Bob, immediately came forward. He offered to move the building to property he owned behind his funeral home and restore it.

"Then the public could use it for anything needed— an art show, the Chautauqua Assembly, a wedding. If I have to pay $60,000.00 to move it, I won't have the money to restore it to its original condition. I want everything to be put back exactly as it was. When you walk through those doors, it needs to look as if you had stepped back to 1931. I take a special interest in restoring the delicate stained glass windows."

Jerry continued, "What I'm hoping is that Miller and the Adkinsons will pay the cost of moving the building because I'm going to spend a quarter of a million dollars to bring it up to the building code. If Miller took $30,000.00 off the cost and the Adkinsons paid $30,000.00 because he'll have to pay to have it demolished anyway, we could use our money to make a gorgeous landmark for the entire community to use."

A handful of citizens agreed with Evans. According to the *Herald*, a teacher at the high school said, "Over the years I have seen one older structure after another taken down to make way for 'progress'. Children need a connection with the past that can be physically touched. To see the church razed to the ground is an unnecessary tragedy. Not a loss of great proportion, but a piecemeal whittling away of the town's legacy that could be preserved."

A member of the new St. Margaret's parish said, "Jerry Evans really seems to have a vision and we would love to help him and do what we can."

These were voices crying in the wilderness, for neither the Catholic Church nor the City Fathers offered materials or money to support Evans' dream.

Jerry Evans had inherited his Grandfather Bob's spirit of community service, but to no avail. The *Herald*, interested in the results of Evans' request, reported the following:

The Herald, unable to contact either Miller or Adkinson, left messages asking if they were willing to act on Evans' proposal to pay relocation costs, but neither had responded when this article went to press. Contact was also made with the Archdiocese of Mobile for commentary; they, too, have not responded.

A *Herald* reporter also contacted the 87-year old 'disabled daughter', Margaret, living in Tucson, Arizona. A university graduate, the mother of three children, she had taught in Holland, volunteered at Mother Teresa's various clinics in India, worked with native teachers in Zambia, crossed the formidable Takla Makan Desert by jeep to Kashgar, lectured in Byzantine History in Istanbul and Greece and was an active volunteer in charitable organizations. Asked by the reporter her views concerning the church, Margaret Hicks Savage replied, "I am delighted that my nephew, Jerry Evans, is interested in this project. The Catholic Church could also promote the preservation of the original structure. It is, in a sense, a historical building being the first Roman Catholic Church in this part of Florida." The work of demolition did not take long. By 2012 a nondescript office building stood across from the Walton County Courthouse on U.S. 90 West. Neither the community nor the Catholic Church participated in making Evans' vision a reality. In the middle of the 20th century and during World War II, scientists took a serious look at the elements affecting a healthy, long life. Various studies with various groups of volunteers showed that diet and exercise played a major role in longevity. It is safe to say that a large percentage of the American population knew nothing of this data. Farm families had a better diet by far than the urban poor. Only in the last half of the 20th century have concerns for healthier living become widespread. Certainly in Bob's family no one thought of the word 'exercise'. Bob, with his favorite diet of Porterhouse steaks, German fried potatoes and cornmeal mush, had gained too much weight for his 5'8" frame. Two or three jiggers of Scotch every evening, plus Cuban cigars smoked constantly did nothing to improve Bob's health.

In October Mr. Beane, an executive in the

corporation that now owned *The Speciality Salesman Magazine*, came to Florida to confer with Bob. There is a photograph of the two men with George Peabody on the steps leading into Bob's office at Alpine Heights. Bob, dressed in a white Palm Beach suit with white leather shoes, leans on his cane between the two men. Each man wears a boutonniere on his coat lapel. Had they been to a luncheon of some importance? Bob, his eyelids hanging heavy over half-closed eyes, looks tired and old, his spirit diminished. His dreams shrank. No longer did he have the mental stimulation of being asked to be the keynote speaker at a national convention. No longer did he fraternize with men holding high offices in the U. S. government. No longer did he travel to New York City, Philadelphia, Detroit or Chicago to meet with men prominent in commerce and industry. Being the 'big fish' in the ' small 'pond' of De Funiak, isolated from the hurley-burley of cities where 'progress' took place in both America and Cuba, he knew he was slipping away from the life he had achieved for himself.

The tango in Havana had been Bob's last dance.

Mae and Bob no longer shared the master bedroom. Margaret and Mae now did so. Bob moved into a bedroom across the hall. A local man, Dee Work, came to be his factotum. Dee also ran errands in one of the family cars, such as collecting Margaret when the school day ended. A small, wiry man, he became virtually invisible in the household but always available when needed for any task.

WHEN Dee Work became a member of the household as Bob's factotum, Mae relinquished her duties of driving Margaret to school. One afternoon on the way home, Margaret, now a second grader, told Dee to stop at the Roadhouse. He complied. She entered the small home-owned café, ordered a steak with fried potatoes, ate, told the owner her daddy would pay and left. When Mae heard the story, she laughed heartily and told the tale to the family, who thought it a capital joke. Margaret never understood what was funny.

Until the last, Bob made sure that his baby daughter received at least as much as was her due. The American Legion in De Funiak made plans for Armistice Day. To raise money for a good cause the committee asked the schools to select high school girls to compete for the honor of being queen. Four pretty girls, and eight year old Margaret, threw their names in the ring. There was no contest, no suspense—Bob bought every ticket and young Margaret became the queen of the Armistice Day celebration on November 10, 1931. Mae chose her cousin's son, Jeff Davis, as Margaret's consort.

The *De Funiak Breeze* carried the following story:
DE FUNIAK FOLK MAKE MERRY
MISS HICKS CROWNED QUEEN OF FESTIVAL

Approximately two thousand persons were on hand tonight as the Armistice Day celebration of the local American Legion got underway. The crowd gathered in the Chautauqua auditorium to witness the crowning of the king and queen of the carnival. Miss Margaret Hicks was crowned queen of the festival. Jeff Davis will reign with her as king. Fifty children took part in the ceremony. The celebration tomorrow is expected to be one of the best in the history of the city...

Shortly before Christmas, 1931, Bob made his will. In the first draft, he appointed Mae as the executrix, but she asked Bob to select someone better qualified. Bob consulted his old friend, Charles Neizer, president of the Ft. Wayne National Bank, who recommended the trust executive, F. A. Schack. Mae, as widow, received the lion's share as was her due. She also had complete control over both of the houses, one in Indiana and the Florida home. The 185 acres on the Gulf of Mexico in Bay County, Florida, Bob personally deeded to her. The oldest son, Elmer Hicks (Rosa's child with Bob), was allocated one dollar as the law required as recognition of a legitimate offspring. The other four children inherited the bulk of the estate equally. The executor filed the will in the offices of the County Clerk of Walton County, Florida.

However, sixty years after Bob's death, his grandson, Richard Cawthon, visited South Whitley for the first time and wrote the following memoir regarding his experiences there, shedding further light on what became of Bob's estate:

Ft. Benjamin Harrison, IN
12 July 1992

Drove to South Whitley, Indiana, today. After sixty-three years Robert E. Hicks is still remembered. Wandered into town and drove about until on the "main drag". It seemed the right thing to do to turn down Columbia. Within a block and a half I detected Robert E's trade mark, the gates. Stopped outside the compound to observe (the gates are at the end of Columbia.) A lady was pulling in to her drive way (Fla. Plates no less – my notes indicate her name may be Chaffney though I'm not sure as to the accuracy of the entry.) I introduced myself as R. E's grandson and asked her if this was the old Hicks' place. She replied "yes", and that Mr. Garmon (the present owner) would likely be glad to see me and to go on in (the compound) and ring his bell.

The gates and compound were in disrepair. The main house had been abandoned. To the right, and across from the main house was a two story frame structure still referred to by the lady I had talked to as "the bungalow". Though the bungalow was open, no one appeared to be at home.

Drove out, stopped at a restaurant to eat and kill a

few hours to see if the Garmon's would return as it was about church time. Upon leaving the restaurant, I went back to the main drag, parked and walked about. Noticed an antique store was open and went in. The proprietors are John and Virginia Weber, Weber's Antiques, 402 State Street, South Whitley, IN 46787. Mr. Weber was sort of a local historian and helped immensely. He referred to the house Mr. Garmon lives in as both the bungalow and the servant house. He confirmed the main house is not now inhabited. Mr. Weber told me the printing plant still stands and was located at the end of Broad St., that the Hicks Tavern was on Columbia, and that Robert E. had rebuilt the First Baptist Church. He also referred to R. E. as a "ten cent" millionaire – big money one day, no money the next (I did not take this as vindictive, this was simply his interpretation of local history.)

I then went to the printing plant. I was taking pictures of this closed down plant when Mr. Lancaster, the caretaker came over from his house. I explained I was R. E's grandson and Mr. Lancaster took me on a tour of the plant. This was a no windows type building and the electricity was off. I did note that there was no water damage inside, the place was a tight as a ship. I was shown two interesting bits of history – basement dirt floor workers toilet and clean up stall area (said to be the original and not used in modern times) – and upstairs two layers of false ceiling and then the original ceiling, each having its own sprinkler system, and the original ceiling complete with its lighting fixtures.

Upon coming out I exchanged a few more pleasantries with Mr. Lancaster and then took a walk around the building.

12 July 1992

Upon coming around front again a neighbor, Mrs. Miers, had come over and in conversation with her Mr. Lancaster had found out that: (a) Garmon purchased the Hicks home from Elmer Hicks (interesting, Elmer was left $1.00 in R. E's Fla. Will – this (the Indiana property) must be Elmer's inheritance by another document or successful court challenge) and (b) the South Whitley Public Library's librarian, Marian Bollinger, is heavy on local history, is about eighty years old and remembers the Hicks (she would be Mama's age group, born circa 1912).

Mrs.Miers suggested I get in touch with Mrs. Bollinger (the librarian) as she (Mrs. Miers) had been on the library board, knew Mrs. Bollinger well, and knew she would be glad to share her knowledge of the Hicks. Mrs. Miers also said she had heard of mama's name, Phoebe Hicks.

Returned to the old Hicks residence. The Garmons were not in. I went to the antique shop to thank John Weber again. I said I would share the few South Whitley photos I had of the Hicks family.

Richard L. Cawthon

A few days later Bob added a codicil to the will disinheriting any of his heirs if one married into the Flournoy family. No reason was given. Colonel Wm. Flournoy had been the lawyer who worked with R. E. L. McCaskill in drawing up the papers for the Hicks-McCaskill Development Company. The family quietly celebrated Bob's 74th birthday on 25 February, 1932. He had 19 more days to live.

On 9 March Phoebe Hughes gave birth to his first grandchild, Barbara Nan, and the only one he ever saw and held in his arms.

On the morning of 17 March Margaret awakened to see her mother leaning against their bedroom door crying. She had never seen her mother cry. A man stood next her mother speaking softly, but Margaret's attention focused on her mom. Why was she crying?

People, quiet and respectful, filled he house. The dining room table overflowed with coffee and tea pots, baked ham, fried chicken, hot biscuits, cornbread, lemon and sweet potato pies and chocolate cake. Where did it all come from so early in the day?

Perhaps Dee Work took on the task of luring

Margaret to the barn to help her saddle Peggy and see her ride down to the store for an ice cream. Anyway, someone kept her busy and away from the house until the hearse came to take away her father's body.

"There's no need for Margaret, young as she is, to go through the trauma of a graveside funeral," Mae explained to a curious cousin, "She'll attend enough funerals in her life. No need to start with this one."

The funeral director conducted the brief, dignified graveside ceremony.

Did Bob's shade go quietly across the River Styx? Did the valiant shades of Odysseus, Hector, Agamemnon and Achilles welcome him? Not always honorable, certainly not always right yet men who had struggled and fought to win the goals they had set for themselves, Bob took his place among them.

THE END

APPENDICES

Obituaries of Robert Emmett Hicks
b. 25 February 1858 d. 17 March 1932
Obituaries can be tricky. If written by the nearest of kin the vital statistics may be accurate, but not always. Both genders have been known to hide the true year of birth from spouses as well as children. A sibling may omit the name of another sibling out of spite or greed. On the positive side, obits may give important genealogical data to great-grandchildren researching the family history. Apart from familial quirks, a journalist may neglect reading, prior to writing the obituary, former articles with well researched data about the deceased. Errors, usually of little importance, can and do occur. Bob's obituaries are a case in point. The eight obituaries listed below are alike in the following omissions:

- Not one gives the birth date or birth place.
- Not one mentions Bob's son who predeceased him.
- Not one has the correct number of his marriages.
- Only one, perhaps out of respect, tells of his Federal crime, imprisonment and presidential pardon.
- Not one refers to his involvement with the Machado government in Cuba.

- Not one mentions his granddaughter, his only grandchild at the time of his death.
- Only one notes the newspapers in Kansas he edited and published.

The Breeze of De Funiak Springs printed this brief article the morning of Thursday, March 17, 1932:
PROMINENT CITIZEN ANSWERS DEATH'S CALL
Robert E. Hicks, prominent and wealthy citizen, died early this Thursday morning at his home on the Old Spanish Trail, west of DeFuniak. A fitting necrological notice will appear next week.

New York Times, March 17, 1932
ROBERT E. HICKS DEAD - FOUNDED MAGAZINE
Was Editor Emeritas of Organ for Specialty Salesmen – Once Managed Kansas Newspapers.
  Special to The New York Times
  Chicago, March 17, Robert E. Hicks, founder and editor of the Specialty Salesman Magazine, died today at his home in De Funiak Springs, Fla. He formerly lived in Wilmette, a Chicago suburb. His age was 74.
  Mr. Hicks was editor of several weekly newspapers in Kansas while a young man. From 1915 until 1928, when he retired, he used his magazine to attack fake mail-order schemes and other swindlers. He brought about a publishers'

conference in 1928 which succeeded in barring many alleged takers from the mails. A widow, three sons and three daughters survive.

On March 18, a day after Bob's death, the following article appeared in the *Chicago Tribune:*

ROBERT E. HICKS, EX-PUBLISHER, DIES IN FLORIDA

Robert E. Hicks, founder and editor of The Specialty Salesman Magazine, died yesterday at his home in DeFuniak, Fla., according to a message received here in Chicago by H. J. Blight, publisher of the magazine. Mr. Hicks was 74 years old. He was editor of several weekly newspapers in Kansas while a young man. About thirty years ago he was indicted for misuse of the mails. After serving part of his sentence when he surrendered twelve years later, and being pardoned by President Woodrow Wilson, Mr. Hicks declared his intention of founding a magazine to expose frauds worked by salesmen of specialties.

From 1915 to 1928 when he retired, Mr. Hicks used the columns of his magazine to attack such swindlers particularly fake mail order schemes. He was the instigator of a publishers conference in 1928 which succeeded in barring many alleged fakers from the mails.

The *De Funiak Herald,* De Funiak Sprs., Florida,

March 24, 1932 reported as follows:

Funeral of Mr. Hicks

The funeral of Mr. Robert E. Hicks was held last Sunday morning at ten o'clock, funeral arrangements being made by Page Funeral Home. A large motorcade of family and friends accompanied the body from the Hicks home to Magnolia Cemetery. [Pallbearers named]. An extended tribute to Mr. Hicks with an outline of his work reaches us too late for publication this week, but will be published in our next issue.

Thirty-two years after Bob's death, Mae joined her husband in Magnolia Cemetery, Walton County, FL: Mae Davis (b. 18 February 1882 d. November 1955) was born in Paxton, FL, the daughter of Louis and Susan Elliott Davis. Mae married Robert E. Hicks in 1921. They built a house in 1929, named Alpine Heights, on the Old Spanish Trail approximately six miles from De Funiak Springs. The house still stands in 2016.

The following letter from Jerry Evans, Bob's grandson, contains some relevant information: *I can hardly wait to purchase a copy of the R.E. Hicks, Sr. biography. Yes, I have in my possession the dining room furniture from the Alpine Heights house. It consists of table (banquet size-four leaves) seats ten a large buffet and a small buffet, a china cabinet and a fire place bench. It is my understanding a gentleman and his three sons from Grand Rapids hand carved three of these identical suites during their life time Mr. Hicks purchased one of them in the 20's. One of the suites was consumed in a house fire in Chicago sometime in the 40's. One of the two remaining suites is in my possession and I do not know of the where-a-bouts of the third.*

The suite was moved from Alpine Heights when Hubert and Helen's new home was completed on North 6th Street in Florala, Alabama. The dining room had to be specifically built to house the massive furniture and resulted in a design modification to the architect's original drawings for the new home. The suite was moved from DeFuniak Springs to Florala sometime, I believe in the late 30's and remained there for fifty years. In 1988 Jerry and Kay Evans who had inherited the Florala House, duplicated that house in DeFuniak Springs. Again, the dining room had to be specifically built to accommodate the furniture. It remained in the DeFuniak Springs home until it was moved to its present location in the all new Jerry Evans Funeral Home in DeFuniak Springs in September of 1999. The pieces are placed in various state rooms and offices throughout the new complex. As in all commercial ventures, the suite was insured against fire and peril. An appraisal by an independent appraiser from neighboring Destin, Florida gave an insurance value of 105-thousand dollars.

The suite is hand carved, highly ornate and is mahogany. Typical of the 1920's the buffets house individual drawers and velvet lined removable wooden silverware caddies in order that "the help" could easily attend to setting formal dining tables with ease and perfection.

Probably meant for more refined homes, Helen Evans could have cared less when she was raising her four little children. Her two oldest, Joe and Dickie, often times screwed metal braces onto the center section of the table to hold their ping pong net in place as they rambunctiously paddled game after game. At Christmas time, Dickie was allowed to set his metal Lionel train set up on the table for the holidays. Kay Evans in the early 70's sought to have the chairs and fireplace bench recovered, but would settle for nothing less than an exact duplication of the original fabric. After months of research and several trips to Atlanta the fabric was secured and the upholstery was completed, however in order to preserve the patina of years and years of memories no refinishing was allowed on any wooden surface *which accounts for 75% of the composition of the suite. In remarkable condition, considering its age and lack of monitored care the suite commands the attention of admiration of all who visit Jerry Evans Funeral Home during services. Its striking presence is a reminder to all who visit of the quality and craftsmanship of the old masters. 5/28/2015*

Bob, as mentioned earlier, had been rescued by volunteers at the Bowery Mission, New York City. When he became a successful publisher, he remembered the Mission, donating money to help maintain it.

In 1935, three years after Bob's death, William L. Stidger wrote a book praising the work of missions throughout the country. His comments concerning Bob follow:

Then there was Robert E. Hicks. He was a convict under indictment for a United States mail fraud. He evaded justice for thirteen years. Then one night in the Bowery Mission, he made a confession of his crime. He was sentenced to serve ten months on Blackwell's Island and later was pardoned by President Woodrow Wilson at the suggestion of friends and the Mission. Hicks was 57 when he left prison but after his release, he made a fortune as a printer. Later he built The Hicks' Tavern at South

Whitley, and sponsored the building of the Baptist Church giving more than $100,000 to good works. - Stidger, Wm. L. *The Human Side of Greatness*, Harper & Brothers Publishers. 1935 New York and London.

The week of Bob's death, the Sunday Diner Grocery advertised the following prices in the local newspaper:

Five cans Van Camp Hominy 25c

Four packages Pillsbury's Grits 25c

Three large cans Mackerel 25c

3 pound pail Honeymoon coffee 50c

Baker's Southern style coconut 10c

One quart jar Sweet Pickles 20c

Four cans Campbell Tomato Soup 25c

Ten bars Octagon soap 25c

May 1925

man sees it. The distinction is clear. In either case he may be the victim of a swindle, but it can be seen here that not all swindles are confidence games.

There are two laws that the confidence man applies in selecting his prospect. Always in approaching his victim the operator appeals to the sucker's cupidity. He shows him how to get something for nothing. That of course can not be done with honest methods; so our nimble-witted friend shuns the honest man. His man may possess any other quality whatever except honesty. An honest person will never enter into such a proposition because of his conscientious scruples.

It is no reflection upon a person's intelligence to fall for a confidence game, except, insofar, of course, as this dishonesty is a reflection upon his intelligence. It concerns his integrity only.

THE UNDERWORLD STANDARD OF MORALS

Those of the underworld have a standard of morals and unwritten laws all their own. If they do not measure up to some other code, it is largely due to different environment. They are not always lived up to any more than any other laws are obeyed, but the penalty for their non-observance is the same as the infringement of all moral laws, the disapproval of others being manifested in various ways, depending upon the degree of the offense, the severest of which is social ostracism.

It is very important that each meets his obligations faithfully. It is seldom that written contracts of any kind are given in exchange for money or valuables in loan or otherwise among them. One's word is considered sufficient; when it is not so considered, the transaction does not take place.

It is an offense of the gravest nature to divulge the secrets of another to any one whomsoever not entitled to receive them, and who might use them to the owner's injury. Any one who is suspected of so doing is said to be "wrong" and "not right." If the fact has been established that he has done so, he is called a "rat." This is the vilest epithet that may be bestowed upon him. He can sink to no lower depths. No one will associate with him, not even other "rats," and he is heartily despised the remainder of his life. On the other hand, when the fact is established that he is "right," nothing is too good for him, and he can have anything in their power to give.

CHAPTER 3

THE BIG STORE RACKET

Trimming a sucker with the racket relating to the big store is known as the "big store work." The same methods are always used with but slight variation in detail necessary to meet different conditions. The store organiza-

ROBERT E. HICKS

"In March of this year (1921) Robert E. Hicks, the Chicago editor and publisher, purchased a complete printing outfit and building at South Whitley, Ind., worth $110,000, for $36,250. This transaction marks a climax in one of the most unusual struggles of self-mastery and success the world has ever known.

Twenty years ago Hicks was a mail order swindler. He almost froze to death during a drunken spree. He had done time in a penitentiary. He was pardoned by President Wilson. He became a noted religious worker, in New York. He has come clean in confessing his wrong-doing."
—Orison Sweet Marden.

Robert E. Hicks is editor and publisher of Specialty Salesman Magazine. He put South Whitley, Ind., upon the map and incidentally in doing so he remarkably demonstrated how overcoming obstacles can cause one to grow in power and character.

Next month's issue will contain an interview of Mr. Hicks wherein he gives you intimate sketches of his life, his struggles, his triumphs, and in his intimate manner his idea of prison evils and the solution.

tion is composed of from four to six persons who own the store. They usually remain in one location and handle any business that may be brought to them. The object of this extraordinary combination is to "trim suckers," or to separate some person not in the combination from his money in a fake athletic contest.

This is how it is done. There are those in this game called "steerers." A "steerer" does not own part of the store. He is a free-lance. He may take his business to any store that may suit his fancy. He goes throughout the

country looking for "prospects." A "prospect" is any person with money who may become interested in swindling some other person. It is said that one of these is born every minute. At any rate the supply seems inexhaustible. They are found among all classes—lawyers, bankers, doctors, merchants, farmers, and he may even be a deacon, Sunday-school teacher or a preacher, and he quite frequently is. Three qualities only are necessary to make a good "sucker," viz., he must possess money, be credulous, and then he has just simply got to be a thief in his heart, for just as sure as two and two make four, if he is not a liar at heart he can never be skinned; because, otherwise, he will have nothing to do with the proposition. He should be susceptible to this particular proposition and believe readily what is told him.

Please bear in mind that the approach (getting acquainted), leading up to the main subject and preparing a way for the opening to spring the proposition, is the most particular part of the entire proceeding, and should be conducted with the utmost caution. If you are going to hook your fish, then you should remember that "fishing is a gentle art when fishing for fish or fishing for men." But when the preliminary proceedings have been negotiated, then comes the proposition. Sometimes a letter is produced purporting to come from the bearer's "brother-in-law." It reads something like this:

"Dear Brother: I am writing you in relation to a real estate deal that I have in view. I have a chance to clean up considerable money if I can get the proper help. Mr. H——, my employer, owns 10,000 acres of land in southern Missouri. It was formerly swampy timber-land but having cut off the timber suitable for lumber, he has no further use for it. He has instructed me to sell it at $2.00 per acre. Recently I learned that the government has dug ditches near this land which has drained the water from Mr. H——'s property and has enhanced its value wonderfully. I have secured a buyer who is willing to pay $8.00 per acre for the property. Let me say, however, that my employer knows nothing whatever about these new developments, therefore, he is still ready to sell at $2.00 per acre. But, George, here is where you come in. Should I sell the land for $8.00 per acre I would be compelled to turn over to Mr. H—— the entire amount because I am employed by the year and do not get a commission on this sale. I want you to secure a suitable and honest business man to whom I will buy an option from me on this land at $2.00 per acre. Afterwards he will re-sell to my buyer at a profit of $6.00 per acre. We shall then divide the profits. Bring no money. I will furnish the money with which to swing the deal. Mr. H—— and I, with a party of business associates, will be in Caldwell, O., soon and you can meet us there and consummate the deal. Now, George, select a man who is not acquainted with my employer,

THE ODD BUCKEYES
OR
THE ADVENTURES OF A WRITER AND A CON ARTIST
by Rodney Peabody

When we up and "Went West Yong Man," I was six and my older, smart alec sister was 10. We chugged by train into South Whitley, Indiana, in the middle of the "wilderness and wild Indians," or so we two kids thought. Dad just smiled when we asked about that.

Somebody Dad knew, met us at the station and walked us four blocks to "Mother's Coffee Shop" for something to eat, as it was past supper time and dark out. It was around the middle of December, 1925.

All our furniture etc. was already in the house Dad had rented, but we, including Mom, had no idea where the house was located.

We came from Elyria, Ohio, where I was born. A small city of 50-60,000 and close to Cleveland. So, when we awoke the next morning, and found ourselves in the wild country of Indians, living in a pioneer village of 1,200, my Sis and I figured there was probably a stockade around the town with a gate to get in and out. Guess I'd read too many wild west stories. I kept looking around for Indians and "Mountain Men," but didn't see a darned one. It was sure different then Elyria, Ohio, though! And we had friends in Lorian, Ohio, right on the Lake Erie shore and spent many a weekend with them and went swimming in Lake Erie–dozens of times with them.

His name was Douglass Mack and he and Dad had started to try writing at about the same time and as a result became good friends.

Dad got started by writing for the New York Central RR Weekly Publication and that gave him an edge on "Uncle" Doug. Uncle Doug taught me to swim at two or three years old, against Mom's screams and protests. He could walk or wade out 100 yards from shore and still be only up to his neck, with me sitting on his neck. Mom had 18 strokes and heart attacks but survived until I could paddle around by myself.

Sis was an expert swimmer and Dad was pretty good and Mom died a thousand deaths, but Uncle Doug finally taught her to swim, too. Boy, how we enjoyed hearing her scream and holler, but she had "guts" and finally got to enjoy swimming.

By the time we went to Indiana, Dad had built up quite a reputation as a writer of sports stories, adventure, even love stories (Ugh!). He was building quite an income from his writing and when he began selling regularly to "Top Notch" magazine (the "Sports Illustrated" of that day), he was raking in a pretty darn good income.

His regular job was a surveyor on the New York Central RR. He was in on building the Bay Bridge and very proud of it. He took all four of us up there on time along with fishing tackle, to show us the "bridge" and to fish off of it. I was three or four years old, and it was almost too much for me to comprehend. Dad helped me land a big perch and I felt so thrilled and proud and so proud of my Dad.

As usual, Mom inadvertently created a crisis. She snagged onto a girant fist of some kind and she was screaming, "George! George! George! (my Dad's name) Help me!" Well Dad scrambled over the ballast stones and got a hold on the line and saved Mom from being pulled into the lake, because she was too stubborn to let goo (there is no question as to where I get my aggressive personality: I'm ¾ like Mom and a ¼ like quiet, calm, Dad or 1/8)

Well, the fish got away! Dad thought it was a large "Sheepshead," that got to 15-20 lbs in size. Then the same way, we left in the early morning from Elyria in the caboose of a "local" train, we went home.

What a thrill for a three-four year old– to ride in a real caboose on a real train! I showed all the trainmen the big perch that I had caught and the "oh'ed and ah'ed" and said it was the biggest perch they'd ever seen, etc. Boy was I in Heaven–I couldn't sleep for a week!

A year or so later, Mom and Dad had a very difficult decision to make. Sis and I could tell something was going on that was very important. What happened was, that a Mr. Bob Hicks, in South Whitley, Indiana, owner and publisher of "The Specialty Salesman Magazine," offered Dad a job as Associate Editor of his magazine, at a very good salary, and that put things in a bind. Dad was on the verge of becoming nationally known for his freelance writing.

Mr. Hicks was an ex-com artist and had been in more jails than Carter had pills! Then he got an "idea." Go straight and expose all the crooked and shady sales companies that were gypping the public. He would publish a magazine full of articles naming all the crooked outfits all of the U.S. and he knew them all!

He used his con artist sills to sell the idea to some moneyed men and gave them shared of stock in the magazine as collateral. What an artist!

After three editions were out, anybody could see it was going to go like a wild fire, but Bob put a sad, beaten, look on his face and went around to all the moneyed men and told them the magazine was going to go under and he would buy back all their stock! They all wasted no time selling back the stock, all but on guy in St. Louis. He had known Bob all his life and he smelled a rat someplace. Only he held just a few shares. Bob now held all the stock to the few shares the St. Louis guy had and he just forgot about him.

We, editions #4 sold out and #5 sold out and they All sold out after that and the magazine had about 15-20 lawsuits going, which didn't hurt at all, publicity wise. Bob created a furor in the Direct Sales Market. He hired the best lawyer in Ft. Wayne, full time, and won every lawsuit he was involved in—but one! And when the Judge pronounced him guilty, he also announced the sentence: one cent fine, and that case got publicity all over the country and was the best thing that could ever have happened.

When he sold out to the Chicago Mob, he told Dad that every time the sun went down, he had made 13,000. Not bad for a broken down con artist.

Dad was Bob's right-hand man by now, and when Bob sold out in 1930, I think, Dad went with the magazine to Chicago, as Editor-in-Chief, with a dandy salary. He commuted by train and was home every weekend.

Then one time he showed up on a Wednesday or Thursday. And we all were aware that something big had happened.

Right in the height of the depression, Dad had walked out. He said to Mom and all of us, "Meg, (his nickname for Mom) I can't work for that bunch in Chicago. They are all a gang of crooks and I can't work for crooks. We will make out someway."

Mom said, "George, I don't want you working for a bunch of crooks. I am glad you walked out and came home!"

You could just see the tenseness and worry leave Dad's face. He was worried Mom would blow up for leaving a high-salaried job. Instead she back him up. He walked over and kissed her and hugged her. While Janice and I just stood looking at each other. We didn't quite understand the enormity of what he had done. Left a top job in Chicago to WHAT?

Well, things work out. Eventually, so did this. Part of this whole deal with Dad and the magazine and Bob Hicks was, before he sold out he took us and his family, wife and 7 year old daughter (his pride and joy!) on a month-long trip to Cuba where Bab and Dad secluded themselves in a hotel room and started writing Bob Hicks life's story.

And what a story! That man was on in a million! I read it years later, and he had pulled every con job there was to pull and invented some new ones. And that was the wrench in the machinery. Dad work on the story for several months while Bob Hicks and family stayed in Florida ad bought up several thousand acres of pine forest and sand and eventually lost his fannie on the deal.

Well, Dad finally had the "Life of Bob Hicks, Ex-Con Artist," all signed and sealed and ready for the printers, when Mr. Hicks had a heart attack and dies– suddenly. He was about 68-72 years old.

That played "hob" with the life story. Mrs. Hicks was horrified when she read the typed, final copy, ready for the printers. She had sort of gone her own way and didn't pay much attention to Bob's activities or former life style. She was his second wife.

When she read about Bob Hicks and his life as a con artist, she literally hit the ceiling and carried on for about a week and destroyed the typed copy and told Dad, "That no way was that biography going to be seen, ever, in print!!!"

Well, that ended the Bob Hicks era of our lives. Dad's ordinal, hand written story is in the Peabody File at the South Whitley, Indiana Library and many people have read it. And many have said, "what a hell of a movie that would have been, with Edward G. Robinson, or George Raft, or Clark Gable, or any of those slick actors in the lead role!" Life can sure be contrary at times. For the want of a horse a nail was lost or however the h–l it goes...

Dad was depressed for a long time, but he got an offer as Editor of the :Opportunity Magazine" in Chicago and knew and liked the publisher, so he took the job and the life of the Peabodys settled into a rather comfortable rut, which was something sort of new to us.

Things went pretty smoothly for us until World War II came along. Mom and Dad has cashed in all their insurance policies to send Sis to college and to live on. Sis almost won a singing contest in Ft. Wayne, Indiana, in 1932. The winner got a free ride at the Julliard School of Music, in Chicago. After the contest, one of the judges came around to Sis, who was crying, and told her that she had, by far, the best voice and delivery in the contest! But she was one high note short of being a true soprano and that put her in the Mezzo-soprano bracket and there was really no future for just another Mezzo. He was real comforting and sympathetic. He said that he was so sorry because she had a beautiful voice.

Sis wound up as wife of the Chief Stores Keeper, to Alcoa Companies, Headquarters at Pittsburgh, world wide and they traveled all over the world. At home she got involved in the music department of a large church in Pittsburgh and wound up as the head of the department and organized on of the best choirs in that part of the state. Also smaller groups, octets, mens groups, she also played the organ and piano, etc. She gave lessons in several instruments and singing–and they weren't cheap. I was extremely proud of her successes. Then one day the doctors discovered cancer. She died in 1970 at the age of 55. It was almost too much to bear.

War stories are passe, but this is just an anecdote. I was in charge of delivering rations to about half of all the Army Air Force, Navy and weather and radio bases in north Africa, stationed at Marakech, Morroco. One day a Master Sergeant walked in with some paper to issue stock of rations. I stood there with my mouth wide open, speechless. He has more medals and stripes than a Zebra, or than Mussolini.

He smiled and said, "Sarge, I need some supplies."

I said, "yes sir Sergeant (Master Sgt.), I'll have your requisition filled right away, got some wheels to load it in?"

He said, "yes, that Buick parked at the dock."

MEIN GOTT IN HIMMEL, a Buick in the Sahara Desert? Well, he was waiting to be shipped home. He has been a secret undercover agent in Africa since about two years before the African invasion; went all around Africa contacting the underground leaders and setting up the invasion. There were several in the group and that's all he would say about the operation. Anyway, for some reason, we became friendly and he took me to the hotel where Roosevelt, Churchill, Montgomery, and Eisenhower, and all the big shots met and made their plans and decisions. Had a huge meeting room and a huge cabinet of booze. The Sergeant said that Churchill drank most of it. The Sergeant job was to oversee everything and drive the Buick wherever someone want to go, and of course, security.

Every so often we would get up in the morning and there would be anti-aircraft guns everyplace. Hundreds of them—everywhere. Well, another big shot meeting and the Sergeant would come in for another stock of the best we had. Yep, a load of big wheels came in overnight on c54s.

One day the Sergeant asked me where I was from. I

told him a little town near Ft. Wayne, Indiana, but that my parents were living in Chicago.

He said, "why that's where I'm from, Chicago, but the big brass made me come to Marakech for a while to cover my trail. Rod," the Sergeant said, " I can't tell you my name, or anymore than I've told you already because there are several people that would love to stick a bayonet in my back. But, I'm going to bend the rules a little. When I get home, I'm going down to Michigan Avenue, to the building where your Dad works and drop in and see him ad tell him all that I'm allowed to, about you and your vital and difficult job and that you're OK. And maybe a few things off the record."

Well, I about went off my trolley. "Sarge," I said, "that's wonderful. My G–d, that office will explode when you walk in with your dress outfit on and all that confetti you have hanging on you. Why my Dad will be flabbergasted! But," I asked, "that won't get you in any kind of a jam, will it?"

"No," he replied, "I'll be free to roam around some in the States, most of the bad guys are not in the U. S. so I'll go talk to your Dad as soon as I can."

After I got home to the States again, Dad told me about it. (He couldn't write much while the hostilities were still on and censorship would have stopped it from getting to me.) But it was just like I imagined. When this 6' 2", handsome, tall, soldier with a real military bearing and air about him, and with all those d–n stripes and bars and medals hanging on him like a Christmas tree, stepped in the door and walked up to the counter, why six or eight girls almost dropped dead. Their eyes bulged out about a mile, so Dad told me.

Finally on of them talked, after clearing her throat about six or eight times, and asked what she could do for him. He said that he wanted to see Mr. Peabody, and one of the office girls finally moved from her frozen stance, and went and got Dad.

When the Sergeant told him his story about being with e in Marakech for a month, and some of the record stuff, Dad told me that he almost cried. Here was a bonafide hero, regular Army career, master Sergeant, coming clear to his office in the Chicago Loop, just to tell some guy his didn't know, about his little old, insignificant buck Sgt. Son, Dad was in chock for two or three days. The office girls never will be the same!

Dad mentioned what a nice gentleman he was, and seemed so pleased that he could tell Dad that I was OK, etc. He just couldn't believe that a soldier of his known and unknown accomplishments, and such high rand, would bother about a little old Sgt. Peabody–no know, or unknown accomplishments. Thank God we had men like that Master Sgt.

By the time I was discharged and back home, Dad

was Editor of the "Masonic Chronicler," and raising a lot of money for a new wing on the Masonic Hospital in Chicago. He was writing letters to the high rollers and a lot of widows with diamonds and pearls and butler, etc.

His stock went up 1,000% with the Shriners when he wrote to an old Biddy that for years had been asked to contribute for their projects and had always turned them down, flat, period. She has million!

Dad wrote her a letter and she coughed up $100,000 for the new wing! The Imperial Potentate and all the ex-Imperial Potentates and other bit shot Masons treated Dad like some kind of god after that! Dad thought it was sor of jumorous, the way they were mesmerized by a $100,000 gift from just his letter when all the big wheels went to see her countless times and could not get a red penny from her!

Well, Dad was a writer, that was his trade. He didn't think it was such a big deal. But, then, THAT WAS MY DAD! He died in 1951 at age 61, of cancer, but he has a full and interesting life.

He was a great success in our eyes–the odd Buckeyes.

THE END

FLIM-FLAM ANOTHER SCAM?
by Rodney Peabody

To set up this perplexing story, I must give you a little background to give iony and humor and a lot of frustration and anger its proper amount of prominence at the final curtain. There was a conartist, who we'll call Mr. Bix, to avoid any rare chance of lawsuits. He came into town, with a wife and three children–two girls and a son. He was broke, fresh out of jail, probably wanted for fraud and related crimes in several states, and frowned upon by the population of South Whitley, IN, population, 1,200.

He was a printer by trade and I think worked some of the time at the A to Z Printing Plant in town. The A to Z and the Gripnut Company feuded for top spot as the No. 1 Factory in South Whitley. Employed about 100 or so.

Mr. Bix stayed around for about a year and then left town for reasons and destinations unknown. Nobody was interested in his fate anyway.

My Dad wrote Mr. Bix's life story, which was unbelievable, and had it ready for the printers, when Mr. Bix had a heart attack and died. The widow, his second wife who had presented him with another daughter, upon reading the proofs blew her stack about a mile high and informed Dad, that, no way would that biography see the light of print and she destroyed the proofs. Evidently, she was not very much aware of Mr. Bix's early life and prison terms, etc.

All the facts and Dad's story or biography is safe in the South Whitley Library vaults—so we'll skip to his last episode with the law, which placed a seven-year ring around his neck at the state prison in Albany, NY.

To give a sample of his brilliance, with his silver tongue and exceptional mind, he managed and maneuvered and finally got the Governor of NY to commute his sentence after seven or eight months. While in prison, he came up with a mind-boggling idea for a magazine. To wit: a monthly magazine to expose all the crooked mailorder, door-to-door, and any other company or fake company that he knew about. And he knew them all. He could smell a con job a mile away!

I'll condense a little here, details are in the book. After a couple years of evangelistic speeches and printed semi-religious pamphlets and mail-outs, he made his play! He went to several moneyed men with his idea—and he knew them all. he exchanges stock in the Specialty Salesman Magazine" for cash money until he had enough for two issues and to buy the A to Z building with was fairly new and in excellent condition And he didn't have a magazine or the presses or personnel, just the key to the door of an empty building. So he borrowed money, somewhere, to buy presses, hire personnel, etc.

The first issue came off the presses and shipped to distributors and, of course, didn't do too well. But, the second issue took off and about triples in sales. So Mr. Bix borrowed some money, Lord knows where. He borrowed enough for the third issue and here's the kicker, you can guess what happened next...

He put on about the third-class suit and dirty hat and a sorrowful look on his face–and $20,000 or $30,000 in his briefcase (it's in the book). He went to all his backers, the moneyed men and told them a sad tale that the "Specialty Salesman Magazine" was probably going to turn "bellyup" and he was going to buy back all their stock while he still had money enough to pay them back. The moneyed geniuses were more than eager to get their money and give him the stock. The felt mighty luck to rescue their money in exchange for worthless stock! Ha, ha, ha!

So, Mr. Bix goes back to South Whitley, IN, with all the stock and just enough borrowed money to put out a third issue. Well, when it hit the newsstands, it sold like hot cakes and the issue sold out completely. Mr. Bix cleared enough for the firth and fifth issues and he was off to the races. Circulation went up like a rocket, and he had all of the stock!

In 1925, Mr. Bix hired my father as Associate Editor and his nephew, Mr. Harold Doran, from Nebraska and hired men and women everyday. The "Specialty Salesman Magazine" became a legend in its own time (to coin a phrase) and put dozens and dozens of crooked business ventures out of business. That was the day of the door-to-door salesman and mail order gimmicks by the hundreds! Mr. Bix could, as I said, smell a con game from here to Nantuckett and he really nailed 'em good and proper. The magazine was sues, of course, by dozens of these crooked companies. Mr. Bix promoted Dad to Editor-In-Chief while he was busy with the law suits. He hired the best lawyer in Fort Wayne, IN, full time and some assistant lawyers.

After the "ball was over" he had won all but on lawsuit. In that one, the judge found him guilty and fined Mr. Bix and the "Specialty Salesman Magazine" just ONE CENT! This case spread like wildfires of the U. S. A. and circulation jumped out of sight. There was even room for another magazine that stared up and became just as successful.

In later years, Dad became Editor of that magazine. It was named "Opportunity" and was 1st class, too, My authority on all these going-on were, of course, My Dad and Harold Doran, who years later taught me to play golf, and on our trips to the golf courses and while playing, Harold would be telling me all this inside stuff about the magazine and personnel. One top man, got his fingers in the till and Mr. Bix sent him to Timbuckto and we never heard anything more about him.

Mr. Bix sold the magazine to a Chicago, IL, bunch in 1930, and he retired. Dad went with the magazine to Chicago. The A to Z building was empty. Everyone was sad about the magazine moving away; a lot of jobs were lost. But—so it goes.

Then, lo and behold, what do you know. A real attractive gentleman drove into town with his car loaded down with some kind of contraptions. It happened that the town board met that night and Mr. Smoothie showed up at the meeting and he really got the floor and gave his spiel. He had invented a new toy and needed a place to manufacture it. He heard about the A to Z building and had looked it over—finding it perfect. The he went to his car and carried one of his contraptions into the meetingroom and set it down for them to examine.

It was a Mustang horse mounted on a "stretched" ordinary tricycle, painted up beautifully. Looked like it would take off running any second. The board members oohed and aahed. Well, it was called and Anacycle and he had patents and all the legal stuff, but not enough money to build them. The price was reasonable and they were well-built with all the rough edges smoothed off inside and out. He had two sizes, three years old to six, and seven years old to ten. Plus, you could make a Zebra out of the horse with the paint job; or you could have a lion, a tiger, or a panther. Just by the paint job you put on it. A beautiful idea. Mr. King was his name(?) and he had 10-12 more assembled and could truck them down from someplace (?), but he had four in his car. He said that he would put them on display around town at various stores on consignment.

So he did. And the kids were absolutely bananas over them. They pestered and pestered until Dad went down and bout one. The truck came in with 30-40 more—instead of 10-12. Mr. King took them to three or four various towns in the area and the same thing happened. Tears and begging were rampant.

So, the town fathers and moneyed men formed a corporation and Mr. King was the president and treasurer. They got a production line started and they were selling hand over fist. We had a bonanza in South Whitley.

Then on Monday morning, Mr. King didn't show up. The back called and said that he'd drawn out, I think, $20,000 and left $300-$400 in the account. That was the last anybody ever saw of Mr. King or the $20,000. Nobody went bankrupt over it, but hurt, yes. That had two experts to consult: J. a Doran and George F. Peabody, but didn't think that was necessary.

Pretty slick SCAM!

THE END

Bix=Hicks

Mr. King had nothing to do with the Hicks family story.

ABOUT THE AUTHOR

Wishing to leave a memorial for her eight great-grandchildren, Margaret H. Savage began at the age of 83 to research and to write the life of her father, Bob Hicks.

As a girl she attended Stuart Hall, Staunton, VA, Gulf Park College, Gulfport, MI, and graduated from the University of Arizona, Tucson.

An inveterate traveler and optimist, she volunteered at Mother Teresa's Hospice, Varanasi, India, taught teachers how to teach in Chingola, Zambia, and lectured in Humanities at the International School in The Hague, Holland.

Now 93, Margaret lives alone writing her memoirs in Tucson.

Made in United States
Orlando, FL
05 February 2023

29542872R00183